BY ALLEN LACY
Home Ground: A Gardener's Miscellany
Farther Afield: A Gardener's Excursions

EDITED BY ALLEN LACY
Gardening for Love: The Market Bulletins,
by Elizabeth Lawrence
The American Gardener: A Sampler

The American Gardener

THE AMERICAN GARDENER

A SAMPLER

*Edited and with
an Introduction by*

ALLEN LACY

*Farrar Straus Giroux
New York*

Introduction copyright © 1988 by Allen Lacy
Compilation copyright © 1988 by Allen Lacy
All rights reserved
Printed in the United States of America
Published simultaneously in Canada
by Collins Publishers, Toronto
First edition, 1988
Designed by Cynthia Krupat

Library of Congress Cataloging-in-Publication Data
The American gardener.
Bibliography: p.
1. Gardening. 2. Gardening—United States.
3. Gardens. 4. Gardens—United States. I. Lacy, Allen.
SB455.A53   1988   635.9′0973   87-37965

See page 367 for copyright acknowledgments

Engravings on the title page and part-title pages are
from Suburban Home Grounds (1870) by Frank J. Scott

For
Kurt, Liesel, and Karl: The Newest Goetherts
and
Elisabeth Woodburn

Contents

Contents

Contents

Contents

The American Gardener

Introduction

Writing in the May 1987 issue of *Harper's*, in a fascinating essay pointing out that through much of our history American attitudes toward gardening have been strongly connected with notions of moral virtue, Michael Pollan remarked in an offhand way that our dependence on British garden designers and the literature they have produced has had a profound effect: there are no great American gardens and there is no great American literature on gardening. In these pages, I hope that readers will find evidence that Mr. Pollan was somewhat overhasty in dismissing the considerable body of writing about gardening by American writers, including Thomas Jefferson, who could write as knowingly about plants and gardens as he could about the human events that necessitate a new political order.

In horticulture, as in much else, the United States and Great Britain have literatures that are intertwined, and yet distinct. It would be absurdly chauvinistic to deny that we can learn much from such British writers of the past as Gertrude Jekyll and Vita Sackville-West—or from such contemporary ones as Rosemary Verey, Christopher Lloyd, or Beth Chatto, among several who could be named—any more than we should forgo the pleasures of reading Charles Dickens or Anthony Burgess. But just as we can enjoy British fiction and still take pride in Melville and Hawthorne, Eudora Welty and William Faulkner, so we can admire Jekyll and her compatriots without forgetting our own writers, such as Celia Thaxter, Alice Morse Earle, Neltje Blanchan, Louise Beebe Wilder, Katharine S. White, and Elizabeth Lawrence. Had no one else in America ever written on gardens, the work of these alone is sufficient to make the point: we do have our native gardening literature, and it's something to take pride in. Furthermore, American writing on gardening is a lively and going concern today, considering the work of Frederick McGourty, Linda Yang, Christopher Reed, Ann Lovejoy, Peter Loewer, and Henry Mitchell, to list some names almost at random.

The reasons that America has developed its own gardening literature, over a period of almost two centuries, are obvious. Bernard McMahon stated them plainly in the preface to his *The American Gardener's Calendar* (1806), an influential work which can lay claim to being the first comprehensive book on horticulture published in this country. "Works published in foreign countries and adapted to climates by no means according with ours, either in the temperature or course of the seasons . . . tend to mislead and disappoint the young *American* Horticulturist, instead of affording him that correct, judicious, and suitable instruction, the happy result of which would give impulse to his perseverance." McMahon, an Irishman who had emigrated to Philadelphia in 1796 at the age of twenty-one, ably provided this instruction in his *Calendar*, which Thomas Jefferson praised as soon as it was published. Jefferson was fully in accord with McMahon's notion that American conditions of soil and climate require a specifically American approach to horticulture. In a letter written from Monticello in 1817 to George Jeffreys, he observed that "there is probably no better husbandry known at present than that of England, but that is for the climate and productions of England."

McMahon's treatise, which went through eleven editions in the first half of the nineteenth century, was widely copied—and even pirated on one occasion. It was relentlessly practical, a compendium of month-by-month advice telling farmers and home gardeners when to plant their cabbages and onions and how to deal with aphids in the hothouse. And it established a tradition of writing on gardening that endures until today. The practical literature on gardening still flourishes, in both books and newspaper columns.

But horticulture is more than a practical matter of facts and information and technique. It has a social dimension, for one thing, as many writers in the middle of the nineteenth century were quick to point out. One of the prime justifications for gardening lay in its utility, as a means toward the moral education of the young, and of young women most especially. This theme is little sounded today, but it remains an important part of the horticultural literature of the past. Horticulture, moreover, has a purely private and personal dimension, putting individual human beings in touch with their senses, connecting them with the liturgy of the successive seasons, uniting them with the flow of time and the force of life. "To dwell," said Martin Heidegger, "is to garden." I take his meaning to be that to garden is not just to be passively in an environment but to make a habitation of the world, during one's allotted span of days. It is this principle that has guided me in putting together this sampler of American writing on gardening, and addressing first the topic "To Make a Garden."

I say sampler, because American garden literature is vast. I make no pretense of having more than nibbled a bit of it, in a fairly unsystematic way, and this book has come into being so that other readers can join me at a feast. It is not comprehensive. It contains fairly little about vegetables and fruits, very large topics indeed in America. (The books and essays published here in the nineteenth century devoted solely to the apple would by themselves fill many library shelves.) It only touches the subject of organic gardening, although my sympathies lie almost entirely with its advocates. I do not deal with Americans abroad, particularly in Great Britain and Europe, or with their observations of gardens there.

This book is divided into seven thematic sections, with the selections in each arranged in chronological order, to provide some sense of historical change.

"To Make a Garden" deals with the reasons people garden— or the reasons they give for gardening, which aren't necessarily the same things. The selections here show a strong tendency in the nineteenth century to justify gardening within a larger moral and educational framework, followed by a period in which gardening is something almost purely personal. Lynden B. Miller's very recent (1986) essay, "Perennials in Urban Areas," represents, however, something of a return to the notion that gardens have a social value, not just a private and personal one.

The next two sections, "Color" and "Fragrance," show two topics of continued interest today, which seem to have first appeared in American writing in the 1890s, and I must confess here to a surprising discovery that took place only in the final stages of assembling the manuscript. It had been my assumption that, within each of the sections, the selections would distribute themselves evenly over the time frame of almost two centuries of American garden writing. This assumption was entirely incorrect. Celia Thaxter's *An Island Garden* (1894)—a delicious book!—was the first place I discovered explicit and direct discussion of color and fragrance. This discovery sent me back into earlier writing, to see if I had missed something, but I came up dry. A flower might be described as blue or red. There might be some mention of pretty colors and sweet fragrance, but only abstractly. Was it possible that an aesthetic sense of the values of color and scent for their own sakes appeared so suddenly and so late in American writing?

There is possibly a faint clue to the answer to this question in an article by a sister in one of the Shaker communities, published in 1906 in *Good Housekeeping* and quoted in U. P. Hedrick's *A History of Horticulture in America*. The passage reads:

The rose bushes were planted along the sides of the road which ran through our village and were greatly admired by the passersby, but it was strongly impressed on us that a rose was useful, not ornamental. It was not intended to please us by its color or its odor. Its mission was to be made into rosewater, and if we thought of it in any other way we were making an idol of it and thereby imperilling our souls. In order that we might not be tempted to fasten a rose upon our dress or to put it into water to keep, the rule was that the flower should be picked with no stem at all. We had only crimson roses, as they were supposed to make stronger rose-water than the paler varieties [. . .] although in those days no sick person was allowed to have a fresh flower to cheer him, he was welcome to a liberal supply of rose-water to bathe his aching head.

Only a few Americans were Shakers, of course, but this native religious sect embodied, in an extreme form, the asceticism that was deeply ingrained in American culture, finding expression in the Sabbatarianism of several Protestant denominations well into the twentieth century. The aesthetic appreciation of color and fragrance for their own sakes, and not for obtaining some kind of moral message or theological parable, is at odds with every form of asceticism. Celia Thaxter, it would seem, no less than Gertrude Jekyll in England,

Introduction

brought something new to horticultural writing—a frank recognition of the claims and the pleasures of the senses.

Particularly as regards color, the question of influence arises. No one writes about anything, including gardening, in a cultural and intellectual vacuum. Thaxter, in writing about her garden, a tiny patch only fifteen by fifty feet, mostly planted in annuals, in front of her cottage on the Isle of Appledore off Kittery, Maine, was obviously influenced by John Ruskin, whom she quotes at length. There is also a clear and mutual influence between her and her friend Childe Hassam, the American Impressionist, who maintained a summer studio on Appledore and whose paintings illustrated the first edition of *An Island Garden*. Certainly Thaxter's book opened the door for a more openly aesthetic tone in American garden writing, which is to be found in the work of Alice Morse Earle, Louise Beebe Wilder, and many others.

American gardeners have a vast selection of plants to grow, many of which are native here but are sometimes ignored in favor of exotic imports, first from Europe and Great Britain in our early history, and then from Asia, as a result of plant collecting there for the past two centuries. But there have always been those among us—including Bernard McMahon, Andrew Jackson Downing, Alice Lounsberry, and Mabel Osgood Wright—who have urged us to pay proper attention to the worthy plants of our roadsides and meadows and woodlands, our goldenrods and asters, our trailing arbutus and our *Shortia galicifolia*, even our poison ivy. A section of essays on what Andrew Jackson Downing called, in the middle of the nineteenth century, "our neglected American plants" is therefore necessarily a part of this sampler.

Ever since Eden, giving plants the names by which they are known has been a prime human occupation, and an important one, considering the need to distinguish between an innocent and useful plant like lettuce and a more wicked one like poison ivy. The section on "naming names" is by no means exclusively American in its concerns, for British and European writers have since early modern times felt the practical and scientific need for giving every plant a precise name that would be universal in character. In the Linnaean system of botanical nomenclature, whereby plants are identified by their genus and species, the demands for clarity, precision, and lack

[7]

of ambiguity are handily met. The scientific names sometimes get changed or revised, as when botanists decide to lump together two previously distinct classifications or to split one class into two or more, or when they discover an older published name for a plant which must be given priority, but still the principle is honored: one plant, one name, and a different name for every plant. Everyone who thinks about the matter must realize that the botanists are right. But everyone must also realize that common names for plants, as messy and confusing as they are, are also highly poetic and evocative and wonderful. No sampler of American garden writing would be adequate without Alice Morse Earle and Louise Beebe Wilder on this topic.

Black widow and brown recluse spiders, biting flies, chiggers, fleas, gnats, mosquitos, ticks, and wasps; in some places scorpions and venomous snakes; poison ivy and bull nettle—America has never been short on things that attack us, making us feel pain, get sick, or even die. Other creatures bedevil our lives as gardeners. Aphids, curculio weevils, horned worms, and other insects go after our to-matoes and our roses, and if the native fauna were not enough, we have imported, either by accident or deliberately, Japanese beetles and gypsy moths to join in the feast. Purslane, crabgrass, dandelions, plantain weed—all these plants of European origin seem almost to find their purpose in infesting our lawns and gardens. Out in the country, deer and woodchucks work their mischief on our crops. Even city dwellers may have their vexing problems with wildlife—I have a friend living on East Fifty-first Street in Manhattan whose back garden was ravaged a couple of summers ago by a raccoon that appeared out of nowhere and then a week later disappeared as inexplicably as he had arrived. Then there are the blights and rusts and smuts and other diseases that plants can, and often do, contract.

When something is damaging the garden, our most natural impulse is to counterattack, to find some punishing remedy, and then to apply it with vigor and thoroughness. American literature on what to do about pests in the garden is enormous and full of ingenuity. Even the strangest of ideas, such as burying a dead cat under a tree or hammering nails into it, can get a hearing. And

Introduction

American gardening, I suppose like gardening everywhere, has been a matter not just of raising plants but also of finding substances to deter or destroy the enemy—everything from wood ashes or salt or whale-oil emulsion to poisons that may be deadly to us as well as to our foes.

Any American gardener of my age, the early fifties, will recall two moments in our history. The first came immediately after World War II, when the promise seemed to be coming true that better living came from better chemistry. The broad-leafed herbicide 2-4D—a viscous liquid that turned water white and gave it a pungent odor that once smelled can never be forgotten—would make weeding the lawn as obsolete as the crank telephone. Soon there were chemicals on the market that would keep crabgrass from sprouting, and others that would doom it if it germinated before the gardener could remember to apply a pre-emergent remedy. Other chemicals guaranteed the annihilation of the insect enemy. I quote here a wonderful passage from *The Better Homes and Gardens New Garden Book* (1951, rev. ed. 1966), which is remarkable for its unalloyed enthusiasm for the chemical arsenal at the gardener's disposal:

The gardener desiring perfect, unblemished fruit and ornamental plants has a pitched battle! He can win only if he is clever and well-informed. May beetle and flea beetle, foliage-feeding insects, visit the plant only to feed. The young develop safely in the soil, often at some distance from the host plant. DDT, or some other poison applied to leaves, will kill these unwelcome guests.

It should perhaps be noted that enthusiasm for horticultural chemicals is by no means an exclusively American phenomenon. The notion of chemical solutions to agricultural problems was well established in Germany by the late nineteenth century—and Vita Sackville-West wrote a newspaper column in the late 1940s describing the pleasure she and some of her guests at Sissinghurst took in spraying weeds with 2-4D and contemplating their imminent demise.

The second moment to remember is the publication of Rachel Carson's *Silent Spring*, which gave the general public its first inkling that DDT and other pesticides might have undesirable and baneful

[9]

effects on all life. *Silent Spring* has of course deeply influenced much recent horticultural writing, teaching the important lessons that some battles are better left unwon and that some apparently good ideas turn out to be dreadful ones.

Foreign visitors to the United States often comment on the peculiar way Americans situate their houses and their gardens in the suburbs where a great many of us live. Our houses are set back on their lots, with lawns open to the sidewalk and the street, and with evergreens corseting their foundations. What privacy there is is to be found in our back yards, which may be hedged or fenced in from those of our neighbors. A drive down almost any suburban street in America is sufficient to show that this ideal has triumphed, that it seems so obviously right and proper as to have no viable alternative. But one of the most fascinating aspects of the history of American garden writing is that this ideal has had not only its proponents but also its strong critics, who argue that a garden is in its essence an enclosure, and that the boundaries between street and residential property should mark the necessary boundary between public and private life. This sampler presents, in its final section, both sides of this debate—and suggests, I believe, that there is good reason to pay sympathetic attention to those writers who, like George Washington Cable and Celestine Sibley, argue the need for privacy and enclosure.

This book has its distant origins in two of the writers I have named. I grew up in Texas among a family of people who gardened and people who read. The books we had on gardening were practical ones, dealing with what to plant and when to plant it, with how deep to dig and when to prune. There were also, of course, seed and nursery catalogues, of no special literary merit. They were instruments of commerce, published by people in the plant trade who wanted to sell their wares and showed no restraint about using incandescent adjectives to do so. Then Katharine S. White came along, with a series of essays in *The New Yorker* which took gardening catalogues seriously as a literary genre. White taught me that it was possible to write about gardening with liveliness and grace, and I watched eagerly for each of her essays to appear, at intervals of about a year, and rejoiced when they were collected after her death and published as *Onward and Upward in the Garden*. More recently, about sixteen years ago, I picked up a tattered copy of Alice Morse Earle's *Old-Time Gardens*. Because it was published in 1901, an "old time" itself, I thought it might be quaint and curious. It turned out to be about as quaint and curious as the Mozart *Requiem* or *The Cherry Orchard*, teaching the lesson that books on gardening, no less than musical and theatrical works, can be classics—not relics of the past, but fresh when first discovered decades after their creator has gone to earth, and fresh on each new encounter. I still read *Old-Time Gardens* and other books by Mrs. Earle, and always with delight. And during the last sixteen years, I have seldom been able to pass by a used-book store, to resist rummaging through its bins, hoping that some new treasure of American garden writing will turn up. Often the search is fruitless, but occasionally it is triumphant, as it was four years ago, when I found Charles Dudley Warner's *My Summer in a Garden* in a junk store in Bell Buckle, Tennessee—or just five months ago, when my friend Hannah Withers of Charlotte, North Carolina, gave me a copy of Celia Thaxter's *An Island Garden*, thinking, absolutely correctly, that I would love it as much as she and her friend the late Elizabeth Lawrence did. As the idea took root, some years ago, that other readers might take pleasure in an anthology or sampler of American garden writing, I began to gather materials more systematically.

Some browsers in this sampler will notice that although it covers almost two centuries of American horticultural writing, two periods dominate the selections—the late nineteenth and early twentieth centuries, and the last twenty-five years, right up to the middle of 1987. This fact corresponds, I believe, to the history of gardening and garden writing in this country. There was, to begin with, a huge surge of interest in gardening in the late Victorian age (which Elisabeth Woodburn has suggested might as easily be known as the age of horticulture), and this interest created an appreciative audience for worthy writing on gardening. Writing in *The Garden Magazine* in December 1905, one Thomas McAdam observed tartly that "ten years ago there were mighty few gardening books that were fit for

Christmas presents." Regarding the gardening books of the past, Mr. McAdam was fairly brutal, except for his good words about those of Andrew Jackson Downing. As for the rest—

there was scarcely a book in the whole collection that a gentleman would care to have in his parlor. They had the look of the barn about them— faded covers, cheap paper, small type, scanty margins and gruesome old woodcuts; they abounded in realistic portraits of hairy caterpillars, apple scab, plum rot, and the like—all in heroic size—and no book was complete without a certain classical picture of the codlin moth's offspring eating the heart out of an apple of iron texture. It used to fascinate me, like the picture of Cortés burning Peruvians at the stake.

No doubt McAdam overstated his case, but the real point of his article is the dawning of a new day in American writing on gardening, the emergence of books that will "help create a race of gardeners." He gives high praise to such recent books as Alice Morse Earle's *Old-Time Gardens* and *Sundials and Roses of Yesterday* and Helena Rutherfurd Ely's *A Woman's Hardy Garden*. Ely's book in particular, a best seller in its day, set the stage for almost three decades of highly distinguished writing on gardening.

By the 1930s, however, there seems to have been a slackening off of garden writing of high and enduring quality. Louise Beebe Wilder and Richardson Wright were still writing their excellent books, and Elizabeth Lawrence would not publish her fine *A Southern Garden*, which is still in print, until 1941. Preoccupied with the Great Depression and then with World War II and its troubled aftermath, America produced little in the way of writing on gardening, in comparison with the first part of the century.

Today, however, we can look back on something of a horticultural renaissance, and the appearance of a new style of horticultural writing that is often highly personal and even confessional, passionate and sometimes opinionated, and sometimes witty and humorous. This book, I hope, gives an adequate sample of the newer as well as the older horticultural writing in this country.

A note on the text. Conventions about plant names change with the times, and they may vary from writer to writer. The general practice today is to put Latin names in italics and cultivar names in

Introduction

single quotation marks. Common names are generally printed without capital letters—e.g., morning glory. But even today some publishers specializing in books on horticulture prefer Morning Glory. Rather than editing for conformity to a single rule of style, I have left spelling, capitalization, and other matters of orthography as each writer preferred. Thus, although most of the writers in this collection write "color" as Noah Webster would have it, Louise Beebe Wilder is permitted to keep to the British practice, with "colour."

Acknowledgments. Behind every book is a long list of persons to whom debts are due. For this book, I am indebted especially to my editor, Pat Strachan, who first saw the possibilities and who encouraged me to spend a summer at the Xerox machine. The book is partially dedicated to Elisabeth Woodburn of Booknoll Farm in Hopewell, New Jersey, who for some years has been my guide into the complex literature of horticulture, in America and elsewhere, but the dedication is insufficient to express my gratitude for her unfailing help. Walter Punch, librarian of the Massachusetts Horticultural Society, was of great assistance, as were Phyllis Ahlsted and Christal Springer of the Stockton State College library. Others who lent encouragement are Allen Bush, Edith Eddleman, Joanne Ferguson, Nancy Goodwin, William Lubenow, Margaret Marsh, Hannah Withers, and Linda Yang—all colleagues in one way or another.

A.L.

New Jersey
September 1987

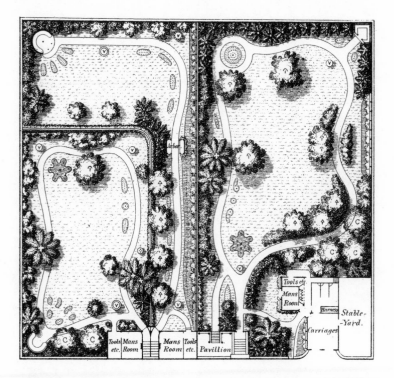

TO MAKE A GARDEN

Henry Ward Beecher
A *Plea for Health and Floriculture*

Every one knows to what an extent women are afflicted with nervous disorders, *neuralgic* affections as they are more softly termed. Is it equally well known that formerly when women partook from childhood, of out-of-doors labors, were confined less to heated rooms and exciting studies, they had, comparatively, few disorders of this nature. With the progress of society, *fevers* increase first, because luxurious eating vitiates the blood; *dyspepsia* follows next, because the stomach, instead of being a laboratory, is turned into a mere warehouse, into which everything is packed, from the foundation to the roof, by gustatory *stevedores*. Last of all come *neuralgic* complaints, springing from the muscular enfeeblement and the nervous excitability of the system.

Late hours at night, and later morning hours, early application to books, a steady training for *accomplishments*, viz. embroidery, lace-work, painting rice paper, casting wax-flowers so ingeniously that no mortal can tell what is meant: lilies looking like huge goblets, dahlias resembling a battered cabbage; these, together with practisings on the piano, or if something extra is meant, a little tum, tum, tuming, on the harp, and a little ting-tong on the guitar; reading "ladies' books," crying over novels, writing in albums, and original correspondence with my ever-adored Matilda Euphrosyne, are the materials, too often, of a fashionable education. While all this refinement is being put on, girls are taught from eight years old, that the chief end of women is to get a beau, and convert him into a husband. Therefore, every action must be *on purpose*, must have a discreet object in view. Girls must not walk fast, that is not lady-like; nor run, that would be shockingly vulgar; nor scamper over fields, merry and free as the bees or the birds, laughing till the cheeks are rosy, and romping till the blood marches merrily in every vein; for, says prudent mamma, "my dear, so you think Mr. Lack-a-daisy would marry a girl whom he saw acting so unfashionably?" Thus, in every part of education those things are pursued, whose tendency is to excite the brain and nervous system, and for the most part those things are not *"refined,"* which would develop the muscular system, give a natural fullness to the form, and health and vigor to every organ of it.

The evil does not end upon the victim of fashionable education. Her feebleness, and morbid tastes, and preternatural excitability are transmitted to her children, and to their children. If it were not for the rural habits and health of the vast proportion of our population, trained to hearty labor on the soil, the degeneracy of the race in cities would soon make civilization a curse to the health of mankind.

Now we have not one word to say against "accomplishments" when they are *real*, and are not purchased at the expense of a girl's constitution. She may dance like Miriam, paint like Raphael, make wax fruit till the birds come and peck at the cunning imitation; she may play like Orpheus harping after Eurydice (or what will be more to the purpose, like a Eurydice after an Orpheus), she may sing and write poetry to the moon, and to every star in the heavens, and every flower on earth, to zephyrs, to memory, to friendship, and to whatever is imaginable in the spheres, or on the world—if she will, in the midst of these ineffable things, remember the most important facts, that *health* is a blessing; that God made health to depend upon exercise, and temperate living in all respects; and that the great objects of our existence, in respect to ourselves, are a virtuous and pious character, and in respect to others, the raising and training of a family after such a sort that neither we, nor men, nor God, shall be ashamed of them.

Now we are not quite so enthusiastic as to suppose that floriculture has in it a balm for all these mentioned ills. We are very moderate in our expectations, believing, only, that it may become a very important auxiliary in maintaining health of body and purity of mind.

When once a mind has been touched with zeal in floriculture

it seldom forgets its love. If our children were early made little enthusiasts for the garden, when they were old they would not depart from it. A woman's perception of the beauty of form, of colors, of arrangement, is naturally quicker and truer than man's. Why should they admire these only in painting, in dress, and in furniture? Can human art equal what God has made, in variety, hue, grace, symmetry, order and delicacy? A beautiful engraving is often admired by those who never look at a natural landscape; ladies become connoisseurs of "artificials," who live in proximity to real flowers without a spark of enthusiasm for them. We are persuaded that, if parents, instead of regarding a disposition to train flowers as a useless trouble, a waste of time, a pernicious romancing, would inspire the love of it, nurture and direct it, it would save their daughters from *false taste*, and all love of meretricious ornament. The most enthusiastic lovers of nature catch something of the simplicity and truthfulness of nature.

Now a constant temptation to female vanity (if it may be supposed for the sake of argument, to exist) is a display of person, of dress, of equipage. In olden times, without entirely hating their beauty, our mothers used to be proud of their spinning, their weaving, their curiously-wrought apparel for bed and board. A pride in what we have *done* is not, if in due measure, wrong or unwise; and we really think that rivalry among the young in rearing the choicest plants, the most resplendent flowers, would be altogether a wise exchange for a rivalry of lace, and ribbons, and silks. And, even if poor human nature must be forced to allow the privilege of criticising each other something severely, it would be much more amiable to pull roses to pieces, than to pull caps; all the shafts which are now cast at the luckless beauty, might more harmlessly be cast upon the glowing shield of her dahlias or upon the cup of her tulips.

A love of flowers would beget early rising, industry, habits of close observation, and of reading. It would incline the mind to notice natural phenomena, and to reason upon them. It would occupy the mind with pure thoughts, and inspire a sweet and gentle enthusiasm; maintain simplicity of taste; and in connection with personal instruction, unfold in the heart an enlarged, unstraitened, ardent piety.

[*Plain and Pleasant Talk About Fruits, Flowers and Farming* (1859)]

Joseph Breck
The Utility of Flowers
The Happy Influence of the Pursuit of Horticulture on the Mind of Man

Not useless are ye flowers; though made for pleasure,
Blooming o'er fields, and wave by day and night
From every source your sanction bids me treasure
Harmless delight.

—HORACE SMITH

Flowers are the expression of God's love to man. One of the highest uses, therefore, which can be made in contemplating these beautiful creations, in all their variety and splendor, is, that our thoughts and affections may be drawn upwards to Him who has so bountifully spread over the face of the whole earth, such a vast profusion of these beautiful objects, as tokens of His love to us. The more we examine flowers, especially when the eye is assisted by the microscope, the more we must adore the matchless skill of the Great Supreme. We must be ungrateful indeed, not to acknowledge His unspeakable goodness in thus providing so liberally for the happiness and pleasure of His children here below.

The Saviour of men, while on earth, often retired to the gardens about Jerusalem to spend a quiet hour with His disciples, or alone, and no doubt took pleasure in contemplating flowers. We all know how He spake of the lily: "Behold the lilies of the field, how they grow; they toil not, neither do they spin; and yet I say unto you that Solomon in all his glory was not arrayed like one of these." How surely would Solomon himself have agreed with this beautiful speech! that his wise heart loved the flowers, the lily especially, is evident from the numerous passages in his song. The object of his love in claiming a supreme dignity of beauty, exclaims: "I am the rose of Sharon, and the lily of the valley." [. . .]

There is a class of men who would pare down everything to the mere grade of *utility*, who think it the height of wisdom to ask, when one manifests an enthusiasm in the culture of flowers, "of what use are they?" With such we have no sympathy. We will not say with the late Henry Colman, in case such an interrogatory being put to us that *"our first impulse is to look under his hat, and see the length of his ears,"* but we are always inclined in such cases to thank God that our tastes do not correspond with their's. "Better," (say these ultra utilitarians,) "devote our time to the culture of things useful and needed to sustain life, than to employ it on things, which, like flowers, are intended only to look at and please the eye." "But why," would we ask, "why should not the eye be pleased?" What pleasures more pure, more warming to the heart, more improving to the mind, more chastening to the affections, than those which come through the eye! Where are more luminously displayed the perfections of the Creator, than in the star spangled heavens above, and the flower spangled earth beneath?

Nonsense,—sheer nonsense to tell us it is useless to cultivate flowers. They add to the charms of our homes, rendering them more attractive and beautiful, and they multiply and strengthen the domestic ties which bind us to them. We would not advocate the cultivation of flowers to the neglect of more necessary objects. Attending to the one, does not involve neglect of the other. Every man engaged in the culture of the earth, can find time to embellish his premises who has the will to do it, and we pity the family of the man who has not. "Rob the earth of its flowers, the wondrous mechanism of the Almighty, and we should lose the choicest mementos left us that it was once a paradise.

"We have no sympathy with those, who would desecrate and pare down the loveliness of earth to the grade of mere utility—who can discover no beauty in the opening bud and blushing flower, and whose exertions are limited on all occasions by a parsimonious idolatry and worse than idiotic privation of sensibility to the maddening love of Gold." The love of flowers is a sentiment common alike to the great and little; to the old and young; to the learned and the ignorant; to the illustrious and the obscure, while the simplest child may take delight in them. They may also prove a recreation to the most profound philosopher. Lord Bacon himself did not disdain to bend his mighty intellect to the subject of their culture.

The great men of our own age as well as those of the past, have given in their verdict in favor of the great utility of the practice of horticulture in refining and elevating the mind. I cannot refrain from alluding to some of the remarks made by Daniel Webster, Caleb Cushing, and other distinguished guests at the remarkable and interesting festival, held by the Massachusetts Horticultural Society at Fanueil Hall, in September 1845. At this grand festival six hundred ladies and gentlemen sat down to a sumptuous feast. The tables, fourteen in number, were arranged lengthway of the hall, while at the end was a raised platform, where were seated the president of the society, Marshall P. Wilder, with the numerous invited illustrious guests. The tables were loaded with every delicacy; but their crowning glory was, the great profusion of delicious fruits and a magnificent display of gorgeous flowers, and the absence of all intoxicating liquors. The scene was exciting and brilliant, enlivened by a band of music, interspersed by appropriate songs, while the eloquent remarks from the distinguished guests, with the numerous sentiments in praise of horticulture, produced a scene never be forgotten.

The Hon. Daniel Webster made the following remarks: "I congratulate you, Mr. President, that our flowers are not

Born to blush unseen
And waste their sweetness on the desert air

"The botany we cultivate, the productions of the business of horticulture, the plants of the garden, are cultivated by hands as delicate as their own tendrils, viewed by countenances as spotless and pure as their own petals, and watched by eyes as brilliant and full of lustre, as their own beautiful exhibitions of splendor.

"Horticulture is one pursuit of natural science in which all sexes and degrees of education and refinement unite. Nothing is too polished to see the beauty of flowers. Nothing too rough to be capable of enjoying them. It attracts, delights all. It seems to be a common field, where every degree of taste and refinement may unite, and find opportunities for their gratification."

Joseph Breck

The Hon. Josiah Quincy, senior, remarked, that in the Horticultural Hall, he had witnessed the wonders wrought by the florist's hand; he had seen there what man could do, by labor and taste, to enlarge, beautify, and multiply the bounties of nature; he had seen how art and wisely employed capital were permitted by heaven, to improve its own gifts, and felt how impossible it was by language, to express the beauty of fruits and flowers, which nature and art had combined to improve. Nor could he refrain from reflecting that all was the work of well directed industry.

The Hon. Caleb Cushing, who had just returned from his mission to China, made the following remarks in relation to woman and flowers: "I am, Mr. President, most thankful for the opportunity to look on a spectacle like this—on the delicate and beautiful fruits and flowers before us. All our associations of beauty and taste are blended with flowers. They are our earliest tokens of affection and regard. They adorn the bridal brow at the wedding; they are woven in garlands around the head of the conquerer; they are strewn on the coffins of the dead. And here is another of their most grateful and beautiful uses—ornamenting the table at a festival, and enlivening the scene and enchanting the eye. In that 'central flowery land,' this is the case at all festivals; flowers there adorn the table, and meet the eye in every direction, on all festive occasions; but they are not there accompanied by what we here enjoy. Here alone—here and in Christian lands—WOMAN enchants and beautifies with her presence, the festive scene. Woman—our equal— shall I not say our moral superior. It is only here, that such a scene can gladden the human eye. I regard this exhibition as a striking proof of the point which education and intellectual refinement have reached in our country; that we have got beyond mere utility, and ceasing to inquire how far it is incompatible with beauty, have found that the beautiful is of itself useful. We have learned to admire art, to appreciate sculpture and painting, and to look upon fruits and flowers, as models of delicacy and beauty."

The Hon. Robert C. Winthrop remarked, that, he "had never cultivated flowers, not even the flowers of rhetoric; as to the sentimentalities of the subject, Mrs. Caudle had quite exhausted them in a single sentence of one of her last lectures, when she told her husband how 'she was born for a garden! There is something about it that makes one feel so innocent! My heart always opens and shuts at roses.' Shakespeare had pronounced it to be 'wasteful and ridiculous excess, to paint the lily, or throw a perfume upon the violet.' And so it would be. The violets had been called, 'sweet as the lids of Juno's eyes or Cytherœa's breath;' and of the lilies it had been divinely said, that 'Solomon in all his glory was not arrayed like one of these.' Both had already a grace beyond the reach of art. But to multiply varieties of fruit and flowers; to increase their abundance, and scatter them with a richer profusion along the way-sides of life; to improve their quality, coloring and fragrance, wherever it was possible to do so; this, the great poet of nature, would have been the last person to call wasteful. Its utility would only be questioned by those who counted it useless to extend the range of innocent recreation and virtuous enjoyment; useless to brighten and strengthen the chain of sympathy which binds man to man; or useless to excite a fresher or more frequent glow of grateful admiration in the human breast, towards the giver of all good." [. . .]

Who, that was blessed with parents that indulged themselves, and children with a flower garden, can forget the happy, innocent hours spent in its cultivation! O! who can forget those days, when to announce the appearance of a bud, or the coloring of a tulip, or the opening of a rose, or the perfection of a full-blown peony, was glory enough for one morning. With tender emotions do I remember the old white rose-bush, trained up to the top of the house by the hand of a dear mother, the abundant and fragrant flowers of which gave delight to all the household, as well as to the neighbors, who received them as expressions of neighborly friendship and goodwill. How many pleasant reminiscenses, crowd upon the memory of one who at the age of three-score and ten, as he looks back on the scenes of his childhood and youth, when from his sainted mother he received lessons of morality and piety, while engaged in the culture of a limited flower garden. Did she forget to love flowers? Were they no source of pleasure to her when old age crept upon her? No, no! At the age of ninety, her table never lacked a bouquet, a pot of fuchsia, or a rose or some other flower, which received her tender care. How many otherwise tedious hours were spent in the contemplation of her little flower garden; and with what cheerfulness did she pass away, from the flowers of earth, to the paradise of heaven, leaving a delightful example, of a happy, cheerful, contented old age, as a rich legacy to her numerous descendants and friends.

But the gratification derived from the garden, is not confined to the young or the old. Who that has been confined to the business of the day, toiling and laboring in the "sweat of his face," does not feel invigorated and refreshed, as he takes his walk in the cool of the evening, with the happy family group about him, and notes the progress of his fruits and flowers? Or, who that breathes the delicious fragrance of the morning leaves glittering with dew, but can look up with greater confidence and love to Him, who has strewed with such liberal profusion in every direction, the evidence of His goodness and love to the children of men!

Man was not made to rust out in idleness. A degree of exercise is as necessary for the preservation of health, both of body and mind, as his daily food. And what exercise is more fitting, or more appropriate for one who is in the decline of life, than that of superintending a well ordered garden? What more enlivens the sinking mind? What more invigorates the feeble frame? What is more conducive to a long life? What can be more grateful to the mechanic or merchant or professional man, than to recreate for a short time in a well selected garden of flowers, neatly arranged and well cultivated?

In reply to the question often asked, "what is the use of flowers?" William Cobbett asks another, "what is the use of anything?" There are many things in this wide world pleasing to the eye of man; many of them expensive and not in the power of all to obtain; but flowers may, without much or no expense, be obtained and possessed by the most humble individual. Their cultivation may be made one unfailing source of happiness to the family. Let parents gather around them every source of innocent amusement and recreation for their children. They should endeavor to make their home attractive and lovely, both within doors and without.

[*New Book of Flowers* (1866)]

Catharine Beecher
and Harriet Beecher Stowe
Gardening and
the Education of Women

There is a great abundance of safe, healthful, and delightful rec-
reations, which all parents may secure for their children. [. . .] One
of the most useful and important, is the cultivation of flowers and
fruits. This, especially for the daughters of a family, is greatly pro-
motive of health and amusement. [. . .] It would be a most desirable
improvement, if all schools for young women could be furnished
with suitable grounds and instruments for the cultivation of fruits
and flowers, and every inducement offered to engage the pupils in
this pursuit. No father, who wishes to have his daughters grow up
to be healthful women, can take a surer method to secure this end.
Let him set apart a portion of his ground for fruits and flowers, and
see that the soil is well prepared and dug over, and all the rest may
be committed to the care of the children. These would need to be
provided with a light hoe and rake, a dibble or garden trowel, a
watering-pot, and means and opportunities for securing seeds, roots,
bulbs, buds, and grafts, all which might be done at a trifling expense.
Then, with proper encouragement and by the aid of a few intelligible
and practical directions, every man who has even half an acre could
secure a small Eden around his premises.

In pursuing this amusement children can also be led to acquire
many useful habits. Early rising would, in many cases, be thus
secured; and if they were required to keep their walks and borders
free from weeds and rubbish, habits of order and neatness would
be induced. Benevolent and social feelings could also be cultivated,

by influencing children to share their fruits and flowers with friends and neighbors, as well as to distribute roots and seeds to those who have not the means of procuring them. A woman or a child, by giving seeds or slips or roots to a washerwoman, or a farmer's boy, thus inciting them to love and cultivate fruits and flowers, awakens a new and refining source of enjoyment in minds which have few resources more elevated than mere physical enjoyments. Our Saviour directs us in making feasts, to call, not the rich who can recompense again, but the poor who can make no returns. So children should be taught to dispense their little treasures not alone to companions and friends, who will probably return similar favors; but to those who have no means of making any return. If the rich, who acquire a love for the enjoyments of taste and have the means to gratify it, would aim to extend among the poor the cheap and simple enjoyment of fruits and flowers, our country would soon literally "blossom as the rose."

If the ladies of a neighborhood would unite small contributions, and send a list of flower-seeds and roots to some respectable and honest florist, who would not be likely to turn them off with trash, they could divide these among themselves and their poor neighbors, so as to secure an abundant variety at a very small expense. A bag of flower-seeds, which can be obtained at wholesale for four cents, would abundantly supply a whole neighborhood; and by the gathering of seeds in the autumn, could be perpetuated.

[*The American Woman's Home* (1869)]

Charles Dudley Warner
The Love of Dirt

The love of dirt is among the earliest of passions, as it is the latest. Mud-pies gratify one of our first and best instincts. So long as we are dirty, we are pure. Fondness for the ground comes back to a man after he has run the round of pleasure and business, eaten dirt, and sown wild-oats, drifted about the world, and taken the wind of all its moods. The love of digging in the ground (or of looking on while he pays another to dig) is as sure to come back to him as he is sure, at last, to go under the ground, and stay there. To own a bit of ground, to scratch it with a hoe, to plant seeds, and watch their renewal of life,—this is the commonest delight of the race, the most satisfactory thing a man can do. When Cicero writes of the pleasures of old age, that of agriculture is chief among them: "*Venio nunc ad voluptates agricolarum, quibus ego incredibiliter delector: quæ nec ulla impediuntur senectute, et mihi ad sapientis vitam proxime videntur accedere.*" (I am driven to Latin because New York editors have exhausted the English language in the praising of spring, and especially of the month of May.)

Let us celebrate the soil. Most men toil that they may own a piece of it; they measure their success in life by their ability to buy it. It is alike the passion of *parvenu* and the pride of the aristocrat. Broad acres are a patent of nobility; and no man but feels more of a man in the world if he have a bit of ground that he can call his own. However small it is on the surface, it is four thousand miles deep; and that is a very handsome property. And there is a great pleasure in working in the soil, apart from the ownership of it. The man who has planted a garden feels that he has done something for the good of the world. He belongs to the producers. It is a pleasure to eat of the fruit of one's toil, if it be nothing more than a head of lettuce or an ear of corn. One cultivates a lawn, even, with great satisfaction; for there is nothing more beautiful than grass and turf in our latitude. The tropics may have their delights; but they have not turf: and the world without turf is a dreary desert. The original Garden of Eden could not have had such turf as one sees in England. The Teutonic races all love turf: they emigrate in the line of its growth.

To dig in the mellow soil—to dig moderately, for all pleasure should be taken sparingly—is a great thing. One gets strength out of the ground as often as one really touches it with a hoe. Antæus (this is a classical article) was no doubt an agriculturist; and such a prize-fighter as Hercules couldn't do anything with him till he got him to lay down his spade and quit the soil. It is not simply beets and potatoes and corn and string-beans that one raises in his well-hoed garden: it is the average of human life. There is life in the ground: it goes into the seeds; and it also, when it is stirred up, goes into the man who stirs it. The hot sun on his back as he bends to his shovel and hoe, or contemplatively rakes the warm and fragrant loam, is better than much medicine. The buds are coming out on the bushes round about; the blossoms of the fruit-trees begin to show; the blood is running up the grape-vines in streams; you can smell the wild-flowers on the near bank; and the birds are flying and glancing and singing everywhere. To the open kitchen-door comes the busy housewife to shake a white something, and stands a moment to look, quite transfixed by the delightful sights and sounds. Hoeing in the garden on a bright, soft May day, when you are not obliged to, is nearly equal to the delight of going trouting.

Blessed be agriculture!—if one does not have too much of it. All literature is fragrant with it, in a gentlemanly way. At the foot of the charming olive-covered hills of Tivoli, Horace (not he of Chappaqua) had a sunny farm: it was in sight of Hadrian's villa, who did landscape-gardening on an extensive scale, and probably did not get half as much comfort out of it as Horace did from his more simply-tilled acres. We trust that Horace did a little hoeing and farming himself, and that his verse is not all fraudulent sentiment. In order to enjoy agriculture, you do not want too much of it, and you want to be poor enough to have a little inducement to work moderately yourself. Hoe while it is spring, and enjoy the best anticipations. It is not much matter if things do not turn out well.

I do not hold myself bound to answer the question, Does gardening pay? It is so difficult to define what is meant by paying. There is a popular notion that unless a thing pays you had better let it alone; and I may say that there is a public opinion that will not let a man or woman continue in the indulgence of a fancy that does not pay. And public opinion is stronger than the legislature, and nearly as strong as the ten commandments. I therefore yield to popular clamor when I discuss the profit of my garden.

As I look at it, you might as well ask, Does a sunset pay? I know that a sunset is commonly looked on as a cheap entertainment; but it is really one of the most expensive. It is true that we can all have front seats, and we do not exactly need to dress for it as we do for the opera; but the conditions under which it is to be enjoyed are rather dear. Among them I should name a good suit of clothes, including some trifling ornament—not including back hair for one sex, or the parting of it in the middle for the other. I should add also a good dinner, well cooked and digestible; and the cost of a fair education, extended, perhaps, through generations in which sensibility and love of beauty grew. What I mean is that if a man is hungry and naked, and half a savage, or with the love of beauty undeveloped in him, a sunset is thrown away on him: so that it appears that the conditions of the enjoyment of a sunset are as costly as anything in our civilization.

Of course there is no such thing as absolute value in this world. You can only estimate what a thing is worth to *you*. Does gardening in a city pay? You might as well ask if it pays to keep hens, or a trotting horse, or to wear a gold ring or to keep your lawn cut, or your hair cut. It is as you like it. In a certain sense, it is a sort of profanation to consider if my garden pays, or to set a money-value upon my delight in it. I fear that you could not put it in money. Job had the right idea in his mind when he asked, "Is there any taste in the white of an egg?"

[*My Summer in a Garden* (1870)]

Helena Rutherfurd Ely
Love of All Things Green and Growing

Love of flowers and all things green and growing is with many men and women a passion so strong that it often seems to be a sort of primal instinct, coming down through generation after generation, from the first man who was put into a garden "to dress it and to keep it." People whose lives, and those of their parents before them, have been spent in dingy tenements, and whose only garden is a rickety soap-box high up on a fire-escape, share this love, which must have a plant to tend, with those whose gardens cover acres and whose plants have been gathered from all the countries of the world. How often in summer, when called to town, and when driving through the squalid streets to the ferries or riding on the elevated road, one sees these gardens of the poor. Sometimes they are only a Geranium or two, or the gay Petunia. Often a tall Sun-flower, or a Tomato plant red with fruit. These efforts tell of the love for the growing things, and of the care that makes them live and blossom against all odds. One feels a thrill of sympathy with the owners of the plants, and wishes that some day their lot may be cast in happier places, where they too may have gardens to tend.

It has always seemed to me that the punishment of the first gardener and his wife was the bitterest of all. To have lived always in a garden "where grew every tree pleasant to the sight and good for food," to have known no other place, and then to have been driven forth into the great world without hope of returning! Oh! Eve, had you not desired wisdom, your happy children might still be tilling the soil of that blessed Eden. The first woman longed for knowledge, as do her daughters of to-day. When the serpent said that eating of the forbidden fruit would make them "as gods," what wonder that Eve forgot the threatening command to leave untouched the Tree of Life, and, burning to be "wise," ate of the fateful apple and gave it to her Adam? And then, to leave the lovely place at the loveliest of all times in a garden, the cool of the day! Faint sunset hues tinting the sky, the night breeze gently stirring the trees, Lilies and Roses giving their sweetest perfume, brilliant Venus mounting her accustomed path, while the sleepy twitter of the birds alone breaks the silence. Then the voice of wrath, the Cherubim, the turning flaming sword!

[*A Woman's Hardy Garden* (1903)]

Hanna Rion
What My Garden Means to Me

The greatest gift of a garden is the restoration of the five senses.

During the first year in the country I noticed but few birds, the second year I saw a few more, but by the fourth year the air, the tree tops, the thickets and ground seemed teeming with bird life. "Where did they all suddenly come from?" I asked myself. The birds had always been there, but I hadn't the power to see; I had been made purblind by the city and only gradually regained my power of sight.

My ears, deafened by the ceaseless whir and din of commerce, had lost the keenness which catches the nuances of bird melody, and it was long before I was aware of distinguishing the varying tones that afterward meant joy, sorrow, loss or love, to me. That hearing has now become so keen, there is no bond of sleep so strong that the note of a strange bird will not pierce to the unsleeping, subconscious ear and arouse me instantly to alertness in every fibre of my being. I wonder if even death will make me insensate to the first chirp of a vanguard robin in March.

During that half-awake first year of country life I was walking with a nature-wise man and as we passed by a field where the cut hay lay wilting, he whiffed and said, "There's a good deal of rag weed in that hay." I gazed on him with the admiration I've saved all my life for wizards and wondered what peculiar brand of nose he had.

Then the heart, the poor jaded heart, that must etherize itself to endure the grimness of city life at all, how subtly it begins throbbing again in unison with the great symphony of the natural. The awakened heart can sense spring in the air when there is no visible suggestion in calendar or frosted earth, and knowing the songful secret, the heart can cause the feet to dance through a day that would only mean winter to an urbanite.

The sense of taste can only be restored by a constant diet of unwilted vegetables and freshly picked fruit.

The delicacy of touch comes back gradually by tending injured birdlings, by the handling of fragile infant plants, and by the acquaintance with different leaf textures, which finally makes one able to distinguish a plant, even in the dark, by its Irish tweed, silken or fur finish.

And the foot, how intangibly it becomes sensitized; how instinctively it avoids a plant even when the eye is busy elsewhere. On the darkest night I can traverse the rocky ravine, the thickets, the sinuous paths through overgrown patches, and never stumble, scratch myself or crush a leaf. My foot knows every unevenness of each individual bit of garden, and adjusts itself lovingly without conscious thought of brain.

To the ears that have learned to catch the first tentative lute of a marsh frog in spring, orchestras are no longer necessary. To the eyes that have regained their sight, more wonder lies in the craftsmanship of a tiny leaf-form of inconsequential weed, than is to be found in a bombastic arras. To the resuscitated nose is revealed the illimitable secrets of earth incense, the whole gamut of flower perfume, and other fragrant odors too intangible to be classed, odors which wing the spirit to realms our bodies are as yet too clumsy to inhabit.

To the awakened mind there is nothing so lowly in the things below and above ground but can command respect and study. Darwin spent only thirty years on the study of the humble earthworm.

To get the greatest good from a garden we should not undertake more than we can personally take care of. I have not had a gardener since the first year when outside help was necessary for the translation of the sumach and briar patches of our Wilderness into arable land. A gardener is only helpful for the preliminary work of spading, after that his very presence is a profanation.

Garden making is creative work, just as much as painting or writing a poem. It is a personal expression of self, an individual conception of beauty. I should as soon think of asking a secretary to write my book, or the cook to assist in a water color painting, as to permit a gardener to plant or dig among my flowers.

[*Let's Make a Flower Garden* (1912)]

Grace Tabor

The Garden's Place in Civilization

There is no ancient gentlemen but gardeners.
—Hamlet

Recognizing the natural—and proper—tendency of those who practice any art to regard that art as peculiarly important, and as a
consequence to exalt its service to the human race until it alone
seems responsible for human progress, I am nevertheless obliged
to assert that here is the one art without which the aforesaid race
could never have emerged at all from primitive conditions! Moreover, it is also true that without it—I am speaking to the broadest
concept of it—mankind would speedily lose everything held dear,
and would slip back into a condition very much more difficult and
more dangerous to survival, as well as very much less worthy, than
that occupied prior to the more or less well-known dawn of civilization.

For what, after all, was that dawn? Where did it break? And
what were the first faint streaks in the sky? That man's first differ-
entiation from the animal came with the fashioning of tools is sufficiently apparent not to be open to argument, of course; but neither
this nor his subsequent rude architecture, nor even the discovery
and use of fire can be said to have carried him very far forward on
the long road he has traveled, since savages to-day employ as much.
No, it was none of these.

It was with the first deliberate planting of a seed and cultivation
of a plant that the darkness of the racial night began really to lift.

[*36*]

And it is to the degree of his loyalty to this first great science-art that man is a success or failure in the world to-day!

Perhaps this seems the usual exaggeration of the devotee; but need I do more than point out the complete dependence of all creation upon a reliable and regular food supply, to prove my case? We have had too recent example of world food shortage to forget altogether how real a menace to every human being individually such shortage may become within an alarmingly short space of time, once production is abandoned. Wherefore we have writ large before us so that he who runs may read, the great and universal obligation of stewardship, wherein each one of us shares, to promote and foster this art in all its branches.

The strongest of all instincts presumably is the instinct of self-preservation—which is the reason that the instinct to grow things lies so deep in the human heart; for the latter is actually merely an extension of the former. Some will say that they lack it altogether, I know; and I grant at once that they seem to. But of these—and to them—let me add that it has never been my experience to find anyone lacking it wholly, once they are given a chance to know what a garden really can be, and can do for them and to them as well as to the world in which they live and have their being. It is the pressure of other things that makes them impatient of Nature's slow processes, or total unfamiliarity with the work, or misconception generally that accounts for indifference. Interest never resists the appeal of the miracles of everyday in the garden, when this has an opportunity to assert itself.

The stewardship of which I have spoken demands that it be given this opportunity; and the active exercise of stewardship begins with the establishment of every home, whether it is large or small. This is the truth that we ought everyone to realize and be governed by.

Yet it is not enough that we act upon an instinct of self-preservation alone, since this would induce each household to be merely food producers—which is neither practicable nor desirable at this late day. The analogy holds, here as elsewhere, between gardening and architecture; since we go a great deal farther now than to provide ourselves just with shelter—the bare necessity—in our exercise of the art of building, so we have arrived at a time when the finer aspects of the art of gardening must prevail. Our one great difficulty in this connection, however, is our tendency to disregard the early, real purpose of it and to devote ourselves to the finer aspects altogether; which is as if we built our houses without roofs because roofs are less interesting and decorative and generally appealing than side walls and doors and fenestration.

The suggestion made by Bacon in his essay on gardens has been quoted so often and universally that I long since foreswore its literal transcription, yet it sums up so much of all that there is to say introductory to the subject that it is almost impossible to do without it! He was so wholly right, and it is so true that, of the twin arts of building and gardening, the latter represents—and requires—the greater perfection. But we have been building stately for long enough now to begin to garden finely; and we are moreover as a nation coming to that self-consciousness which inspires real effort in the arts, in the desire to express itself. Hence we are ready to produce something worthy in gardens—and when I say worthy I mean just that, in every sense and all senses of the word. We are ready not only to assume the obligations of our stewardship of such land as we acquire, but we are ready to spare no pains to embellish and make beautiful as well as to make productive. We are ready at last to justify possession of our bit of earth, inasmuch as we are ready to make the most of it in the fullest sense.

Distinct from its aspect as a civilizing factor, therefore, is the garden's aspect as an evidence of the progress of civilization. It established it in the first place; and now it is the measure by which it may be gauged. Crude people garden crudely—this is as true of individuals as it is of races—while people of high culture and highly evolved discrimination and sense of harmony, garden finely. By their gardens indeed shall we know them; for a garden is surely the fruit of its creator's mind and will reveal the inner man as nothing else he can make. Which is another striking thing about them—they will not deceive nor give out a false impression. Hence if it is desired to produce a certain impression through the home and its gardens, it is necessary to start in the very heart of things and become what that impression signifies. In no other way will it be possible to convince; we must be, in other words, what we want our garden to make us seem.

Happily this works both ways; for the garden itself is the best means of becoming genuine—of getting right oneself. Just why this is so does not always appear on the surface of things—but I suspect it is because everything dealt with in the garden is so genuine, and because it is in itself such an elemental occupation. There is virtue in earth contact and there is inspiration in the observation of plant unfoldment, whether we are mystical, empirical, or rationalistic in our temperament—whether we believe it or not, in short. And what is more, it *works*, whether we believe it or not. So we have only to give it the chance; the rest will come.

In its application to the individual and the individual garden all that I have just said resolves itself into one sound maxim for a starting point, namely:—the garden is at once the opportunity and the achievement, the cause and the result. If this is understood nothing more need be said in urgence of its claims; the rest will come along in due season and order.

[*Come into the Garden* (1921)]

Linda Yang
Blueberries on a Mid-City Terrace

Blueberries the size of *marbles* growing in mid-Manhattan? On a *terrace* on the 19th floor? Tell any farmer and he'd probably laugh right out loud. But it's true and I should know, because I grow them. And actually, if you think about it, highbush blueberries are really ideal shrubs for "gardens" like mine—a terrace on a high-rise apartment building.

First of all, they will grow in areas of limited sunlight; mine receive only about 5 hours or so a day. This is a major advantage since, in the city, large buildings loom overhead, frequently blocking the sun for part of the day. They prefer acid soil; another situation well-suited to town, since the pollution "fallout" eventually turns the soil acid anyway (certainly in this part of the country). The periodic pruning required to keep them at peak production level is also useful for keeping them reasonably short and thus content with minimal growing space.

In addition to being an edible (thus "useful") plant, blueberries add much to the terrace garden as ornamentals. In late spring and early summer, cascades of graceful, white, lily-of-the-valley-type flowers appear. From these flowers, as if by magic, come the silvery-gray berries which ripen to a purple-blue. (The "magic" is obvious to those who take time to watch . . . yes, bees are at work, right in the middle of this concrete jungle.)

Then comes autumn and the leaves turn shimmering tones of crimson and orange. With the onset of dormancy and winter, snow accentuates the jagged branch forms, which are now punctuated with bud hints of next year's flowers and fruit. This is just a reminder to "one who is city-pent" that ever-changing nature does exist, after all.

But what about the cultivation of these ornamental-edibles? Two plants at least must be grown to insure pollination. And since I can't rely on any fellow "gardeners" nearby, I grow two myself. One an early-season producing strain, the other a late. A large half-barrel, roughly 24 inches in diameter and height, is all the room I can give them to grow in, but fortunately their root growth is not so rapid that they mind. This tub size is also sufficient to insure winter survival in this zone.

I started with well-established balled-and-burlapped stock which was at least three years old. To prepare the barrel for the plants, I made several holes in the bottom for drainage, and then covered them with two inches or so of rocks and gravel. The soil I mixed then was a friable, rich combination of top soil, compost, peat moss and perlite.

Each fall, I restore the nutrients by cultivating lightly with dehydrated cow manure, bone meal and more compost, when I can get it. (As with nearly all materials, I am at the mercy of my nurseryman as my only source of supply.) As the cold weather intensifies, I add several layers of holiday evergreen boughs to the tub. When the spring comes, these boughs, which provide winter cheer throughout the garden, are removed, but the needles they've dropped are worked into the soil. At this time, I cultivate again, now adding ground phosphate rock to further insure good flower and fruit production.

In addition to the winter covering of evergreens, I maintain a year-round mulch of medium-size bark chips. These are attractive as well as most practical for terrace gardens, since they are not so light that they are blown off the tubs. They aid greatly in conserving moisture, thereby helping solve one problem which is probably worse for "upstairs gardeners" than for those with plants *in* the ground. The bark chips also keep the weeds minimal . . . and we *do* have weeds, suburban opinions to the contrary notwithstanding.

The bark chips are practical, too, since they can easily be moved aside for the bi-yearly soil cultivation, which is imperative. Although organic, their rate of decay is so slow that I tend not to expect it. However, should they be accidentally worked into the soil, at least I know they will *eventually* disintegrate.

In the summer, the plants must be watered nearly every day. And periodically, I treat them to a fertilizing of fish emulsion mixed into the water. I find that the odor of this, as with the cow manure, is an intoxicating and joyful experience, not generally understood or appreciated by my fellow apartment residents. I greatly treasure the nostalgic thoughts of the countryside they produce . . . rarely being sure if it's real or imagined. (I have, after all, lived in cities all my life!)

Since it is necessary periodically to test for the 4.5 to 5 pH soil condition that blueberries require, I have made use of various soil testing methods. However, a few years ago, I decided to attempt a *continual* monitoring by growing a small, flowering hydrangea in the same tub. Hydrangeas respond to acid soil by producing *blue* flowers. If the soil becomes alkaline, the flowers turn pink. Now, by simply checking the blossoms on the hydrangea, I know instantly if my soil is acid enough for the blueberry shrubs. Since hydrangeas in this area die back to the soil line each winter, the plant remains small enough so that it does not compete with the blueberries for growing space.

Every second or third year, during the spring cultivation session, I make a point of digging *very* deeply into the tub in order to sever and remove several bunches of roots from the plants. This is a modified form of "root pruning" which, in combination with the yearly branch pruning, is my secret for the long-term survival of *all* the woody plants in containers on my terrace. A fresh mixture of soil and peat moss is then worked into the space where the roots were removed.

At least every other week, during the active growing period, I give both the upper and lower leaf surfaces a forceful hosing with a strong stream of water. This serves to control the buildup of soot or other city pollutants which clog the pores and reduce the availability of sun. But in addition, the hosing keeps unwanted pests to a minimum. With the exception of several bouts with leaf rollers, my blueberries have remained quite free of disease and other problems. As an added precaution, however, I do use a dormant oil spray in late fall or very early spring.

I don't lose too many berries to visiting birds, possibly because they prefer the easy pickings at the feeders I keep well stocked nearby. When they do get greedy, however, I find that several long strips of flexible aluminum foil, hung from several branches, keep them away.

I often wonder, as my children bring in *bowls* full of berries, can any country gardener possibly understand a city slicker's ecstasy upon stepping forth from his apartment and picking *fresh* fruit for breakfast?

[*Organic Gardening* (1975)]

Robert Finch
Going to Seed

There is something to be said for letting a garden go to seed. In fact, I have never quite understood such figures of speech as "gone to seed" and "looking seedy." Metaphorically, they are used to imply stagnation and decay, but in nature seediness is a condition of ripeness and fruition. Where, after all, would we be if nothing went to seed?

On this late September afternoon my garden whirls and bursts with seed. All through the summer the pole bean vines rose and swung in light breezes like a green harp on the nylon webbing strung over their wooden frames. I picked and picked the pods, ripe notes off a staff, until, as Frost with his apple-picking, "I was overtired / Of the great harvest I myself desired." Now the long, wrinkled, paper-pale, knobby pods yield hundreds of smooth, shiny, dimpled, coffee-brown beans, more than enough for next year's planting. If I were more skilled in letting things alone, I would probably not even have to plant next spring.

The broccoli, too, has gone to seed, or at least to blossom. The secondary shoots, left uncut, have sent up spindly, curved nosegays of small, lovely, four-petaled yellow flowers visited now by black-and-yellow bumblebees with bright orange pollen sacs strapped like saddlebags to their rear legs. Examining the flowers I find that they are arranged around each curving stalk in a climbing rotation, one every 144 degrees, so that the pattern is repeated every fifth blossom, or two rotations around the stem—an unexpected detail of perfection and order I should never have noticed if I had cut them as edible bud-clusters. How many other plants do we eat before they blossom?

The garden has managed to reach this unaccustomed state of seedfulness because for the last month I have not found much time for it. Had I done so it might by now have been composted, limed, rototilled and planted with winter rye in the prescribed manner, and I would never have known its rich autumn face.

Instead, lying in neglect, it has taken on a character of its own, separate from me, shaped upon the framework I gave it in the spring, but infused and animated now by another force. To a certain extent we raise a garden as we might a child, putting in the seed, nourishing it and gathering nourishment from it, pruning and weeding its growth, protecting it, loving it, worrying over it. But at some point we must let it go, and now I take a bittersweet pleasure in seeing some of my lineaments in it as it takes its own way.

There are more than beans and broccoli going to seed here. In one unmulched corner of the garden some tall, spike-leaved field thistles have invaded the perimeter. Their slender, five-foot stalks bear candelabra of white, hairy seed-tufts, milkweed-like seeds that drift across the garden like a dry snowfall, and rise up through the pitch pine branches toward white clouds and blue sky with that breath of adventure of all seasonal migrants in them.

Goldfinches visit the garden daily for these seeds, mostly the dull, yellow-green females, perhaps still feeding their late broods. They alight on the main stalks, then walk out on the side stems, curving and bending them down like boys on birches until they reach the seed-tufts. There they work at them industriously if inefficiently, shaking them loose in scattered, fugitive bursts, sending ten aloft for every one they take, dispersing the seeds even as they harvest them. Once I saw a female, finishing up a tuft, take off after the last escaping seed-ball. After a few yards' chase she snatched it on the wing like a nighthawk taking a moth.

Finches feeding on garden thistles are, I suppose, a common enough sight this time of year, but it underscored the matrix of functions that each organism, plant and animal, performs in nature. Who can say what the *main* function of any form of life is, what it is good for, or meant for, beyond perpetuating itself? We should not blame ourselves for using the earth's resources. That is not only human nature, but the nature of all things. We have no monopoly on exploitation; all life is opportunist. We ourselves, our bodies, our homes, our crops, waste and pollution are all exploited by innumerable other organisms. The error is in assuming that *our* use of any one life-form is (in the language of property-tax laws) "the highest and best use," and justifies the usurpation of all others. In the face of nature's own manifest multiple-use policy, such an attitude is not only dangerous but constitutes a self-defeating presumptuousness. Only through expensive, inefficient systems and carefully blindered outlooks can we manage to believe that anything grows in an exclusively human shape. Nature puts democracy to the acid test, which is perhaps one reason why Americans have for so long remained insensitive to its basic principles.

Too often, in such fevers of exclusiveness, even a garden can become a source of, rather than a refuge from, haste and anxiety. In the heat of summer I sometimes find myself rushing overheatedly from row to row, looking for signs of invasion from the surrounding woods and fields that suddenly take on the aspect of a storehouse of infinite evils.

But now in September the garden has cooled, and with it my possessiveness. The sun warms my back instead of beating on my head. No longer blindingly bright, it throws things before me into sharp relief and deepening color. The harvest has dwindled, and I have grown apart from the intense midsummer relationship that brought it on. Except for a small row of fall lettuce put in in late August, I have no vested interests now and can take what falls as manna rather than hard-earned bread.

There is a pleasure, a late-season wine, in returning here after an absence more as an observer and discoverer than a would-be master. The great August flood of foliage has subsided, and I walk through the rows finding unexpected delights and surprises: here an overlooked onion, there a delicate flowering weed, and even a volunteer cantaloupe that sprouted from a compost seed, now reaching rough-skinned fruition in the potato patch. The pairs of white cabbage butterflies still continue their pirouetting duets among the broccoli, but I am no longer compelled to join their dance, pinching their voracious green larvae off the growing plants each day. I can again take simple aesthetic pleasure in watching them, a pleasure deepened by a once and future attachment I have acquired with them.

Robert Finch

I grow old, I grow old, the garden says. It is nearly October. The bean leaves grow paler, now lime, now yellow, now leprous, dissolving before my eyes. The pods curl and do not grow, turn limp and blacken. The potato vines wither and the tubers huddle underground in their rough weatherproof jackets, waiting to be dug. The last tomatoes ripen and split on the vine; it takes days for them to turn fully now, and a few of the green ones are beginning to fall off.

The garden air is full of the sound of crickets, the year's clock made audible, ticking off the days. I have learned that it is the black field crickets that have eaten my tomatoes in late summer, but there is still such a red flood ripening on the window sills that I do not begrudge them what they take now.

I listen to their high tripping trills, short zigzag chirps, and the searing metallic drone of the conehead grasshoppers. They provide a rhythm and a beat for the garden, their song growing slower yet somehow more urgent as the sun slants further southward through the late September skies. They themselves have no hope of surviving the season, yet they raise their communal voices in a contradictory shout, as though to warn others: "We are running down, running down!" Spawned in summer, they are a fall sound, like the dry seed husks scraping together, the empty shells, the expended world of autumn sinking to order—dry, like death.

Yet mixed with the dry cricket song is the rich smell of marigolds which form a flow of colors around the perimeter of the garden— burnt sienna, deep orange, butter gold. The marigolds were planted late this year, but they seem more fitting as autumn flowers, when all things, even sunsets, eschew pastels. The garden is like a fire going out, dying from its center, but burning clear to the last.

It is two o'clock. The great oak to the west begins to cast its shadow across the garden as it did in March when I planted the first snow peas. Now it falls across me like a cool shroud. The warmth has gone out of the air, retreating back across space to the sun itself. Afternoons are starting to disappear once again. It is time to go in.

[*Common Ground* (1981)]

Jay Neugeboren
Reflections on a Family Garden

In 1970 my wife, Betsey, and I bought a house in North Hadley, Massachusetts, a beautiful old colonial house that had been the village's parsonage, serving the Second Congregational Church from 1835 to 1948. The house sat on a small rise—the best sledding hill in our village of about four hundred and fifty—overlooking North Hadley Pond. Beyond the pond is Mount Warner, where, from the window of my office (the room once used by the minister to marry people and to sit with their bodies after death), I could see cows grazing in the meadows, among the apple trees. Behind the house and its attached three-story barn was an acre or so of weeds and overgrown fields, untended for at least a dozen years—goldenrod, blackberries, raspberries, blackeyed Susans, rhubarb, self-seeded maple and butternut and sumac and oak. In the fall of 1971 we began clearing the land, marking and transplanting those plants we wanted to save. We plowed the back acre under, and then spent the ensuing winter planning our arboretum.

When spring came we harrowed, raked, seeded grass, dug holes, and began planting a carefully landscaped garden, one that was to be a memorial to Betsey's parents. We put in 135 different trees and shrubs that first spring; we also laid out 5 perennial gardens, planted hundreds of bulbs and flowers, and, in the northwest corner, alongside the old iron fence that separated our property from the town's ancient graveyard, we put in a small vegetable garden.

Now, a decade later, the arboretum has filled in, and year-round it gives us an endless series of fascinating vistas, changing color, lush textures. It contains about 350 different trees and shrubs, 4 dwarf conifer gardens, and 9 perennial beds. We work at it steadily, and we also use it. From the end of one winter to the beginning of the next, Betsey paints in it—flowers mostly—four or five times a week. And four or five times a week we sit in it after lunch and go over our work together.

During these years—both of us working at home, both of us sharing in chores (cooking, cleaning, splitting wood, canning, sewing)—we also raised three children. Our eldest, Miriam, was eighteen months old when we bought the house. She loved, that first spring, to ride in the wheelbarrow as we transported trees and mulch from one end of the property to the other, and to play hide-and-seek in the holes we'd dug. Our two boys, Aaron and Eli, were born in 1973 and 1974. The three of them now help with the chores and play there. They rake and weed and carry compost, they play dodge ball and kickball and tag, they bury one another under mounds of leaves and war against each other with willow switches. With the years we find that we've come to date moments in their lives and ours from events in the life of the arboretum. We smile, for example, when we recall that it was because Betsey grew dizzy and faint while moving an enormous, root-balled eastern redbud that we first discovered, in the spring of 1972, that she was pregnant with Aaron.

For several years before moving to North Hadley, we lived in a tiny three-room house in Spéracèdes, a French village set in the foothills of the Maritime Alps, about twenty miles inland from Cannes and the Mediterranean. Spéracèdes was about the same size as North Hadley; its landscape, however, was dominated not by maple, spruce, and oak but by olive, cypress, and stone pine, by mimosa, broom, and tamarisk. The years there were good ones for us—we found that we liked being together and working together. Back in the United States, we talked of trying to re-create, somehow, not only the easy yet intense personal life we led there but the very surroundings that had added to our pleasure. Western Massachusetts was not, of course, southern France; still, while clearing the back acre we began to search through nurseries and catalogs for trees and shrubs that, without marring what was unique about the New England landscape, might remind us of our life in Spéracèdes.

Then, on December 26, 1971, Betsey's mother died, leaving a cousin her only living relative. Her father had died in 1964. On our

return to Indiana for her mother's funeral, we visited Betsey's childhood home in Greenwood, a home her father, who grew up on farms
in Illinois and Iowa, had built himself. On a half-acre behind the
Greenwood house, he had, in the early 1950s, planted trees and
shrubs, and Betsey was astonished at how large many of them now
were. Nothing, she said, had given her father more pleasure after
a day's work than to go off to the backyard and tend his trees and
vegetable garden, and it pained her that he had never lived to see
them grow to maturity.

Home in North Hadley, we talked often of the brief hour we
had spent at Betsey's childhood home, and we began planning in
earnest to turn our back acre into a garden that would require (at
least) one lifetime's work and care. It comforted us that winter to
spend endless hours discussing what trees and flowers and shrubs
we wanted to plant. In keeping with the spirit of the Jewish prayer
for the dead—the *kaddish*—which never mentions death, we decided to plant a garden that would reflect our faith in life's continuity.

During that first winter in North Hadley, I came to call Betsey
"the rabbi of trees," for she would sit for eight to ten hours a day
in her upstairs studio, surrounded, like a Talmudic scholar, by gardening encyclopedias and catalogs, going from one to the other,
correcting the books that were wrong or confused. Did any two
catalogs agree on the nature and nomenclature of the dwarf Hinoki
false cypresses? Why was the Japanese black pine (*Pinus thunbergii*)
often confused with the Austrian black pine (*P. nigra*)? She argued
fiercely with those authorities that said we could not grow certain
shrubs or trees in our hardiness zone; and she spent hours visiting
local gardens and nurseries, finding out where the rarer trees and
flowers could be obtained. (We had actually lived in an arboretum,
just before our stay in France—the Planting Fields Arboretum in
Oyster Bay, New York—while I taught at a branch of the state
university.)

That first winter we laid out on paper where our trees and
shrubs and flowers would go. What Betsey wanted, above all, was
visual interest during all seasons: she wanted the vistas to be interesting from any spot within the garden, at any time of year; and
she wanted the larger trees to have room to grow in so that one
could enjoy their unique shapes and colors and textures.

We worked first with what we had. The back acre (plowed under, limed, and fertilized the previous fall) was virtually square, approximately two hundred feet on each side. It was bordered on the south (the left, when one looked down upon it from the back of the house) by a stand of blackberries a hundred and fifty feet long and, in places, twenty feet thick. Along the far western edge of our property the previous owners had planted three weeping willows, which were about twelve feet high. We left those, and we also left, in the southwest corner between the willows and the blackberries, a thicket of sumac that offered a brilliant blaze of color in autumn.

We wanted several wild areas at the borders of our property to separate it from fields where local farmers grew onions, potatoes, asparagus, corn, squash, and pumpkin. We left a miniature forest of self-seeded sumac, oak, catalpa, elm, strawberries, and raspberries at the northwest corner, across from the sumac. Still, the Connecticut River was only a few hundred yards away, and our young trees would need protection from the strong northwest winds that blew in from the river. So we decided to edge the property on the north and west with evergreens, planting about three dozen different trees that would eventually grow close enough to one another to provide a windbreak, at the same time giving us privacy. But although we enjoyed, that first year, looking down a row of lovely specimen trees—Fraser fir, Balsam fir, Colorado blue spruce, weeping white pine, and Lawson false cypress—the visual effect was more pleasing in the mind's eye than it turned out to be on land, where the separate trees looked forlorn and vulnerable. By the second spring we were filling in the spaces with arborvitae, hemlock, pine, spruce, forsythia, and old-fashioned rose, thereby extending the sense of a somewhat wild forest enclosing a more landscaped park.

We left the center of the arboretum fairly open, a mall of grass about fifty by a hundred and twenty feet long, running east and west. This was an entryway to the arboretum from the rear of the house and a place for the children to play. An old, thirty-foot-high 'Baldwin' apple tree stood to the right of the mall, its huge limbs arched out over the grass. Fifty feet south, on the other side of the entranceway, we planted a dwarf-conifer garden of about fifteen specimens and, beyond that, toward the blackberries, a large perennial garden. Walking toward the arboretum from the house, then, on a slight downward-sloping incline, one would see the open green expanse at the center, the 'Baldwin' to the right, and the dwarf conifers and perennials to the left. Even at full growth and bloom, the two gardens would be low enough to allow a view of the trees and shrubs beyond.

On our maps and diagrams we marked, next to each planting, the eventual height and breadth of each tree at maturity. In planning the placement of our 135 trees, we started with the larger specimen trees that, for size and viewing, needed space: a purple weeping beech (*Fagus sylvatica* 'Purpurea Pendula'); a Sargent weeping hemlock (*Tsuga canadensis* 'Pendula'); a dawn redwood (*Metasequoia glyptostroboides*); a weeping white birch; a Japanese maple; a 'Kwanzan' cherry.

The challenge, of course, came in creating a garden that would be interesting year-round: the straight, red branches of the red-stemmed dogwood (*Cornus alba* 'Sibirica') might provide a fine contrast to the bare and drooping branches of the weeping crab apple (*Malus* 'Red Jade') in winter, both silhouetted against snow; but in summer and fall? And if we wanted to have a more or less constant bloom from early spring to late fall, from Korean azalea to witch hazel, then blossoming time had to be taken into account also.

At night Betsey would show me her maps and diagrams, go over the problems she'd encountered, the discoveries. She prepared lists that charted, month by month, the calendar of bloom for trees as well as for perennials, and she prepared other lists on which she noted the color and texture of conifers. For example, the golden-thread sawara false cypress (*Chamaecyparis pisifera* 'Filifera Aurea') was almost iridescent green in spring, yellow green in summer, and bronze gold in winter. She thought of the arboretum as being made up of islands—small groupings of trees, some with softly curving perennial beds between them—and she wanted islands in one part of the arboretum to echo islands in other parts. Thus the circle of dwarf fruit trees near the weeping cherry in the southern section would have a diagonal echo in a somewhat larger and more irregular circle of trees and shrubs on the northern side of the mall: weeping white birch, Mugo pine, redbud, potentilla, spirea 'Anthony Waterer,' among others. Between this grouping and the vegetable garden, the airy, light-green curls of the corkscrew willow (*Salix Matsudana* 'Tortuosa') would contrast richly with the deep-green, fan-shaped twigs of a *Chamaecyparis obtusa* 'Nana Gracilis,' while at the same time leading the eye to the slender, silver gray leaves of a nearby Russian olive (*Elaeagnus angustifolia*). Between the Russian olive and the corkscrew willow were a saucer magnolia (*Magnolia soulangeana*) and a rhododendron 'Nova Zembla,' both with dark, leathery, green leaves. And the rough bark of the Russian olive was somewhat similar in texture to the bark of the nearby 'Baldwin' apple. The relationships, in different seasons—of leaf, color, bark, flower, shape, scent, texture—were infinite, subtle, complex, and each time we made a decision about the placement of one tree, or one grouping, it seemed to raise new questions and problems about areas we thought already settled.

Though the Russian olive bore no fruit (I pruned it to one trunk the third year after we planted it), it looked remarkably like the olive trees we had loved in Spéracèdes, especially when the wind lifted its fuzzy leaves and delicate white flowers and gave them a silvery cast. We were nearly two zones colder than New York City or Greenwood (and much colder, of course, than Spéracèdes); still, we were able to find plants that, like the Russian olive, gave us visual reminders of our previous lives. Though neither broom (*Cytisus praecox*) nor tamarisk (*Tamarix ramosissima*) nor silk tree (*Albizia julibrissin*) were supposed to be hardy in our zone, and though none looked exactly like their French counterparts (the broom blossoms, for example, were peach colored instead of yellow orange), by placing them in protected areas and by shielding them in the winter and early spring with mulches, burlap cages, hay, and leaves, we were able to keep them. The same, though without as much difficulty, with trees we remembered from our childhoods in Brooklyn and Indiana: the double-flowered 'Kwanzan' cherries and Austrian pines I recalled from the Brooklyn Botanic Gardens (I was born two blocks away); and the redbud and gray birch and 'Crimson King' maple that had grown in Greenwood.

If we began by thinking of our garden as somehow naturalizing our past, we also came, with the years, to think of it as being the focal point of our present, as representing the hope for our future. We stocked our garden with plants common to Hadley, to New England: rose-shell azalea, red-stemmed dogwood, mountain laurel, Virginia juniper, Canadian hemlock; with plants that, for the most

part, thrived here; pin oak, lilac, iris, forsythia. In a time when
many of our friends and relatives seemed to be living mobile, transient lives, we decided to cultivate our own garden: to stay in one
place for as long as we could and, quite literally, to set down roots
for ourselves and our children.

That spring, as we began the actual work on the garden—rolling
the land during a misty rain, seeding it, staking it out, digging holes,
planting trees and flowers, traveling to different parts of New England to obtain hard-to-get plants—I would sometimes wonder how
a boy from the streets of Brooklyn, who hardly knew a pine from
an oak and could not tell a linden tree when he saw one (though
he played, most of his childhood, in the courtyards and alleyways
of Linden Boulevard), could be on his hands and knees, planting
and weeding and mulching, making trip after trip across our land
for wheelbarrows of compost and mulch, digging hole after hole,
setting in tree after tree, tearing away burlap from root balls, putting
in topsoil and composted manure and peat moss, pruning back
branches, stamping down soil, watering, mulching . . .

The work was hard that first year, and sometimes less than
rewarding. We had been thinking until then of what the arboretum
would look like at maturity. Like the evergreen border on the north
and west, however, the trees looked astonishingly small and frail
when they were in. Though we bought the largest trees and shrubs
we could, paying premium prices so we could enjoy them that much
sooner, the arboretum sometimes resembled an enormous perennial
garden not yet in bloom, with here and there a stick or flower jutting
up out of the sparse new grass. Indeed, the major chore that year
and for the next few was to keep the young trees weeded and
mulched, so that we could see them and not bump into them or
run them over when mowing.

We discovered that the land—Connecticut Valley river bottom—was especially rich and wet and black in the southwest (near
the willows, which thrived), while diagonally across, in the northeast
corner (near the vegetable garden), it was sandy, acidic, and choked
with witchgrass (against which we are still, inch by inch, battling).
We began to make changes dictated by the soil, by the availability
of trees, and, of course, by how things looked once the plants were
actually in the ground.

Just as I had come late to gardening, so Betsey had come late

to painting. Trained as a librarian, she had never painted a picture
(other than in art period at school) or taken an art course until 1965,
the second year of our marriage. Then, while working at the Brooklyn Public Library as children's librarian, she decided to take her
first art course. And yet, she said one evening while we were walking
in the arboretum, she could recall, as a child, going out into her
backyard by herself many times and sitting on the grass and staring
at a single flower as hard as she could, sometimes for a half-hour or
longer. When she began to paint flowers and to exhibit and sell
them here and in France and in New York, she painted them, for
the most part, singly. In the afternoons, when we talked about our
work, she would describe the flowers she painted—some of them
just peeking their heads above the bottom of the paper, others
seeming to hide in corners, still others set boldly in the center—as
if they were individuals with particular personalities. Why she placed
a flower on the page where she did, and why she chose the particular
configurations she chose—though she could give explanations af-
terwards, having to do with light and weather and time of year, with
the particular quality of a flower on a particular day—was largely
instinctive. She would sometimes stare into a small section of a
perennial bed for an hour or more before she began her work, and
when I once pointed out to her an obvious parallel between the
open spaces she left on her paper and the open spaces of our arboretum, the analogy surprised her as it delighted. For it was the
open spaces—in the paintings and in the garden—that led the eye
to individual shrubs and trees and flowers, that let the eye see the
particularity of a single blossom on a 'Kwanzan' cherry, that let the
eye admire the curious mixture, in an iris, of sensuality and reti-
cence, strength and delicacy.

Through the years, though we came to add items to our arboretum, to make changes—though we came, in fact, to think of
our entire 2½ acres as our arboretum, the back acre its focal point—
the basic plan proved to be a good one, and most of our plantings
thrived. During the first few years, overwhelmed a bit by the work,
by the competing demands of trees and children, flowers and career,
I would resist walking in the arboretum with Betsey in the evening.
It was difficult to enjoy the trees and flowers when I was so aware
of all that I had not yet done—pruning, weeding, transplanting,

mulching, composting, tagging. When I was doing the work myself, I was happy, free. To move down a line of flowers, inch by inch, pulling weeds, and to be able an hour or two later—who could tell how much time had passed?—to look back and see the flowers standing by themselves against the brown soil, gave me feeling of joy different from any I had known.

I had always been impatient, and I was surprised and pleased to find that I could learn to move slowly and steadily, that I could, in my middle years, learn to be patient. If one wanted quick results, one did not create an arboretum. And though, year by year, I became better and better at what seemed more natural for Betsey, it did not occur to me for quite some time that there were analogies between my gardening and my writing. When asked about my writing, I now found myself explaining that having an idea one year that becomes a story three years later, and is published two years after that, is a little like putting in a fruit tree that might not bear for a half-dozen years. And making a novel—working for several years through ten to twelve drafts to give life to something that, in the end, might not even be published—isn't that a bit like planting seeds that, despite all one's labors, might never germinate?

Our garden came into being out of our experience of loss, and that experience was, of course, repeated within the garden itself. The silk tree and the broom lasted for a half-dozen years or so and then succumbed. An Atlas blue cedar, a blue-angel holly, a deodar cedar, a cryptomeria were defeated by weather, disease, insects, animals. Field mice, wintering in mole holes, ate our lily bulbs; a woodchuck ravaged our vegetable garden for two consecutive summers. We made mistakes: the plant food we gave our perennials and new 'Pride of Hadley' tulips leeched into the root system of a magnificent twenty-year-old Japanese spider-leaf maple (*Acer palmatum* 'Dissectum Ornatum') we had planted to honor the publication, in 1974, of a new novel. That, and an excessively hot and early spring followed by a killing frost, made the tree swell and split its bark, and though we kept it alive by pruning, painting, tree-wrap, and burlap cages, it died two years later. Along the cemetery fence behind the vegetable garden I set up what I called my Infirmary; if all our efforts seemed in vain and a plant was near death, I would dig it up, transplant it to the Infirmary, cut it way back, feed it, water it heavily, mulch it well, and pray. Sometimes—as with a star magnolia, a purple-leaf sand cherry, and a *Viburnum carlesii*—I was successful, and a few years later the tree would return to the arboretum.

Although Betsey had begun painting in oils, from the time we put in our arboretum she painted only in watercolors. She sensed that she could better delineate the beauty and impermanence of the life in our garden—the fragility of buds and blossoms, the evanescence in a spray of spring flowers—through the spontaneity and transparency of watercolors. Though she tried from time to time to paint larger configurations of plants that were hardier—the conifers, the beeches, the willows—she was drawn back again and again to those flowers, like the oriental poppies and day lilies that lived and died in a single day, whose very beauty seemed to tell of—to contain—their passing.

It is now ten years since we put in our garden: four hundred trees, several hundred paintings, four books, and three children later. I can finally enjoy walking in the arboretum with Betsey at evening, discussing the trees, petting them, examining them, deciding what, if anything, we need to do for them. The arboretum seems to have filled in with magical speed, and within it we feel protected. We now have gardens within our garden, a climbing rock near the weeping birch, bowers, and stone benches (transported from tumbling old stone walls in the woods) within the bowers, where we sit and talk and rest.

I'm no longer overwhelmed by the work in the garden, because, though there is always work and there are always losses and we are always making changes (we put in a second dwarf-conifer garden as a thirteenth-anniversary present to ourselves, and, since then, two smaller ones, nearer the house), we realize that, as with our children, much of the essential work has already been done.

Is the analogy too exact? We gave the trees what they seemed to need for growth—we fed them and protected them, cared for them when they were ill, and took pleasure in them when they were healthy—and now they are pretty much on their own. Barring the trauma caused by a severe winter, a sudden disease, or an unnaturally warm and early spring, they should live out their lives naturally, with minimum intervention from us. We may not be here to see the purple weeping beech grow to maturity fifty or so years from now, but perhaps our children will, and that seems all right, too. The shape that tree will then have has been largely determined, of course, by its particular nature—by who it is, as it were—but also by the love and care we've lavished upon it, by the direction our pruning has given it, by what we trust has been a nurturing influence.

As with our trees and flowers and shrubs, so with our paintings and books and stories and children. We help create them, and then, if we are lucky, they go on to have lives of their own, lives that, we hope, will be as special and blessed as our own.

[Horticulture (1982)]

Henry Beetle Hough
A *Counsel of Prudence*

Betty Bowie and I were married in 1920 and came to live in Edgartown, Massachusetts, on the island of Martha's Vineyard, where we edited and published the *Vineyard Gazette*, weekly on Fridays. When someone asked, "Do you help your husband?" she was properly furious, for she had marched down Fifth Avenue in the great suffrage parade and was always a creative and independent spirit, as in the matter of the lilies of the valley.

Betty managed our purchase of the old pasture land, a piece of property not far from the town center on one side or from the open country and woods on the other. This would become our house site, but long before we got around to any building, or could even find the money to begin, she remembered the lilies of the valley at her childhood home in Uniontown, Pennsylvania.

She wrote to an aunt in Uniontown asking her to pack up some of the plants and mail them to us. It was springtime and they were in bloom, but we had hope; Betty said the chance of shipping was worth taking, for these lilies of the valley had been in her family a long time, maybe from year one of the initial Bowie settlement. The sentimental importance was greater than the practical.

The lily of the valley plants were travel-worn when they arrived, although they had been packed with the diligence of an inexperienced person, which is often greater than that of the experienced. However, diligence is not always the point, for horticultural things want a certain latitude so that they can shrug and shift around a bit for themselves.

Betty and I comforted the new arrivals as well as we could,

and she set them out under the branches of a native maple tree at the west side of our house site, near the lane. The transported ancestral lilies of the valley were adamant about dying. They wouldn't. They regained their modest vigor and flowered and were wonderful with fragrance whenever the signal of spring came around. They never required any real attention—just as well, for Betty and I were occupied with any number of outdoor projects. During one era I undertook to hybridize two worthy rose plants—any two, but old ones preferably—to produce a new beauty, which I would call the 'Betty Bowie' rose. I still have the camel's-hair brush with which I planned to transfer pollen, but whether pollen was actually transferred I cannot remember. Most of my projects were interrupted, as this one was, but I did have the name for my hybrid, and not all rose hybridizers wind up that far ahead.

Betty died in 1965. The lilies of the valley still bloom in her memory, spreading through the fence toward the lane, under the widening canopy of maple foliage overhead. Our house has been standing so long now that it's ranked as an old house. Trees that I planted nearby, especially two elms, tower over the roof. Yet nothing outranks, in value and my affection (when I happen to think about them), the lilies of the valley on the lane.

Betty used to show them to visitors, and we noticed that their faces always lighted up with surprise and then admiration. With an alertness of discovery. It can be a delight to see such sparkle in the eyes of human beings, male or female, of any age whatever, and to hear the quickly indrawn breath before any words of exclamation.

The reason for all this is that our lilies of the valley are pink, and who ever heard of pink lilies of the valley? Some people have, but most haven't. The existence of these flowers is no guarded secret. We were then, and I am now, aware of not being alone in possessing them, but I think they do not loom large in the collective mind of the gardening community.

Lilies of the valley, *Convallaria majalis*, from the Latin for valley and the Greek for lily: to me the expression "of the valley" is unfailingly sentimental, with a magic to which I yield. This definition somewhat ameliorates the severity of the encyclopedia's definition: "A group of only one species of hardy herbaceous perennial." I found this in our public library in my research, which began with an 1896 volume, *Illustrated Flowers*, by Nathaniel Lord Brittain,

[60]

Ph.D., and Hon. Addison Brown, who recorded as a fact that the lily of the valley is white.

I carried forward my research at the public library and found references to Fortin's Giant Lily of the Valley, large-flowered and white. Later on, I found the brief statement that "Rosea is a form with pink flowers," and the more I looked at this diminishing postlude, the smaller the type appeared.

At another time, glancing through a catalog of what seemed to be a rather obscure nursery, I found the pink form listed. For all I know, "rosea" may be available elsewhere, and my point here is not of any rarity or mystery or simple absentmindedness or condition of not noticing. It is the point that anyone who wanted pink lilies of the valley could have had them without the strain of organizing an expedition to some distant mountain fastness. It would appear that no one has wanted them, so steadily have they dropped from sight.

Betty's pink lilies of the valley came to her by inheritance through many generations (inheritance is one of the best-recognized ways of coming by unwanted things). Sentiment is strong enough, and if the past instead of dying merely hangs far off, phantom-like, such things may acquire a singular value.

In conversation sometimes, Betty would say, "Well, it's a sort of muddy pink." I agreed, with some qualifications. No matter, the faces of our visitors always did light up. And how, I have asked myself at times, do you tell a muddy pink from some other pink? Qualities in nature are not subject to too much challenge.

At times, it has seemed to me that the fragrance of the pink lily of the valley has been superior to that of the white. But was the sunlight ever before as moderating as this? What degree of moisture is in the air?

My own experience with lilies of the valley as such—the always-familiar white—goes far back into my childhood. My mother was the gardener in our family. We lived winters in New Bedford, Massachusetts, and summers my mother, my brother, and I moved to our old house on a modest height in North Tisbury, overlooking a mile-long woodland descent to Vineyard Sound. My father joined us weekends and for his vacation.

In order to minimize the danger of late frosts or to find some advantage, my parents changed the location of the garden fairly often. For a while we planted a wide border along an old stone wall on the south, but this was exposed to northeast winds. Then we tried the experiment of a garden at the foot of a steeply inclining slope, a genuine lowland near an ancient crab-apple tree that bloomed and fruited abundantly; it was also near the moist, ferny margin of a swamp. This place was wonderful except that it was out of view from our house and also subject to early frosts, the earliest and the latest frosts known, it seemed to us.

This is not really a digression, for wherever we had a garden, from year to year, for a greater or shorter time, the lilies of the valley kept right on growing and blooming in spite of our inattention or forgetfulness.

Their generations still survive and increase handsomely, competing with and turning to their own advantage the neighboring, hospitable wild growth. The greatest abundance of lilies of the valley at North Tisbury today is in an area occupied mostly by blueberry bushes, bayberries, blackberry runners, and wild roses, with branches of young oak trees.

Now I come to the matter I have been holding off as long as possible. What should Betty say to these guests of ours, their faces lighting up in delight at having discovered fragrant lilies of the valley that were unexpectedly, superbly, pink, when they asked if they might have just a plant or two to take home for gardens of their own?

As nicely as possible, politely, but with unmistakable finality, Betty said No. She spoke not from a selfish instinct of possessiveness; anyone who cared to do so was free to get pink lilies of the valley somewhere else. It wasn't likely that many people would, though.

Betty understood that long, cherished neglect had provided for the pink lilies of the valley a fragile rarity. Very likely, these flowers were once of a prevalence now forgotten, and being common, they had little worth or distinction.

And here is an errand of this essay, a plea to undiscerning collectors who do not recognize privacy as a right of many flowering plants. I commend a counsel of prudence. Will not, for instance, this surprising shade of pink soon become nondescript or muddy if it is established in a nicely ordered garden?

I am rather against collectors who tend to quantify. They are likely to throw away too much after the first day or the first week.

In terms of loveliness and fragrance the white lily of the valley needs no accessory, and in choice gardens here and there can find no existing rival. White is indeed what lily of the valley should be—except where chance or antiquity has intervened. I think of those white carpets of blossoms on a cold spring morning in North Tisbury, the rim of golden sunlight just breaking across Norton's Hill, and I wouldn't want a strain of pink annoying the purity and compatibility of earliness, low temperature, and delicate scent of the spectacle slowly revealed under the bayberry bushes and low-branched oaks.

In abundance, pink lilies of the valley would lose a moral superiority, their one advantage to connoisseurs, and value in the marketplace. We shield them not as DeBeers limits an oversupply of diamonds but in such modesty as we can, to which the very modest rank they hold, and truth itself, entitles them.

[*Horticulture* (1985)]

Lynden B. Miller
Perennials in Urban Areas

Like people everywhere, and perhaps more than most, city dwellers want and need gardens and growing things. New Yorkers are no exception. Naturally there have always been the usual geraniums, impatiens, and begonias in municipal plantings, but these days perennials are the hottest thing in town; even the Mayor of New York has a brand-new perennial border at Gracie Mansion.

You can find perennials everywhere: in back-yard gardens, on rooftops and penthouses high above the ground, in volunteer-run community gardens, on Fifth Avenue, and inside huge office buildings. The largest permanent public display of perennials is in large herbaceous borders in a formal garden in Central Park. There is a wide range of sites where perennials are to be found in New York, and their appearance and popularity underscore the fact that they have a special significance for people who live in a noisy, crowded city. Not only are they interesting and attractive to look at but, if properly chosen and well cared for, they can symbolize permanence and renewal in an otherwise often chaotic atmosphere.

One of the most moving examples of city dwellers' need and determination to have gardens is in the community gardens springing up all over New York City. Community gardens are volunteer-run oases created on empty sites leased from the city or a developer for an unknown period of time. City gardeners must be a determined group. In order to make a community garden out of a vacant or abandoned lot, they must tackle bureaucracy, red tape, rubble, and garbage before beginning to plant. There are over four hundred community gardens in New York City involving eleven thousand people assisted by nine public and private agencies which supply soil, seeds, and know-how.

Community gardeners, who are often totally inexperienced at first, start out, as so many have before them, with vegetables, then annuals, and finally more and more of them have been turning to perennials. Hope Community Garden, for instance, is located in East Harlem, a poor neighborhood of mostly blacks and Hispanics. With the help of a city agency called Green Thumb, neighbors created a tiny oasis between tenement buildings. First came a fence; then an artist painted a mural of trees, flowers, and tiny skyscrapers on the wall, and even gouged out a waterfall, which is operated by a hose coming out of a window. Water cascades down the wall into a concrete-edged stream surrounded by irises, peonies, roses, day-lilies, *Heuchera*, and *Lythrum*.

On the west side of Manhattan is a very large community garden which combines vegetable plots in one area with flower gardens in another, each tended by a different gardener. On a summer day there are many annuals that provide color against the surrounding apartment buildings, but the move is now toward perennials. The impetus for this came from one accomplished gardener, who created a rockery out of construction rubble and quietly proceeded to grow over one hundred different kinds of perennials and alpines. At first her fellow gardeners, many of them totally inexperienced with plants, simply couldn't understand how she could grow things that didn't blaze with color all summer, but slowly they have become converted and are now enthusiastically exchanging plants and reaping the great satisfaction of having beloved plants return each year in spite of their battles with not only the elements but dogs, children, trash, and other vicissitudes of life in the city.

As is always possible with these gardens, a developer recently bought the land from the city and began to bulldoze the carefully tended plots. Community pressure was such that he finally agreed to leave one-third of the space for a future garden and provide funds for rebuilding it. He apparently finally realized that this lovely space and its caretakers would enhance his property values.

Along the Hudson River in what was once an unused strip of compacted soil in a run-down park is Riverside Community Garden. A group of forty seasoned community gardeners, displaced by a developer from another site, formed a group called the Garden

People and persuaded a reluctant and skeptical Parks Department to let them grow flowers. Oriental poppies, astilbes, iris, peonies, clematis, artemesias, foxgloves, and coreopsis are now flourishing, to everyone's delight. Asked for a list of plants, they found to their pride and amazement that they were growing almost 150 different kinds of perennials in the many separately run plots within the garden.

Gardening in a big city is not easy. Signs in Spanish and English ask people not to pick or take the flowers, and designs must be worked around the gratings of underground railroad tunnels. Despite all this, the gardens are ravishing and gardeners persevere. Most people are thrilled by the display, and even the city's Parks Department was inspired to hire a gardener to bring the surrounding park back to life.

Rockefeller Center is one of the major tourist attractions in New York and has changing displays in its Channel Gardens located just off Fifth Avenue. Where once red salvia was the rule, last fall thousands of ornamental grasses were the attraction, and one spring eight hundred lovely perennials bloomed there for three weeks. Designed by Professor Richard Iversen from Farmingdale University, who is researching the forcing of perennial plants, the series of pools were lined with aruncus, campanulas, geraniums, salvias, verbascum, foxgloves, and artemesias, all ordered and grown a year in advance. After the exhibit, the plants were given to community gardeners around the city. To find this sensitive and charming display in such a prominent place is evidence of the great surge of interest in perennials.

High above the ground at Rockefeller Center are four large roof gardens. Designed in the 1930s to be looked at from above by office workers who never enter them, these elegant green spaces give rest and relief from the city, and when they were recently restored, thousands of daylilies and *Sedum* 'Autumn Joy' were added. Another rooftop surprise was a meadow in the sky of wildflowers seeded with iris and grasses one hundred feet off the ground. Inside the IBM headquarters at the commercial center of the city under a glass roof covering forty-foot bamboo trees are large planters, which often contain lavish displays of such perennials as delphiniums, platycodon, astilbes, achilleas, etc. Quite a sight to see as the traffic surges along outside. Even on Fifth Avenue, instead of the usual taxus and azaleas, luxury apartment buildings are commissioning plantings that include carefully chosen perennials that can withstand severe winds, extreme cold and heat, and not be too time-consuming, such as Siberian iris, *Lythrum* 'Morden's Pink,' and daylilies.

The most lavish display of perennials in Manhattan is in New York's largest garden: Central Park. A six-acre formal space within the park called the Conservatory Garden is located at 105th Street and Fifth Avenue, on the edge of East Harlem. Designed in the 1930s to evoke the great estate gardens of the wealthy living outside the city, it was originally tended by fourteen gardeners and much visited. But it fell on bad times during New York's fiscal crisis and was virtually forgotten by the rest of the city. Its restoration began in 1982 with funds donated by the Rockefeller Center, and since that time over $200,000 more has been raised by the Central Park Conservancy, a nonprofit organization, to prune lovely old trees and shrubs, replace lawns, fix fountains, redesign the perennial section of the Garden, and, most importantly, to hire a full-time horticulturist to tend the large herbaceous borders.

New Yorkers are now flocking to the thousands of perennials displayed in seemingly casual abandon. Large drifts of plants are arranged both to give interest and to bloom from late March to November, and also to form pleasing compositions of form and foliage even when not in flower. Another aim of the design, which was originally intended to evoke English gardens such as Sissinghurst and Hidcote, was to introduce city dwellers to the many delights of perennials with which they might not be familiar by growing thalictrums, Japanese anemones, perennial geraniums, and many kinds of salvias among almost two hundred different species. Easily recognizable plants, such as peonies, iris, and phlox, are interspersed with those chosen just for their lovely foliage, such as *Syllabum marianum* or the blue Lyme grass, *Elymus arenarius*, hostas, and the variegated Solomon's seal. Many gray-leaved plants were used—artemesias, santolinas, *Salvia argentea, Perovskia*—to give atmosphere and spill out of the beds onto the paths, their silver color making all the greens in the garden more vivid. The end result is a peculiarly American garden of plants, now in its fourth season, doing well in this situation so close to the city streets and greatly loved and appreciated by its visitors.

When it was first suggested that herbaceous borders be put into the park near East Harlem, almost everyone prophesied that no one would appreciate them, that all would be taken or destroyed. And of course they were wrong. When I first started working there in 1982, the Garden was listed as one of the two places most avoided in Central Park. In the past there had been annuals and bulb displays there, but it was really the perennials and the presence of the gardener who brought the people back from all over the city to this lovely place. People return again and again to this elegant oasis, exclaiming as they do, "How marvelous! It looks quite different from when I was here last!" We work hard with our visitors to increase their appreciation of the plants and the work that goes into their care. Trained volunteers who also work on the borders take people on popular tours of the garden, and we work closely with school groups, patients from nearby hospitals, and citizens' groups. We feel that the more people understand about the special nature of the plants, the more they will respect and care for them. We do lose a certain number of plants, especially in the spring, and we have found that *Sedum* 'Autumn Joy' and *Ruta graveolens* are much sought after and are almost impossible to keep in the Garden. This is part of gardening in a big city. Less easy to take is the stealing of special rare plants, such as *Crambe cordifolia*, by horticulturists. However, heartbreaking as it is for those of us who tend them, it is also perhaps evidence of the great interest and demand for perennials. In the end, the loss is so minuscule in terms of the whole garden that one simply has to persevere.

There seems to be considerable support for the theory that plants are good for people, and I see this every day in my work in Central Park. Even those most unsophisticated about plants, and who will never know a *Thalictrum* from a *Lamiastrum*, seem to respond to the patterns and rhythms of a garden. Graffiti have virtually disappeared, trash ends up in trash cans. Even teenagers full of untapped energy have learned to come into the Garden and actually sit down.

In a speech to the American Horticultural Society in 1985, Charles Lewis said, "Plants take away some of the anxiety and tension of the immediate NOW by showing us that there are enduring patterns in life." In the Conservatory Garden visitors return to greet old friends in the borders and exclaim over new ones blooming since their last visit. People seem to take strength and pride in the Garden's very existence, and it is the perennials particularly that have given an important message to those who live in a busy city: one of beauty, hope, and renewal.

[Perennial Plant Association Symposium (1986)]

COLOR

Celia Thaxter
The Poppies of
the Isle of Appledore

Eschscholtzia—it is an ugly name for a most lovely flower. California
Poppy is much better. Down into the sweet plot I go and gather a
few of these, bringing them to my little table and sitting down before
them the better to admire and adore their beauty. In the slender
green glass in which I put them they stand clothed in their delicate
splendor. One blossom I take in a loving hand the more closely to
examine it, and it breathes a glory of color into sense and spirit
which is enough to kindle the dullest imagination. The stems and
fine thread-like leaves are smooth and cool gray-green, as if to temper the fire of the blossoms, which are smooth also, unlike almost
all other Poppies, that are crumpled past endurance in their close
green buds, and make one feel as if they could not wait to break
out of the calyx and loosen their petals to the sun, to be soothed
into even tranquillity of beauty by the touches of the air. Every
cool gray-green leaf is tipped with a tiny line of red, every flower-
bud wears a little pale-green pointed cap like an elf, and in the early
morning, when the bud is ready to blow, it pushes off the pretty
cap and unfolds all its loveliness to the sun. Nothing could be more
picturesque than this fairy cap, and nothing more charming than to
watch the blossom push it off and spread its yellow petals, slowly
rounding to the perfect cup. As I hold the flower in my hand and
think of trying to describe it, I realize how poor a creature I am,
how impotent are words in the presence of such perfection. It is
held upright upon a straight and polished stem, its petals curving
upward and outward into the cup of light, pure gold with a lustrous

satin sheen; a rich orange is painted on the gold, drawn in infinitely fine lines to a point in the centre of the edge of each petal, so that the effect is that of a diamond of flame in a cup of gold. It is not enough that the powdery anthers are orange bordered with gold; they are whirled about the very heart of the flower like a revolving Catherine-wheel of fire. In the centre of the anthers is a shining point of warm sea-green, a last, consummate touch which makes the beauty of the blossom supreme. Another has the orange suffused through the gold evenly, almost to the outer edges of the petals, which are left in bright, light yellow with a dazzling effect. Turning the flower and looking at it from the outside, it has no calyx, but the petals spring from a simple pale-green disk, which must needs be edged with sea-shell pink for the glory of God! [. . .]

I think for wondrous variety, for certain picturesque qualities, for color and form and a subtle mystery of character, Poppies seem, on the whole, the most satisfactory flowers among the annuals. There is absolutely no limit to their variety of color. They are the tenderest lilac, the deepest crimson, richest scarlet, white with softest suffusion of rose; all shades of rose, clear light pink with sea-green centre, the anthers in a golden halo about it; black and fire-color; red that is deepened to black, with gray reflections; cherry-color, with a cross of creamy white at the bottom of the cup, and round its central altar of ineffable golden green again the halo of yellow anthers; purple, with rich splashes of a deeper shade of the same color, with grayish white rays about the centre; all shades of lavender and lilac; exquisite smoke-color, in some cases delicately touched and freaked with red; some pure light gray, some of these gray ones edged with crimson or scarlet; there are all tints of mauve. To tell all the combinations of their wonderful hues, or even half, would be quite impossible, from the simple transparent scarlet bell of the wild Poppy to the marvelous pure white, the wonder of which no tongue can tell. Oh, these white Poppies, some with petals more delicate than the finest tissue paper, with centres of bright gold, some of thicker quality, large, shell-like petals, almost ribbed in their effect, their green knob in the middle like a boss upon a shield, rayed about with beautiful grayish yellow stamens, as in the kind called the Bride. Others—they call this kind the Snowdrift—have thick double flowers, deeply cut and fringed at the edges, the most opaque white, and full of exquisite shadows. Then there are the

Icelanders, which Lieutenant Peary found making gay the frosty fields of Greenland, in buttercup-yellow and orange and white; the great Orientals, gorgeous beyond expression; the immense single white California variety. I could not begin to name them all in the longest summer's day! The Thorn Poppy, Argemone, is a fascinating variety, most quaint in method of growth and most decorative. As for the Shirleys, they are children of the dawn, and inherit all its delicate, vivid, delicious suffusions of rose-color in every conceivable shade. Of the Poppy one of the great masters of English prose discourses in this wise. Speaking of the common wild Poppy of the English fields, which grows broadcast also over most of Europe, he says: "The splendor of it is proud, almost insolently so," which immediately brings to mind Browning's lines in "Sordello,"—

> *The Poppy's red effrontery,*
> *Till autumn spoils its fleering quite with rain,*
> *And portionless, a dry, brown, rattling crane*
> *Protrudes.*

Papaver Rhœas is the common wild scarlet Poppy that both these writers describe. John Ruskin says: "I have in my hand a small red Poppy which I gathered on Whit Sunday in the palace of the Cæsars. It is an intensely simple, intensely floral flower. All silk and flame, a scarlet cup, perfect edged all round, seen among the wild grass far away like a burning coal fallen from Heaven's altars. You cannot have a more complete, a more stainless type of flower absolute; inside and outside, all flower. No sparing of color anywhere, no outside coarsenesses, no interior secrecies, open as the sunshine that creates it; fine finished on both sides, down to the extremest point of insertion on its narrow stalk, and robed in the purple of the Cæsars." [. . .]

I know of no flower that has so many charming tricks and manners, none with a method of growth more picturesque and fascinating. The stalks often take a curve, a twist from some current of air or some impediment, and the fine stems will turn and bend in all sorts of graceful ways, but the bud is always held erect when the time comes for it to blossom. Ruskin quotes Lindley's definition of what constitutes a Poppy, which he thinks "might stand." This is it: "A Poppy is a flower which has either four or six petals, and two or more treasuries united in one, containing a milky, stupefying fluid in its stalks and leaves, and always throwing away its calyx when it blossoms."

I muse over their seed-pods, those supremely graceful urns that are wrought with such mathless elegance of shape, and think what strange power they hold within. Sleep is there, and Death his brother, imprisoned in those mystic sealed cups. There is a hint of their mystery in their shape of sombre beauty, but never a suggestion in the fluttering blossom; it is the gayest flower that blows. In the more delicate varieties the stalks are so slender, yet so strong, like fine grass stems, when you examine them you wonder how they hold even the light weight of the flower so firmly and proudly erect. They are clothed with the finest of fine hairs up and down the stalks, and over the green calyx, especially in the Iceland varieties, where these hairs are of a lovely red-brown color and add much to their beauty.

It is plain to see, as one gazes over the Poppy beds on some sweet evening at sunset, what buds will bloom in the joy of next morning's first sunbeams, for these will be lifting themselves heavenward, slowly and silently, but surely. To stand by the beds at sunrise and see the flowers awake is a heavenly delight. As the first long, low rays of the sun strike the buds, you know they feel the signal! A light air stirs among them; you lift your eyes, perhaps to look at a rosy cloud or follow the flight of a caroling bird, and when you look back again, lo! the calyx has fallen from the largest bud and lies on the ground, two half transparent, light green shells, leaving the flower petals wrinkled in a thousand folds, just released from their close pressure. A moment more and they are unclosing before your eyes. They flutter out on the gentle breeze like silken banners to the sun, and such a color! The orange of the Iceland Poppy is the most ineffable color; it "warms the wind" indeed! I know no tint like it; it is orange dashed with carmine, most like the reddest coals of an intensely burning fire. Look at this exquisite cup: the wind has blown nearly smooth the crinkled petals; these, where they meet in the centre, melt into a delicate greenish yellow. In the heart of the blossom rises a round green altar, its sides penciled with nine black lines, and a nine-rayed star of yellow velvet clasps the flat, pure green top. From the base of this altar springs the wreath of stamens and anthers; the inner circle of these is generally white, the outer yellow, and all held high and clear within the cup. The radiant effect of this arrangement against the living red cannot be told.

The Californias put out their clean, polished, pointed buds straight up to the sun from the first, but all the others have this fashion of drooping theirs till the evening before they blow. There is a kind of triumph in the way they do this, lifting their treasured splendor yet safe within its clasping calyx to be ready to meet the first beams of the day.

The Orientals are glorious, even in the victorious family of Poppies. Ruskin has a chapter on "The Rending of Leaves." I always think of it when I see the large, hairy, rich green leaves of this variety, which are deeply "rent," almost the whole width of the leaf to the midrib. These leaves grow somewhat after the fashion of a Dandelion, spreading several feet in all directions from the centre, which sends up in June immense flower-stalks crowned with heavy apple-like buds, that elongate as they increase in size, till some morning the thick calyx breaks and falls, and the great scarlet flags of the flower unfold. There is a kind of angry brilliance about it, a sombre and startling magnificence. Its large petals are splashed near the base with broad, irregular spots of black-purple, as if they had been struck with a brush full of color. The seed-pod, rising fully an inch high in the centre, is of a luminous, indescribable shade of green, and folded over its top, a third of its height, is a cap of rich lavender, laid down in points evenly about the crown. On the centre of this is a little knob of deep purple velvet, from which eleven rays of the same color curve over the top and into each point of the lavender cap. And round this wonderful seed-pod, with its wealth of elaborate ornament, is a thick girdle of stamens half an inch deep, with row upon row and circle within circle of anthers covered with dust of splendid dusky purple, and held each upon a slender thread of deeper purple still. It is simply superb, and when the great bush is ablaze with these flowers it is indeed a conflagration of color. "The fire-engines always turn out when my Orientals blaze up on the hillside," writes a flower-loving friend to me. No garden should be without these, for they flourish with the least care, are perfectly hardy, and never fail to blossom generously.

[An Island Garden (1894)]

Alice Morse Earle
The Blue Flower Border

Blue thou art, intensely blue!
Flower! whence came thy dazzling hue?
When I opened first mine eye,
Upward glancing to the sky,
Straightway from the firmament
Was the sapphire brilliance sent.

—JAMES MONTGOMERY

Questions of color relations in a garden are most opinion-making and controversy-provoking. Shall we plant by chance, or by a flower-loving instinct for sheltered and suited locations, as was done in all old-time gardens, and with most happy and most unaffected results? or shall we plant severely by colors—all yellow flowers in a border together? all red flowers side by side? all pink flowers near each other? This might be satisfactory in small gardens, but I am uncertain whether any profound gratification or full flower succession would come from such rigid planting in long flower borders.

William Morris warns us that flowers in masses are "mighty strong color," and must be used with caution. A still greater cause for hesitation would be the ugly jarring of juxtaposing tints of the same color. Yellows do little injury to each other; but I cannot believe that a mixed border of red flowers would ever be satisfactory or scarcely endurable; and few persons would care for beds of all white flowers. But when I reach the Blue Border, then I can speak with decision; I know whereof I write, I know the variety and beauty of a garden bed of blue flowers. In blue you may have much difference in tint and quality without losing color effect. The Persian art workers have accomplished the combining of varying blues most wonderfully and successfully: purplish blues next to green-blues, and sapphire-blues alongside; and blues seldom clash in the flower beds.

Blue is my best beloved color; I love it as the bees love it. Every blue flower is mine; and I am as pleased as with a tribute of praise to a friend to learn that scientists have proved that blue flowers represent the most highly developed lines of descent. These learned men believe that all flowers were at first yellow, being perhaps only developed stamens; then some became white, others red; while the purple and blue were the latest and highest forms. The simplest shaped flowers, open to be visited by every insect, are still yellow or white, running into red or pink. Thus the Rose family have simple open symmetrical flowers; and there are no blue Roses—the flower has never risen to the blue stage. In the Pea family the simpler flowers are yellow or red; while the highly evolved members, such as Lupines, Wistaria, Everlasting Pea, are purple or blue, varying to white. Bees are among the highest forms of insect life, and the labiate flowers are adapted to their visits; these nearly all have purple or blue petals—Thyme, Sage, Mint, Marjoram, Basil, Prunella, etc.

Of course the Blue Border runs into tints of pale lilac and purple and is thereby the gainer; but I would remove from it the purple Clematis, Wistaria, and Passion-flower, all of which a friend has planted to cover the wall behind her blue flower bed. Sometimes the line between blue and purple is hard to define. Keats invented a word, *purplue*, which he used for his indeterminate color.

I would not, in my Blue Border, exclude an occasional group of flowers of other colors; I love a border of all colors far too well to do that. Here, as everywhere in my garden, should be white flowers, especially tall white flowers: white Foxgloves, white Delphinium, white Lupine, white Hollyhock, white Bell-flower, nor should I object to a few spires at one end of the bed of sulphur-yellow Lupines, or yellow Hollyhocks, or a group of Paris Daisies. I have seen a great Oriental Poppy growing in wonderful beauty near a mass of pale blue Larkspur, and Shirley Poppies are a delight with blues; and any one could arrange the pompadour tints of pink and blue in a garden who could in a gown.

Let me name some of the favorites of the Blue Border. The earliest but not the eldest is the pretty spicy Scilla in several varieties, and most satisfactory it is in perfection of tint, length of bloom, and great hardiness. [. . .]

The early spring blooming of the beloved Grape Hyacinth gives us an overflowing bowl of "blue principle"; the whole plant is imbued and fairly exudes blue. Ruskin gave the beautiful and appropriate term "blue-flushing" to this plant and others, which at the time of their blossoming send out through their veins their blue color into the surrounding leaves and the stem; he says they "breathe out" their color, and tells of a "saturated purple" tint.

Not content with the confines of the garden border, the Grape Hyacinth has "escaped the garden," and become a field flower. The "seeing eye," ever quick to feel a difference in shade or color, which often proves very slight upon close examination, viewed on Long Island a splendid sea of blue; and it seemed neither the time nor tint for the expected Violet. We found it a field of Grape Hyacinth, blue of leaf, of stem, of flower. While all flowers are in a sense perfect, some certainly do not appear so in shape, among the latter those of irregular sepals. Some flowers seem imperfect without any cause save the fancy of the one who is regarding them; thus to me the Balsam is an imperfect flower. Other flowers impress me delightfully with a sense of perfection. Such is the Grape Hyacinth, doubly grateful in this perfection in the time it comes in early spring. The Grape Hyacinth is the favorite spring flower of my garden— but no! I thought a minute ago the Scilla was! and what place has the Violet? the Flower de Luce? I cannot decide, but this I know— it is some blue flower.

Ruskin says of the Grape Hyacinth, as he saw it growing in southern France, its native home, "It was as if a cluster of grapes and a hive of honey had been distilled and pressed together into one small boss of celled and beaded blue." I always think of his term "beaded blue" when I look at it. There are several varieties, from a deep blue or purple to sky-blue, and one is fringed with the most delicate feathery petals. Some varieties have a faint perfume, and country folk call the flower "Baby's Breath" therefrom.

Purely blue, too, are some of our garden Hyacinths, especially a rather meagre single Hyacinth which looks a little chilly; and Gavin Douglas wrote in the springtime of 1500, "The Flower de Luce forth spread his heavenly blue." It always jars upon my sense of appropriateness to hear this old garden favorite called Fleur de Lis. The accepted derivation of the word is that given by Grandmaison in his *Heraldic Dictionary*. Louis VII of France, whose name was then

written Loys, first gave the name to the flower, "Fleur de Loys";
then it became Fleur de Louis, and finally, Fleur de Lis. Our flower
caught its name from Louis. Tusser in his list of flowers for windows
and pots gave plainly Flower de Luce; and finally Gerarde called
the plant Flower de Luce, and he advised its use as a domestic
remedy in a manner which is in vogue in country homes in New
England to-day. He said that the root "stamped plaister-wise, doth
take away the blewnesse or blacknesse of any stroke" that is, a black
and blue bruise. Another use advised of him is as obsolete as the
form in which it was rendered. He said it was "good in a loch or
licking medicine for shortness of breath." Our apothecaries no longer
make, nor do our physicians prescribe, "licking medicines." The
powdered root was urged as a complexion beautifier, especially to
remove morphew, and as orris-root may be found in many of our
modern skin lotions.

Ruskin most beautifully describes the Flower de Luce as the
flower of chivalry—"with a sword for its leaf, and a Lily for its heart."
These grand clumps of erect old soldiers, with leafy swords of green
and splendid cuirasses and plumes of gold and bronze and blue,
were planted a century ago in our grandmothers' gardens, and were
then Flower de Luce. A hundred years those sturdy sentinels have
stood guard on either side of the garden gates—still Flower de Luce.
There are the same clean-cut leaf swords, the same exquisite blossoms, far more beautiful than our tropical Orchids, though similar
in shape; let us not change now their historic name, they still are
Flower de Luce—the Flower de Louis.

The Violet family, with its Pansies and Ladies' Delights, has
honored place in our Blue Border, though the rigid color list of a
prosaic practical dyer finds these Violet allies a debased purple
instead of blue.

Our wild Violets, the blue ones, have for me a sad lack for a
Violet, that of perfume. They are not as lovely in the woodlands as
their earlier coming neighbor, the shy, pure Hepatica. Bryant, calling the Hepatica Squirrelcups (a name I never heard given them
elsewhere), says they form "a graceful company hiding in their bells
a soft aerial blue." Of course, they vary through blue and pinky
purple, but the blue is well hidden, and I never think of them save
as an almost white flower. Nor are the Violets as lovely on the
meadow and field slopes, as the mild Innocence, the Houstonia,

called also Bluets, which is scarcely a distinctly blue expanse, but rather "a milky way of minute stars." An English botanist denies that it is blue at all. A field covered with Innocence always looks to me as if little clouds and puffs of blue-white smoke had descended and rested on the grass.

I well recall when the Aquilegia, under the name of California Columbine, entered my mother's garden, to which its sister, the red and yellow Columbine, had been brought from a rocky New England pasture when the garden was new. This Aquilegia came to us about the year 1870. I presume old catalogues of American florists would give details and dates of the journey of the plant from the Pacific to the Atlantic. It chanced that this first Aquilegia of my acquaintance was of a distinct light blue tint; and it grew apace and thrived and was vastly admired, and filled the border with blueness of that singular tint seen of late years in its fullest extent and most prominent position in the great masses of bloom of the blue Hydrangea, the show plant of such splendid summer homes as may be found at Newport. These blue Hydrangeas are ever to me a color blot. They accord with no other flower and no foliage. I am ever reminded of blue mould, of stale damp. I looked with inexpressible aversion on a photograph of Cecil Rhodes' garden at Cape Town—several solid acres set with this blue Hydrangea and nothing else, unbroken by tree or shrub, and scarce a path, growing as thick as a field sown with ensilage corn, and then I thought what would be the color of that mass! that crop of Hydrangeas! Yet I am told that Rhodes is a flower-lover and flower-thinker. Now this Aquilegia was of similar tint; it was blue, but it was not a pleasing blue, and additional plants of pink, lilac, and purple tints had to be added before the Aquilegia was really included in our list of well-beloveds.

There are other flowers for the blue border. It is pleasant to plant common Flax, if you have ample room; it is a superb blue; to many persons the blossom is unfamiliar, and is always of interest. Its lovely flowers have been much sung in English verse. The Salpiglossis is in its azure tint a lovely flower, though it is a kinsman of the despised Petunia.

How the Campanulaceæ enriched the beauty and the blueness of the garden. We had our splendid clusters of Canterbury Bells, both blue and white. I have told elsewhere of our love for them in childhood. Equally dear to us was a hardy old Campanula whose full name I know not, perhaps it is the Pyramidalis; [. . .] nothing in the garden is more gladly welcomed from year to year. It partakes of the charm shared by every bell-shaped flower, a simple form, but an ever pleasing one. We had also the *Campanula persicifolia* and *trachelium*, and one we called Bluebells of Scotland, which was not the correct name. It now has died out, and no one recalls enough of its exact detail to learn its real name. The showiest bell-flower was the *Platycodon grandiflorum*, the Chinese or Japanese Bell-flower. Another name is the Balloon-flower, this on account of the characteristic buds shaped like an inflated balloon. It is a lovely blue in tint. The Giant Bell-flower is a *fin de siècle* blossom named *Ostrowskia*, with flowers four inches deep and six inches in diameter; as purple, but as brightly blue as Scilla. The dwarf Ageratum is also a long-blossoming soft-tinted blue flower; it made a charming edging in my sister's garden last summer; but I should never put either of them on the edge of the blue border.

The dull blue, sparsely set flowers of the various members of the Mint family have no beauty in color, nor any noticeable elegance; the Blue Sage is the only vivid-hued one, and it is a true ornament to the border. Prunella was ever found in old gardens, now it is a wayside weed. Thoreau loved the Prunella for its blueness, its various lights, and noted that its color deepened toward night. This flower, regarded with indifference by nearly every one, and distaste by many, always to him suggested coolness and freshness by its presence. The Prunella was beloved also by Ruskin, who called it the soft warm-scented Brunelle, and told of the fine purple gleam of its hooded blossom: "the two uppermost petals joined like an old-fashioned enormous hood or bonnet; the lower petal torn deep at the edges into a kind of fringe,"—and he said it was a "Brownie flower," a little eerie and elusive in its meaning. I do not like it because it has such a disorderly, unkempt look; it always seems bedraggled.

The pretty ladder-like leaf of Jacob's Ladder is most delicate and pleasing in the garden, and its blue bell-flowers are equally refined. This is truly an old-fashioned plant, but well worth universal cultivation.

In answer to the question, What is the bluest flower in the garden or field? one answered Fringed Gentian; another the Forget-me-not, which has much pink in its buds and yellow in its blossoms;

another Bee Larkspur; and the others *Centaurea cyanus* or Bachelor's Buttons, a local American name for them, which is not even a standard folk name, since there are twenty-one English plants called Bachelor's Buttons. Ragged Sailor is another American name. Corn-flower, Blue-tops, Blue Bonnets, Bluebottles, Loggerheads are old English names. Queerer still is the title Break-your-spectacles. Hawdods is the oldest name of all. Fitzherbert, in his *Boke of Husbandry*, 1586, thus describes briefly the plant:—

Hawdod hath a blewe floure, and a few lytle leaves, and hath fyve or syxe branches floured at the top.

In varied shades of blue, purple, lilac, pink, and white, Bachelor's Buttons are found in every old garden, growing in a confused tangle of "lytle leaves" and vari-colored flowers, very happily and with very good effect. [. . .]

In *The Promise of May* Dora's eyes are said to be as blue as the Bluebell, Harebell, Speedwell, Bluebottle, Succory, Forget-me-not, and Violets; so we know what flowers Tennyson deemed blue.

Another poet named as the bluest flower, the Monk's-hood, so wonderful of color, one of the very rarest of garden tints; graceful of growth, blooming till frost, and one of the garden's delights. In a list of garden flowers published in Boston, in 1828, it is called Cupid's car. Southey says in *The Doctor*, of Miss Allison's garden: "The Monk's-hood of stately growth Betsey called 'Dumbledores Delight,' and was not aware that the plant, in whose helmet- rather than cowl-shaped flowers, that busy and best-natured of all insects appears to revel more than any other, is the deadly Aconite of which she read in poetry." The dumbledore was the bumblebee, and this folk name was given, as many others have been, from a close observance of plant habits; for the fertilization of the Monk's-hood is accomplished only by the aid of the bumblebee.

Many call Chicory or Succory our bluest flower. Thoreau happily termed it "a cool blue." It is not often the fortune of a flower to be brought to notice and affection because of a poem; we expect the poem to celebrate the virtues of flowers already loved. The Succory is an example of a plant, known certainly to flower students, yet little thought of by careless observers until the beautiful poem of Margaret Deland touched all who read it. I think this a gem of modern poesy, having in full that great element of a true poem, the most essential element indeed of a short poem—the power of suggestion. Who can read it without being stirred by its tenderness and sentiment, yet how few are the words.

> *Oh, not in ladies' gardens,*
>   *My peasant posy,*
> *Shine thy dear blue eyes;*
> *Nor only—nearer to the skies*
>   *In upland pastures, dim and sweet,*
> *But by the dusty road,*
>   *Where tired feet*
> *Toil to and fro,*
>   *Where flaunting Sin*
> *May see thy heavenly hue,*
>   *Or weary Sorrow look from thee*
> *Toward a tenderer blue.*

I recall perfectly every flower I saw in pasture, swamp, forest, or lane when I was a child; and I know I never saw Chicory save in old gardens. It has increased and spread wonderfully along the roadside within twenty years. By tradition it was first brought to us from England by Governor Bowdoin more than a century ago, to plant as forage.

In our common Larkspur, the old-fashioned garden found its most constant and reliable blue banner, its most valuable color giver. Self-sown, this Larkspur sprung up freely every year; needing no special cherishing or nourishing, it grew apace, and bloomed with a luxuriance and length of flowering that cheerfully blued the garden for the whole summer. It was a favorite of children in their floral games, and pretty in the housewife's vases, but its chief hold on favor was in its democracy and endurance. Other flowers drew admirers and lost them; some grew very ugly in their decay; certain choice seedlings often had stunted development, garden scourges attacked tender beauties; fierce July suns dried up the whole border, all save the Larkspur, which neither withered nor decayed; and often, unaided, saved the midsummer garden from scanty unkemptness and dire disrepute.

[*Old-Time Gardens* (1901)]

Candace Wheeler
Mrs. Thaxter's Island Garden

Many gardens may have been planted to secure an effect of gradu-
ation in color, but my first thought of it came to me years ago in
a place I like to remember. A great part of the beauty of Mrs.
Thaxter's house in the Isles of Shoals was made up of flowers. It
was far more enjoyable than her garden, where the flowers grew
luxuriantly at their own sweet wills, or at the will of the planter,
never troubling their heads about agreeing with their neighbors. I
remember it as a disappointment that a woman with so exquisite a
sense of combination and gradation in the arrangement of flowers,
should have so little thought of color effect in her garden.

But in the house! I have never anywhere seen such realized
possibilities of color! The fine harmonic sense of the woman and
artist and poet thrilled through these long chords of color, and filled
the room with an atmosphere which made it seem like living in a
rainbow.

The tops of the low bookcases, that filled all the wall space not
opened in windows to the sea, were massed with her beloved flowers. I remember she told me that at four in the morning, when the
sea and sky seemed to be spread for her alone, she was always out
gathering them. I like to think of her there—the tall, white figure
standing under the sky and beside the sea which laps her much-
loved Isles of Shoals, among the flowers in the early morning, which,
although bare of humanity, she found full to the brim of the beauty
which her soul loved.

Later her friends always found her in her room, with books
and piano and flowers, making a harmony together which must live

in many hearts until Heaven substitutes something as good and
without decay.

I remember that the grand piano, which at ten in the morning
was always giving out harmonies under the hands of some of Mrs.
Thaxter's friends whose natural speech was music, stood against the
end of the chimney-piece, and that pictures hung above it and leaned
against it. Just at the end where it touched the low shelf of the
chimney, there commenced a bank of small white poppies, very
tender in color and effect, with half-transparent leaves, showing all
the veins and fibres of structure, like a baby's skin, and speckled
by the anthers which stood like a fringed crown around the seed-
cups. Next to these came pale-tinted poppies, and pink ones with
white edges, and then the satisfying conch-shell pink, and deeper
ones, and deeper still, until it ended in the peculiar *pink-red* which
is found only in the poppy tribe.

There were pictures everywhere on the walls; but over the
white end of this bank of flowers—the tender, half-transparent white
of which I have spoken—hung a little picture of the sea, one of
Childe Hassam's,—as blue as the sea itself, with a blue made up of
a thousand tints and shadows and reflections such as the sea holds
and keeps the secret of for the most part, but which it has given to
this painter, and to a few others who love it. This bit of blue above
the white was the note of contrast which made the perfection of the
whole.

Everywhere around the room roses were sweeping into depths
of roses, and nasturtiums going from palest yellow into winelike
claret, and blue of asters into darks of purples, and sweet-peas stood
in groups on the tables and by the windows; but my eyes always
came back to the soft gradation over the chimney-piece, with the
bit of blue sea over the white. Both blue and white were so tender
and mixed in quality, and yet so strong in contrast, they might have
been born of the bass and treble notes which went floating over
them from the great piano.

It was in this room, and enjoying its color as I have enjoyed
few things in life, and conscious all the while of its impermanence,
conscious that in lastingness of quality it was scarcely more than a
dream of color, that I began to think of making a summer dream of
it in my garden. It is a summer dream, and yet a reality—not only

to me but to other garden lovers; but I still enjoy the remembrance of its source, and shall, perhaps, enjoy it beyond the limits which separate earthly and heavenly gardens.

[*Content in a Garden* (1902)]

Mrs. Francis King
A Charming Happening
in the Borders

A charming happening has just taken place in the borders. The bush honeysuckles of Michigan were never more gloriously covered with their veils of white and rose than this spring. It may have been the gradually warming season, the uninterrupted progress from leaf-bud to blossom; in any case, the tale is the same all about us—the loniceras have been remarkably fine. Below a towering group of *Lonicera*, var. *bella albida*, whose flowers in early June are just passing, crowds of the swaying long-spurred hybrid aquilegias bloom and blow. Most of us now know the unusual delicacy and range of color in these charming flowers—faint pinks, yellows, blues, and lavenders—all pale and poised as they are.

But oh! to catch beyond, under the shadow of the honeysuckle boughs, as I did but now, the sight of masses of blooming pink scillas, *Scilla campanulata*, var. *rosea*, at precisely the moment and in precisely the place where its modest beauty was most perfectly displayed—to have this as a surprise, *not* a special plan—here was a pleasure of a quality all too seldom felt and known. Nothing could carry on and repeat the tones of the pink and lavender aquilegias as does this loveliest of late scillas. In appearance more like a tall lily-of-the-valley than any other flower I can call to mind, in tone so cool a pink that it is perfect in combination with the blue, lavender, or pink columbines. It is enchanting as their neighbor and far more interesting thus used than in the more commonplace proximity to its cousin or sister, the lavender *Scilla campanulata*, var. *excelsior*, blooming at the same time. To me it would be dull to see sheets of these two spring flowers near each other or intermingling. Dull, I mean, compared with such a possibility as the combination I have tried to describe and which was simply one of those heavenly accidents befalling all too rarely the ardent gardener.

On this June day the buds in my garden are almost as enchanting as the open flowers. Things in bud bring, in the heat of a June noontide, the recollection of the loveliest days of the year—those days of May when all is suggested, nothing yet fulfilled. To-day I have been looking at something one of these photographs feebly tries to show—tall spikes of pale-pink Canterbury bells, the flowers unusually large, standing against a softly rounding background of gypsophila in bud; to the left of the campanulas, leaves of *Iris pallida Dalmatica*, so tall that their presence is immediately felt; a little before, but still to the left of the pink spikes and the iris, perhaps a dozen tall silvery velvet stems of *Stachys lanata*, whose tiny flowers give but a hint of their pale lavender as yet, and are lost in the whiteness of the young leaflets, and—and this is the thing which really creates the picture—three or four spreading branches, a foot from the ground and directly below the campanulas, of *Statice incana* Silver Cloud, tiny points of white showing that the whole dense spray will soon be full of flowers.

Below and among the campanulas (which I keep in bloom a very long time by a careful daily taking off of every shrivelling bloom) stand salmon-pink balsams, these to replace with their two-foot masses of flowers the campanulas when the latter's day is over and to rise above the gray-white leaves of the stachys when its blooming time is also past. This stachys is a lovely adjunct to the garden. The texture of its leaves is a matter of surprise to every one who touches them. Most people would call stachys "woolly," but I do not like this word—(is it because I live in the West?)—and why apply an unpoetic word to any one of the lovely inhabitants of our gardens?

It came about that a space before the bush honeysuckles—the pink flowering variety, *Lonicera Tatarica*, var. *rosea*—in a border, needed filling with lower shrubs. The piece of ground to be furnished was perhaps fifteen feet long by three wide, though irregular in both width and outline. Last autumn *Rosa nitida* had been there set out, planted about three feet apart. Bare ground for this year and next was sure to spoil the look of things while these roses were yet young, and a covering for it was thus managed. Canterbury-bell plants were distributed in small groups among the roses, especially toward the back of the border; and English irises, Rossini and Mr. Veen, were tucked in in longish colonies before and among the campanulas. In ordinary seasons these irises might not have bloomed with the campanulas, but this year it was Monte Cristo-like—the flower and the hour!—with a resultant superb effect of color. Mr. Veen, a true violet iris, Rossini, a purplish-blue, were good together to me, who differ from Miss Jekyll in possessing a penchant for blue combined with purple or with lavender.

To compare a bloom of one of these irises with a spray of the Dropmore anchusa is to get an extremely vivid and interesting idea of the effect of colors upon each other. Taken alone, *Iris xiphioides*, var. Mr. Veen, is a blue without very much purple in its tone; beside the anchusa all the blue vanishes—the iris is a distinct purple; place it beside Rossini, it becomes blue again; and grow masses of Rossini below the anchusa, especially the variety Opal, and there is one of the most beautiful juxtapositions possible in flowers—so far as I know an original combination of color and one to charm an artist, I believe. Anchusa of a year's standing, a three-foot anchusa, might be best to use in this way. The two-foot iris would prove a good companion.

There follows, soon after the gray-and-pink combination in my garden of which I spoke a few paragraphs back, the combination of pink *Campanula medium* and *Stachys lanata*, a time when one of the loveliest of all double poppies lights up the little place with color. For this poppy—an annual—there is no registered name. It is double, extremely full, perhaps three feet in height, and of a delicious rosy-pink, exactly the pink of the best mallows, or of the enchanting half-open rosebuds of the ever-lovely rambler Lady Gay. To see three or four of these poppies in full bloom among the white mist of gypsophila, either single or double, the oat-green of the poppy leaves below, is to see something more delicately beautiful than often occurs in gardens. Many packets of the seed of my poppy are always in readiness, as I have a superabundance of the same; and if ten people read these words, and if, peradventure, there be ten gardeners with vision to see through the veil of these sentences the rose-pink beauty of this flower, let them ask for a bit of this seed, for it is theirs for the asking!

The love of flowers brings surely with it the love of all the green world. For love of flowers every blooming square in cottage gardens seen from the flying windows of the train has its true and touching message for the traveller; every bush and tree in nearer field and farther wood becomes an object of delight and stirs delightful thought. When I see a rhubarb plant in a small rural garden, I respect the man, or more generally the woman, who placed it there. If my eye lights upon the carefully tended peony held up by a barrel hoop, the round group of an old dicentra, the fine upstanding single plant of iris, at once I experience the warmest feeling of friendliness for that householder, and wish to know and talk with them about their flowers. For at the bottom there is a bond which breaks down every other difference between us. We are "Garden Souls."

[*The Well-Considered Garden* (1915)]

Louise Beebe Wilder
Magenta the Maligned

Beauty deprived of its proper foils ceases to be enjoyed as beauty, just as light deprived of all shadow ceases to be enjoyed as light.

—RUSKIN

The above quotation supplies the reason that magenta is so universally despised and shunned. Not only is it deprived of its proper foils, but it is nearly always set down beside those colours surest to bring out its worst side. I am very fond of this colour as worn by flowers and have taken some trouble to bring it into harmony with its surroundings. Combative it is, but to be won; fastidious as to its associations, but gentle and beautiful when considered. Surely any one who has seen the sumptuous rim of colour following the banks of the Hudson River and its tributary streams in certain sections where the Rose Loosestrife, a flower of the purest magenta, has naturalized itself, will not deny the possibility of beauty in the use of this colour. Besides the Loosestrife many of the finest hardy plants garb themselves in the maligned hue, and Mr. Schuyler Mathews in his *Field Book of American Wildflowers* gives 73 familiar wild flowers that are enrolled under the magenta banner. But in all my gardening experience I have met only one person who confessed admiration for this colour and I have come across but one garden writer who boldly put down in print his admiration for it. Indeed nearly every writer upon garden topics pauses in his praise of other flower colours to give the despised one a rap in passing. Mr. Bowles writes of "that awful form of floral original sin, magenta"; Miss Jekyll calls it "malignant magenta"; and Mrs. Earle, usually so sympathetic and tender toward all flowers, says that even the word magenta, seen often in the pages of her charming book, "makes the black and white look cheap," and again "if I could turn all magenta flowers pink or purple, I should never think further about garden harmony, all other colours would adjust themselves."

In the thoughtlessness of colour arrangement that prevailed in the gardens of our grandmothers, magenta was recklessly handled— so many sweet and willing flowers wore the now despised hue— but no one felt the horror of such great masses of magenta Phlox and Tiger Lilies, of magenta Foxgloves and scarlet Sweet William that I remember in the charming box-bordered garden of my grandparents in Massachusetts. But now, with this new vision of ours for colour harmony, there is no reason why we should, on account of the past sins of our forefathers and the present sinning of our nurserymen in miscalling it, banish this rich and distinctive colour with all the fine plants that it distinguishes, without some effort to provide for it the proper foils to fully develop its beauty.

I would ask any one possessing Dr. Ridgeway's *Colour Standards and Colour Nomenclature* to open the book at Plate 24 and look at magenta in all its tender gradations of tint and shade. There is but one magenta, but about it are the gentle sisters of the discredited clan: Liseran purple and rose purple, dull and dusky purple, Indian lake, dahlia carmine, auricula purple, pale and deep Rosalane pink, all of which we are accustomed to lump as magenta. And on Plate 12 of that same chart there are yet others that come under the unjust ban: the mallow pinks and purples, amaranths and aster purple. These are beautiful colours as seen against the soft gray background of the page. Perhaps if we could strike out the word magenta, so laden with custom-made stigma, and use only these other colour names, all pleasant sounding and suggestive, we should lose much of the antipathy now felt for the flowers that wear it.

When the early writers had magenta to name they usually wrote it as "a little purple mixed with red," and to give it a more poetic but none the less exact description we might reverse Dante's idea of the colour of Apple blossoms—"more than that of roses but less than that of violets."

In my garden I have been able to match but one flower to the magenta of the colour chart. This is the Rose Loosestrife (Lythrum Salicaria). It is pure magenta, but in eight catalogues examined it is described as rose pink, or bright pink. One seedsman ventures so near the taboo name as to call it rosy-purple, another flies from it to the length of describing an improved variety as "glistening cherry red." Even in the *Cyclopedia of Horticulture* it is described as "rose colour."

It is small wonder that when our minds are set upon, and some garden space prepared for, glistening cherry red, or the ever-cordial and agreeable rose colour, we are exasperated by the arrival of plants that in their flowering show the strange off-tones of the magenta group. It is not among the accepted colours of the garden; we do not plan for it, nor seek it, though it is often thrust upon us; so what chance has the poor colour to come again into its own, for it is believed to have been the "royal purple" of the ancients.

> *Custom hangs upon us with a weight*
> *Heavy as frost and deep almost as life.*

It is the custom to despise magenta. It is hustled out of our gardens and out of our consciousness and no one has eyes to see the imperial scarf of magenta Phlox that stoops to bind the dusty roadside, or the riot of tender colour in the neglected cottage dooryard where Petunias have sown and resown themselves and flutter about the gray and rotting porch and squeeze through the gray and rotting palings of the fence in exquisite harmony with the weathered wood.

I am so fond of this colour and its kindred tints and shades that to come across in *The Garden*, December 11, 1915, the following article by Clarence Eliot in its praise, was a great pleasure and I cannot refrain from using it in defence of my beloved magenta blossoms.

In some circles it needs as much moral hardihood to say that one likes magenta as it does to confess that one dislikes cold baths. Some folks seem hardly to like to use the word magenta, as though it were unclean, and resort instead to "rosy-purple." This seems as bad as softening "cold bath" into "soapy-tepid." As a matter of fact, however, real true magenta is a very rare colour among flowers. Callirhoe pulchella is one of the truest examples, and the glossy silky texture of its petals seems to enhance the glowing brilliance of the colour. The most splendid examples of magenta I have ever seen were Bougainvillea cascading over white walls in Madeira,

and great trailing slabs of some Mesembryanthemums on the cliffs at the entrance of the harbour of Bonificio. But alas, these two effects cannot be repeated in this country [England] except perhaps on the "Cornish Riviera."
. . . I have often thought I should like to try a border of strong magentas with a good many violets and purples and lilacs, a few pinks of the type of Lavatera Olbia, that is with just a suspicion of blue in them, and perhaps a very few white flowers.

Here is Mr. Eliot's list of flowers for a magenta border of which he says, "Comparatively few of them are of the true colour, yet most or all of them are reds and pinks that would accord."

Aubrietias Fire King and Leichtlinii, Epilobium Dodonaei, Calamintha grandiflora, Lythrum alatum, Dianthus Seguieri, Lychnis viscaria splendens, Thymus serpyllum coccineus majus, Betonica grandiflora superba, Cortusa mathiola (shade), Primulas pulverulenta and Veitchii, Lathyrus latifolius (grown on pea sticks), Lavatera Olbia (and nearer it Nepeta Mussini), Lythrum virgatum Rose Queen, Lythrum Salicaria superbum; Phlox Le Mahdi, Albert Vandal, Reichgraf von Hochberg and Rosenberg for strong colours; and Phlox Eugene Danzanvillers, Phlox pilosa, Phlox subulata compacta, Monarda violacea superba, Verbena venosa (tender but beautiful), Lunaria biennis, Callirhoe pulchella, and Mesembryanthemum tricolor.

To this good list I must add a few of my own favourites: the exquisite, sprawling Callirhoe involucrata, Lychnis Coronaria the Mullein Pink, Kansas Gay Feather, purple Foxglove, Azalea amoena, Rhododendron catawbiense, the splendid Ironweed, Lychnis alpina, Spiraea Davidii, Centaurea dealbata, Desmodium penduliflorum, and some fine Michaelmas Daisies of the novae-Angliae ruber type.

I am well aware that this list will simply stand as a warning to most gardeners, but while my aim is not so high as Mr. Eliot's in hoping to inspire a magenta border, yet I do hope to start even a small revulsion of feeling in favour of this tender, hushed colour, to give it in these pages as I have in my garden some of the associations that silence its combativeness that it may raise its erstwhile imperial head, not as of old in the terrible if joyous racket of Tiger Lilies and Sunflowers, but in assured and reposeful harmony.

The first time I saw magenta flowers used with thoughtful consideration was in the wondrous gardens of Drummond Castle in

Scotland. There a double border running on either side of a grass walk for nearly a quarter of a mile, between dark, severely clipped Hollies and Yews, was planted in blocks of about twelve feet in two alternating colours—blue and magenta! I do not now recall all the plants used in the border, but among them were Loosestrife and Monkshood, Spiraea Rutlandi and Veronica, magenta and bluish-violet Phloxes. Standing at one end and looking along the narrowing perspective one's eye was carried from great richness of effect to an indescribable softness that finally seemed to melt away like a trail of smoke.

The best colours to associate with magenta are deeper and paler tones of itself, the dim blue of such as Monkshood, pale buff, sky blue like that of Salvia azurea, white, the mallow pinks—that is, those pinks that have a bluish cast, lavender, and gray foliage. Indeed, I think it safe to say that all colours are in harmony with it save strong yellow, red, scarlet, orange, cherry, and the salmon pinks.

Magenta does not come into conspicuous life in the garden before June, when enter Foxgloves and Sweet Williams. Before this, however, we have little patches of it here and there where creeping Phloxes and Aubrietias, Lychnis alpina and Viscaria splendens wind the border verges with a soft-hued scarf in front of sweeps of nodding, pale-coloured Star Daffodils and hoary-leafed Nepeta gleaming the lovelier for the shadow of a full-flowered Cherry-tree. Many Rhododendrons and Azaleas affect the colour. In a friend's garden Azalea amoena is broadly massed against dark evergreens, producing a most striking effect.

All the gray-foliaged plants are particularly happy with the dear magenta culprits, and gray stone is a perfect background for them. The tall magenta Foxgloves we plant with Southernwood or Wormwood and perhaps a few soft blue Peach-leaved Bellflowers or lavender Canterbury Bells. Mullein Pink (Lychnis Coronaria) is splendid with the gray leafage and lilac flower spikes of Nepeta Mussini, or shining through a haze of Gypsophila with a background of creamy Mulleins. This plant which, as near as I can match its velvet depths, answers on the colour chart to aster-purple, is described in various catalogues as "blood red," "purple or scarlet," "beautiful pink," "bright rose," "rosy crimson," and "red"; no two alike and all keeping well out of the danger zone of truth. It is an old-fashioned plant seldom seen in new-fashioned gardens, but its glowing colour and gray velvet leafage should give it entrance everywhere. I am glad to say that it seldom fails to win admiration from visitors to my garden. The white form is fine but far less beautiful.

The Rose Loosestrife blooms for about six weeks at midsummer and is one of the best hardy plants of its season. There are several "improved" forms that, while not changed in colour perceptibly, are perhaps of a slightly purer tone. [. . .] It is lovely in groups with Aconitum Napellus and Gypsophila. The creamy forms of Anthemis tinctoria are quite safe to plant with it as is the soft lavender of Erigeron speciosa. No plant is finer for water-side planting. I would suggest massing it at the water's edge where we may have the added beauty of wind-stirred reflections, and against it bold groups of deep blue water Iris.

A little later in the summer come the Gayfeathers (Liatris), whose impetuous, hurtling aspect has suggested to the children the name of "sky rockets." These grown in groups behind Lyme Grass or Rue and mingled with clumps of white Moon Daisies are very effective. They are prairie plants requiring a dry soil and a sunny aspect. Later we have the delightful Trefoil or Bush Clover (Desmodium penduliflorum) with slender, wandlike branches closely hung with tiny winged blossoms in two shades of magenta. It grows in my garden against a stone wall in company with the opaque lavender flowers of Clematis Davidiana and plenty of pale yellow Snapdragons. Later still there is Vernonia arkansana, to be worn in the garden like a festal plume, with Phlox Peachblow and Lyme Grass to set off its peculiar glowing colour. And last of all we have the Michaelmas Daisies, with many a good member that may be said to belong among these unappreciated treasures.

I do not deny that there are poor and wishy-washy tones of magenta and that these are not desirable; but where the colour is frank and pure and used with a right intermingling of green and other soft friendly hues, there is none more beautiful and distinctive. It requires only such consideration as we give as a matter of course to blue or scarlet, but which is certainly not vouchsafed magenta in the gardens of to-day.

[*Colour in My Garden* (1918)]

Elizabeth Lawrence
November—and the Barbaric Scarlet of Tithonia

Today is the fourteenth of November. I have been sitting in the sun eating my lunch and staring at the barbaric scarlet of Tithonia Fireball against the cold blue sky. The low retaining wall of the terrace is a study in values: bright silver leaves of *Veronica incana*, dull grey mounds of santolina, scattered flowers of white verbena against dark foliage. The path to the summer house, framed in a green arch, is as gay as ever from a little distance, even though the edging of *Zinnia linearis* and sweet alyssum proves, on closer view, to be a little ragged. Against the dark temple fir the scarlet berries and glossy foliage of the Formosa firethorn have assumed the brilliance that they will carry well into the winter. Along the fence there are still a few pale butterfly flowers on the climbing rose, Mermaid. The flowers of the tall yellow crotalaria and of the dwarfer bronzed one have become discolored during the cold nights, but one plant— protected by the hedge—still lifts tender yellow spires against the green. Throughout the garden the ageratum volunteers have come into their own, covering bare beds with the intense blue that they take on with the first cool weather. The strawberry pink reflection of a neighboring maple lies on the black water of the pool. Already the leaves are falling from the trees.

Any night now frost may blacken the last crotalarias, zinnias, marigolds, and chrysanthemums. But, when the dead branches have been cleared away, there will still be the green of the ivy, the grey of santolina, and the scarlet fruit of the firethorn. Already sweet violets are in bloom, and before long there will be buds on the Paper White narcissus and the Algerian iris.

[*A Southern Garden* (1942)]

Harland J. Hand
The Color Garden

The color motif of my El Cerrito, California, garden developed because of a very practical problem with a path. I had made a dirt path that wound down the steep slope of the garden. But it was always full of weeds and the packed soil made them very difficult to remove. To eliminate this problem, I made steps and stepping-stones of concrete, doing them in place, directly on the soil. When the concrete was finished, I became intrigued by the color relationship between it and the surrounding plants. There seemed to be something very special about the way the colors sharpened and gave drama to each other. To my eye, the concrete registered as a very light color, while the contrasting color of the plants, for the most part, seemed very dark. The significant thing was that the dark plants, though they actually were a middle tone, clearly registered as a dark color in contrast to the very light color of the concrete.

The relationship of these dark and light colors reminded me of the grey granite glacial formations of the high Sierra. The area of the mountains near Silver Lake with its strong color contrasts between the very light grey granite and the dark islands of conifers, was one giant, dramatic dark and light garden. I decided to use the strong dark and light contrast of that powerful landscape as the color motif of my garden.

I knew that light colors along a path would make for greater visibility at night, so I planted plants with light grey leaves near the sharpest curves. I discovered that, where I had placed these grey leaved plants next to the light grey concrete, the two colors combined to make one shape. When I widened and narrowed the light shape of the path by placing grey leaved plants next to it, I discovered a rhythmic pattern beginning to appear. I found that I could control the way my eye flowed over the garden by the way I varied these light shapes. So I began to add more and more concrete. I made paths through every area of the garden. If they led my eye too swiftly, I could vary the pace by narrowing them in some places and abruptly widening them in others. I eventually made such a network of light colored paths that they isolated mounds of soil, plants and native rock into islands of middle tone. Where these darker islands became too regular in size and shape, I made variations by running another path through them. For even greater variation I reversed the colors completely by tearing out some dark islands and replacing them with light colored, level rooms with concrete slabs for a floor, and concrete benches for furniture. The additional concrete strengthened and massed the light shapes so much that the whole garden appeared more and more dramatic. The islands of dark seemed to grow out of a bedrock of light colored concrete slabs, benches and paths.

I added concrete pools, placing them so that they appeared to flow into each other. This helped to give a suggestion of a riverbed and, through the exploration of this idea, I established a flow of dark and light color throughout the entire garden. The more concrete I put in, the more the garden appeared to be a light colored rock outcropping with islands of dark plants, much like that Sierra landscape.

I am constantly on the lookout for items that help widen and enrich the light colored concrete areas. I am continuously searching for grey leaved plants. Most such plants have special structures that make them grey. These structures give a texture to the leaf or stem surfaces that can further vary the color by producing tiny textural shadows that change with the season and time of day. The furry rabbit ears of *Stachys olympica* have dense soft hairs which give the leaves a very light, almost white color that, when seen next to the concrete, is very unexpected. The white powdery covering of *Echeveria elegans* provides a delicate pale, grey-green that seems juicy in contrast to the hardness of the grey concrete. The leaves of some tansies are like tiny feathers. They are usually soft and downy, giving a color that is actually an off-white. When planted next to the heavy concrete they make a contrasting combination that is very nearly unbelievable. The short hairs on snow-in-summer (*Cerastium tomentosum*) make their leaves a dull greenish grey. I have found many plants that can be used to enhance or enlarge the light grey shapes of the concrete, but the above are my favorites.

White flowers give contrast to the light colored areas. They provide highlights that push forward to enliven the greys and grey-greens. They are especially effective when the white flowered plant itself has grey leaves. The small, airy, white flowers of snow-in-summer and the small white daisies of certain of the low growing chrysanthemums are both ideal for providing subtle highlights within the light colored shapes of the garden because both of them have grey leaves.

Other materials that act as light shapes or as part of a light shape are gravel (the coarse grey pebbles used as an aggregate for concrete), sculptures of birds and animals made of concrete or pottery, rocks (especially worn river rock) and driftwood.

The islands are made primarily of evergreen plants with some native rocks placed among them. Plants in leaf usually register as a middle tone which, in the color relationship of my garden, is dark. Most azaleas, rhododendrons, fuchsias, junipers, citrus, ferns and camellias are middle tone. I use some deciduous shrubs and trees for their middle tone leaves in summer and for their medium brown, airy branches in winter. These plants include lilacs, magnolias, roses, plums, prunes, apples, peaches, maples and many others. Like the woody plants, most herbaceous ones also have foliage that is middle tone. Agapanthus, hellebores, iris, lilies, arums, orchids, bergenia and geraniums (pelargoniums) are some examples. Some very low rock garden plants that fit this category include thyme, achillea, armeria, violets, iberis and some succulents. I also enjoy annual plants of this color range because they give quick color to a newly planted garden before perennials have time to mature. These annuals may include petunias, lobelias, verbenas, salpiglossis, marigolds, poppies, nicotiana, ageratum, violas and pansies.

Whereas white flowers give contrast within the light shapes by acting as highlights, very dark colored plants give contrast to the middle tone areas by suggesting deep shadows. Those plants that register as extremely dark are rather rare; however, some examples are purple leaved plums, Irish yew, Hinoki false cypress (*Chamaecyparis obtusa*), *Agave victoriae-reginae*, and especially *Aeonium arboreum* 'Schwartzkopf' with its maroon black leaves. Of course, the darkest color would be formed by the shadows on these dark plants. Some plants with strong architectural form, such as the conifers, also produce shadows of dark color, but shadows change during the day and so will not always give very dark color where it is needed. To help make up for this illusiveness, I set life sized figures of birds and animals, painted black, in places that need a bit of strong dark color for emphasis.

I try to group the plants within the middle tone islands so that they work like a well balanced flower arrangement. The tallest are off center, with middle-sized ones on the outside and low plants arranged around the edges so that they tie into the level of the concrete surfaces. This can allow the color to actually surround the viewer, especially in places where trees with overhanging branches are used.

Plant groupings within the islands also depend upon two practical considerations; one, the amount of shade in case there is a large tree; and two, the varying amounts of water because of sprinkler problems. Shade plants are grouped in the shade, bog plants in the drainage runs, and some scree plants or California natives in the areas missed by the sprinklers. By working the practical problems and color composition together, I have been able to include thousands of interesting plants. They produce very satisfying color relationships even in the most difficult problem areas.

To unify the color and to give a natural flow of color throughout the garden, I place some dark items in the light colored areas and some light colored things in the dark areas. Between and around the concrete structures I spot a few plants of the dark leaved *Armeria juniperifolia* (white or pink flowered), *Veronica repens* (dark leaves and white flowers), *Iberis sempervirens* 'Snow Flake,' *Achillea tomentosa* and other low rock garden plants that have dark color but do not restrict the flow of traffic through the rooms and paths.

I mix some grey things into the dark islands to help tie them to the surrounding masses of light color. I use such plants as white roses, magnolia, agapanthus and lilies. The white flowers provide a very sharp contrast to the dark foliage within the islands. Grey artemisia, salvia and oat grass are tall enough to hold their own when spotted within the islands. Grey driftwood pilings from San Francisco Bay are placed so that their light shapes soar out of the middle tone carrying the light color up and above my head. I use vines such as clematis, pandorea, billardiera, wisteria and climbing roses to soften the stark forms of the pilings. The white flowers and dark leaves of *Clematis* 'Henryi' against a grey driftwood piling is an astonishing combination.

The total effect of the dark and light design is planned to be one that not only leads the eye through the garden but it also moves out of the garden to the dark wooded ridges above and below, then on to the light grey buildings in the flatlands, to San Francisco Bay and the city beyond. Since the garden occupies a ridge, an enormous sky that fluctuates between darkness and lightness envelops it. Strong dark and light seems to be the dominant color motif for the whole Bay Area.

The most satisfying aspect of the dark and light motif of the garden is that it forms a base for fully orchestrated color. Any color that I want to use can be worked into it because every single color has its dark and light aspect. For example, yellow is a very light color and works fine within the light areas. Other colors such as blue, violet, green, orange and red are middle tone and work nicely within the dark islands. Pale colors (tints of the above) usually register as light. Shades (very dark colors) register from middle tone to near black. Each color can fit somewhere within the dark and light plan.

Besides fitting into the dominant color motif of the garden, each plant color has a special relationship with other colors. Colors do things to each other that are sometimes unexpected. For example, yellow; the yellow flowers of *Gazania uniflora* against its silvery leaves and the grey concrete make every color in this combination both brilliant and subtle. Because of the grey of the concrete, the yellow of the flowers is vibrant and because of the yellow the grey of the concrete takes on a strange blue-violet cast. A spot of purple violas nearby makes those same yellow flowers look like jewels in a silver mounting.

Another striking example of what a single hue can do is shown by the small rose 'Garnet'. Its dark red flowers and dark reddish-green leaves against the light grey of pebbles and concrete make a combination that is bold yet deeply subtle. The eye will move toward this combination wherever it may be placed in the garden. This same rose makes blue ageratum shimmer intensely, and when I use it in a dark island with orange-red rhododendrons, magenta azaleas and dark pink roses, it makes a deep, blended, glowing combination. If I use this same maroon-red rose with warm and cool reds, it produces a kind of "red on red" relationship with such depth of color that I stand fascinated in front of it. When orchid, pinks and oranges are combined with the dark red of this rose, there is a feast of Persian color.

Within the middle tone of the dark islands, I experimented with all kinds of color relationships. To me, the most important idea that I discovered was that the closer the colors are in brightness and value (lightness and darkness), the more iridescent and glowing they all become and the less likely they are to cancel each other out. This is especially true of cool colors. Blues, violets and deep greens make a particularly rich combination within the middle tone of the islands. These are the peacock colors and are particularly useful both as background and as foreground color.

There are two devices that I often use to develop a satisfying color impact; one is to use many plants with similar colors together; the other is to use small amounts of warm colors to bring out cool colors that are often lost in a planting, I usually combine them with similar colored flowers that are bold and rather vulgar in their impact. For example, I plant dull pinkish flowered plants such as *Enkianthus campanulatus* or *Tamarix parviflora* (the spring blooming tamarix) with the large flowered pink and red reticulata camellias, pink rhododendrons, pink azaleas and pink primroses. In this combination of similar warm colors, the small dull pink flowers brighten considerably and in turn they soften the impact of the large flowers. To make the whole combination bright and rich, I add just a little cool color; a few violets and blue muscari are all that is needed.

Another special way of increasing the impact of small but richly colored flowers is to plant them near a bench or walkway where they can be viewed up close. The big vulgar-flowered plants can be subdued by planting them in more distant positions. Their boldness can attract the eye to areas that it might otherwise skip over.

Although flowers of nearly every color appear throughout my garden, each area is dominated by a special color combination wherein the abundance of one color unifies the others. For example, near the house is a quiet area with an abundance of white flowers throughout the entire year. Some white flowers that bloom in the spring are camellias, calla lilies, iberis 'Snow Flake,' *Magnolia soulangiana* 'Alba,' primroses and heather. Following these come azalea 'Snow Bird,' the flowering peach 'Iceland,' white flowering broom and *Wisteria floribunda* 'Longissima Alba' with the white *Clematis* 'Henryi' growing up the same pole and in bloom at the same time. In late spring and early summer, roses ('White Masterpiece,' white polyanthus and a white climber), white Japanese iris, abutilons, fuchsias, and late rhododendrons keep the area white. The roses continue through the rest of the year along with white hydrangea, *Gypsophila* 'Bristol Fairy,' *Bouvardia* 'Albatross,' white fuchsias and many others. To help soften the whites, of course, there is the grey concrete and grey-leaved plants. For subtlety and richness I add just a few very light colors such as 'The Fairy,' a pale pink rose, cream colored alyssum and bright yellow *Achillea tomentosa*. To brighten the whites I use dark foliaged plants and spots of dark red and dark blue. A 'Garnet' rose tree, deep magenta primroses, *Rochea coccinea*, gerberas and others provide the spots of dark red. The spots of dark blue include agapanthus, *Felicia amelloides*, several campanulas and *Sisyrinchium bellum* among others. Because this area near the house is dominated and unified by an abundance of white, I call it the White Garden.

The Yellow Garden is one of warm colors with yellow dominating over oranges, golds and warm reds. A few small, white flowered plants are added for subtle highlights with a few spots of blue and violet to make the warm colors of this area glow like fire.

The Blue Garden (it has cool colors dominated by blue) was completed in the spring and in order to bring it into full color as soon as possible, I put annuals among the newly planted perennial plants which will eventually take over. I planted annual lobelia in dark blue, light blue and mauve; petunias in purple, steel blue, dark blue, light blue, a few magenta and three bright red ones; to this mixture I added blue ageratum; blue and violet verbena with some blue violas and pansies for the more shaded parts. This planting was done in April, and in June there was a great show of billowing color. The whole combination glowed brilliantly even from a distance, especially after I added two fiery orange-red gerberas.

* * *

Some sections of the garden are planted so that different color combinations will dominate at different times during the year. To bring this about, I attempt to manipulate the color in order to produce a special kind of expression, like music, that is revealed in time sequences. The blue sequence starts in January with blue muscari, blue and violet primroses, blue Peruvian scilla, violets and purple violas—all showing a little color. These bloom more and more profusely, especially the muscari, until they hit a peak in late March. Then the blues subside slightly and are gradually overwhelmed in late April and early May by a spectacle of reds, pinks, orchids and yellows (azaleas and rhododendrons mostly) with just enough blue and violet left to intensify them all. By late May the warm colors quiet down and the blues commence their main surge to dominate, beginning with blue-violet Siberian iris, then Japanese iris, with some blue agapanthus just starting to flower. I have agapanthus that are very tall, others that are shorter; some have heavy flowered heads and others airy ones. They are planted abundantly in clumps and drifts all through the garden. The agapanthus increase their flower production through June, becoming a crescendo of blue that has its climax in July and August. At this same time, blue-violet pleroma, blue *Solanum rantonnetii*, fuchsias in many shades of blue and violet, summer violets, several lavenders, campanulas, dark blue felicias, blue-violet and mauve *Tradescantia virginiana*, blue veronicas, blue-violet and mauve clematis and many others are all blooming profusely, adding to the intensity of the blue which flows off in every direction taking the eye through every vista of the garden. After this climax the blue subsides again, but this time it gently gives way to a saturation of greens.

The greens of my garden play a background theme with a climax in early fall. There are fewer flowers blooming between September and February, so during this time the garden becomes a saturation of greens with a few spots of other colors to brighten and enrich them. The middletone greens that form most of the islands include green-greens, rusty-greens, blue-greens, yellow-greens and others, all in rich variety of leaf and stem texture. The yellow-greens of golden cypress, golden juniper and tree ferns furnish the highlights. The dark, blackish greens of Irish yew, Hinoki cypress, rosemary and some of the azaleas and rhododendrons add the deepest shades.

During the late season, spots of red roses intensify the greens as do the pinks of fuchsias, roses, abutilons and geraniums. Yellow flowers add bright highlights and with the yellow-greens, seem like beams of sunlight on a dull day. Blue and violet flowers inject a touch of mystery and richness to the tapestry of green. Plants with colored leaves such as purple-leaved plum, red phormium and a rainbow of succulents continue a kind of subdued opalescent color that does not end.

During the late season, when flowering has subsided, I am most aware of the placement of color in the garden. At this time, it seems clearer to me just how color can distort the feeling of space. Warm colors seem to advance like the warmth of a fire and cool colors seem to recede like the sky on a cold clear day. The warm color of the yellow garden, which is some distance from the house, seems close and makes the cool colors of the blue garden beyond seem so far away that to prevent its seeming to recede completely from the rest of the garden, I had to plant the everblooming, salmon-pink rose 'Margo Koster,' beyond it.

Another aspect of color that comes out of this advancing and receding is a kind of *trompe l'oeil*. For example, in order to give unity and rhythm of color to the garden, I place a color, such as yellow, in three different positions so that one yellow plant is close, the second is middle distance and the third is in the background. If I stand so that the three yellow plants line up and appear to merge into one yellow shape, I will be slightly confused because I cannot quite figure the position of what now seems to be a single yellow shape. But if I move a few feet to one side, the single shape will again separate into three distinct shapes, each with a clear position in space. Purposefully arranging colors so that they alternately confuse and clarify spatial relationships is a device that can add an interest going beyond the mere presence of the items in the garden. This is one of those illusive things that can give a special magical vitality to a design.

Color relationships are constantly changing as the viewer moves through the garden. Where a color is seen as the focus of attention from one position, from another position this same color is seen as part of the background for another color. This aspect can produce some unexpected color relationships that can add richness and unity to the entire garden. For example, one spring day while sitting on a bench at the top of the garden, I was surprised to discover that the colors from that view lined up like a rainbow (but not in that order); blue iris were closest, purple iris next, then magenta azaleas, red rhododendrons, then an orange-red azalea, orange aloes and finally yellow alyssum in the far distance. This had not been planned, but it did unify several areas of the garden.

Pools provide endless color variation because the effects of water are everchanging. The pools in my garden were conceived as having color that would reverse the space of the dark islands, that is, be a dark hole instead of a dark mound. Each one was to be a ring of light grey concrete around dark water, a kind of variation of the concrete slab. For the most part the pools actually do what I had planned. However, the extent of the color variation provided by the water goes beyond these ideas, because water reflects everything around it and changes color with the time of day and with the position of the viewer as he moves around. Because of the organisms that grow in it, water can usually be seen as a dark color, but at times it becomes a very intense light-colored surface, especially when it reflects the sky or light colors nearby. By its reflections, water provides echoing color that can rhythmically repeat any color that is around it. A solitary green fern is reflected in the water and so seems less isolated; or a clump of yellow alyssum is reflected in the water and the yellow becomes doubly abundant. A reflection can also increase the amount of a color to the point where the balance of the color relationship is destroyed.

Not only does light affect the reflections on water and thus change color relationships, but changing light affects the color in the whole garden. Morning light tends to cool all the colors, while afternoon light tends to warm them. The changing position of the sun moves the shadows around so that plant colors are bright and advancing one moment and dull and receding the next. Shadows can change a shape that is light colored one moment into one that is middletone the next.

Every single part of the color garden must be maintained because there is not a square inch that is without color. Dead flowers must be picked off, proportions controlled by pruning and by the removal or the installation of plants. Diseased plants have to be treated, weeds removed and paths and rooms must be swept of garden debris. The colors can be dull and depressing one moment and, with a little cleaning, become bright and delightful a short while later.

I do not believe that full control of the color in natural light can be achieved. However, it is fascinating to be able to understand what happens to color in the garden and to try to make the most of every circumstance.

[*Pacific Horticulture* (1978)]

Henry Mitchell
Marigolds and Mass Madness

Marigolds are bright and beautiful if, like cousins, you don't have too many of them at once.

Hardly any flower makes sense when bedded by the thousands, though that is the way you commonly see flowers used in parks. Nobody expects much imagination or thought in public plantings, however; and the theory—as I understand it—is that if you're driving along at seventy miles an hour, it makes no great difference what the flowers are or how they are grouped.

But in home gardens, needless to say, there is no reason to mass flowers of the same kind endlessly—there is no reason to have solid beds or (here I commence to meddle) for that matter solid edgings of a single brassy flower. The mere fact that you get a lot of seeds in a packet doesn't mean you have to plant all of them. They keep quite nicely for next year. A handful of marigolds, stuck in here and there among violet or blue or yellow petunias, can be festive, whereas a solid mass of marigolds, apart from being overwhelming, looks dull.

It is the principle of the skyrocket, of course, that applies here. Rockets seize all eyes when they burst in gold rain against a dark sky. But if you make the sky solid with gold (as the sun does at noon) then you rather lose the effect of skyrockets. Similarly, a touch of scarlet is one thing in a necktie, but something else again when shirt, pants, socks, shoes are all vermilion. Without further laboring the point, therefore, let me respectfully command you to plant your marigolds for brilliant accents, not for masses.

One can never say that some particular way of using color is "right" and other ways are "wrong." Rather it is a fact that drama and delight are lost by using colors some ways, and enhanced by other ways. Now I have a friend who would be happy if all the world were turned purple, and that person actively dislikes all yellows. Strange. But then people are. And who would wish to argue with somebody strangely constituted colorwise? Such persons should go right ahead with color arrangements that please them, however odd. But relatively normal gardeners usually respond with the greatest pleasure when colors are used not necessarily sparingly, but rather carefully. In general, the more brilliant the color the less of it you need. Or, put another way, the more brilliant it is, the sooner you have a belly full of it.

This does not mean (as the timid suppose) that the garden should have nothing but gray and puce in it. Quiet colors can be notably boring. I have a gang of dark violet petunias in pots. When I group these all together they are fairly dull, however safe from the reproach of vulgarity. But these dark petunias are wonderfully alive if two pots of raw brilliant pink petunias are stuck in among them. The pink is assertive and loud and restless, but when used sparingly with dark purple it is magical and splendid.

Among roses you can hardly help noticing that whole family of neon-electric vermilion-orange-pink. There is nothing wrong with the color as a color—it is clear, brilliant, sparkling, and if it makes you rather sick it is because too much of it is used. If there is a paved walk in the garden, it is possible to set up poles near the end of it, covered with vines, a shady bower with the walk continuing through it. If there is a garage, as there often is at the back of a garden, try covering the walk with vines (up in the air, of course) so that you see the walk in blazing sun, then dark under the vines, then (at the far end) in brilliant sun again. At that far end, you can have good effects from roses of the most day-glow brilliance. They are set off by the dark bower in front of them. There such a rose as 'Tropicana' may show itself off. It can be handsome with purple-leaf plants around it, or with plenty of gray leaves. But it seems to me a mistake (the rose itself is a mistake, as far as I am concerned, because I have no aptitude for these neon colors in roses, but there they are) to use such a color in beds of rose and pink and crimson and yellow roses, for there the strident color wars with and dominates everything within sight.

Dark crimsons, by the way, and intensely rich violets and mahogany and bronze—what sumptuous colors they are. And yet in a garden they invariably give a heavy dull effect when used by themselves, and what is strangest of all they become invisible at thirty feet. You discover, after a bit, that, rich as those colors are, they do not give rich effects, except when used with other colors. Straw yellow—a color that hardly anybody starts off admiring—is one of the most useful of all colors, as you will quickly see if you try it with the rich bronzes and crimsons. It makes them come alive, and so does fairly pale magenta.

Yellow irises (to give an example here) are great favorites of mine, and once I thought they would look fine contrasted only with sky-blue and white irises. Theoretically they should have looked good, since the colors were all pure and sparkling. To my surprise, the effect (which I feared might be too brassy, contrasting the yellow and blue) was distinctly tame and yawnworthy.

"I warned you to use plenty of wisteria lavender and sweet-pea pink," said an experienced gardener at the time, surveying my dull effect and quite pleased (for gardeners are not angels, let me tell you) to see it had worked out as badly as she had predicted.

As it happens, that mauve-magenta-sweet-pea pink is a color I cordially dislike. But the next year I included the lavenders and off-pinks, as instructed by my friend, and over my dead body of course. Needless to say, the same yellows and blues came brilliantly alive.

One of the most glorious of all colors is royal purple, and fortunately you find it in irises as in no other flower. I have noticed that men tend to go hog-wild with it, as I have so often done, and then wonder (as I did) why the effect was not as opulent as they thought it would be. One of the great disappointments of my life was the discovery that rich purple loses its effect unless used very sparingly. A few blobs of rich purple is fine—but if planted as freely as I would like, it becomes lifeless, however gorgeous the color may seem in an individual flower.

Thus experience forces us to learn a little, and after years of muddling about we usually discover (often late in life) what "everybody" has always known:

Soft and non-brilliant yellows and soft unspectacular lavenders and grayed blues and clear but not aggressive pinks are endlessly satisfying. Then you add extremely little deep purple, virtually no mahogany red, virtually no bronze (though it is beyond any gardener's strength to omit them entirely) and the result suddenly becomes marvelous.

White is commonly recommended—by the blind, I have often suspected—as a great pacifier of warring colors. I find it eggs on the warriors rather than reconciles them. White can behave like a spotlight, throwing everything else out of key. Of course there are many whites, some on the yellow side, some on the blue side, and the yellowish whites are the easiest to live with.

No harm at all is done if the colors don't seem quite right to you at first. Simply move the plants around until you like them better. When you shift things about you get a good many surprises, and commonly one partner of an especially satisfying color group will promptly die, or else grow out of bounds. That sort of thing we all know very well. No matter. We just keep at it, and presumably we will get it all worked out the year after we die.

But along the way we really do learn that marigolds gain enormously in impact when used as sparingly as ultimatums. We learn the pitfalls of too much brilliance, in which the gorgeous ones cancel each other out. In colors, as in humans, we learn there is much to be said for the modest, the pure, and (God save us all) the relatively dull.

[*The Essential Earthman* (1981)]

Frederick McGourty
Combining Perennials

In the United States, the cultivation of plants takes many forms. There are African violet hobbyists, gladiolus growers, hosta lovers, bonsai buffs, greenhouse plant gurus, orchid and rhododendron specialists, primulologists, cannaphiles, devoted students of the genus *Saxifraga*, gerbera groupies, and many veterans of the vegetable patch. More than sixty plant societies are active these days, not to mention ten societies devoted specifically to irises.

On occasion, I have attended the meetings of such organizations and found them fascinating, not only for the animated and detailed discussion of special plants, but also for the human participants, many of whom are quite special in their dedication. If a hemerocallis meeting had taken place on the last voyage of the *Titanic*, its members would have been oblivious to the main problem at hand, at least until the last stanza of "Nearer My God to Thee" was sung. Lifelong friendships are made at such get-togethers, and a certain number of lasting enmities, too. I remember one speaker showing 140 consecutive slide close-ups of gentians. As a result, I have developed what will probably be a lifelong coolness toward this otherwise innocuous group of plants.

But is all this emphasis on individual plant groups really gardening? Perhaps it is, if we consider gardening in a very strict sense, as the collecting of cultivars. To me, however, the subject has always implied something more: the creation of aesthetically pleasing arrangements of plants, as well as the culture of those plants. It is the combination of different forms—the coarse with the refined, the light with the dark—as well as their synergistic effects, that truly make a garden distinct from a collection of plants.

The late Vita Sackville-West put it another way. She once remarked that successful gardening was largely a matter of good marriages, albeit arranged ones for the most part. She was referring, of course, to plant combinations. Some are not lasting affairs, despite impeccable lineage and spectacular honeymoons. A shocking number were just never meant to be because of the roving nature of one of the partners. In some cases, there can be no recourse but divorce, by the yanking out of one or more of the incompatible parties. (*Ménage à trois*—or *quatre*—requires extra-special circumspection in the floral kingdom.)

Our own garden is full of divorces, as are the gardens of friends who also care about the compatible display of plants. We don't like to talk about skeletons in the family closet, at least not in print. If we are dealing with trees and shrubs, permanent scars can be inflicted on the landscape by the wrong combinations. Fortunately, with perennials the simple corrective is a trowel. Perennials can be moved! Many of them have traveled long distances in our own garden. Had they belonged to an airline travel club, I am sure a few would have won a trip to Hawaii by now.

The mixing of flower colors from different parts of the spectrum, such as yellows and pinks, frequently causes squabbles. Oranges and pinks always bring about pitched battles while the gardener looks on helplessly. Counseling doesn't work under such circumstances, though buffering the contending parties with plenty of silver foliage, white or blue flowers, or green foliage can turn adversity into diversity.

Timing is of the essence in avoiding some fierce battles. Each year there is a near-collision in one of our lightly shaded borders between two sound perennials—*Astilbe* 'Rheinland,' which has lovely 18-inch-tall steeples of clear pink flowers, and the common 'Enchantment' lily, whose flower color has been described as vermilion or nasturtium-red by polite authors. Actually, it is traffic-cop orange, which is a hard tint to use in the garden, though there is hope if one keeps it several hundred feet from the house. Fortunately, in the half-dozen years of this partnership, the astilbe has finished doing its thing two or three days before the lily starts. Someday the weather conditions may cause the blooms to overlap, and if they do, I will be prepared to scythe the astilbe in one fell swoop. Being a peace-keeper forces one to make difficult decisions.

In some parts of the country, climatic conditions may routinely cause the astilbe and lily to overlap. Clearly, some of the floral combinations that work for us in New England don't in Georgia or California, even though the plants may grow well there. The United States is a large country, and gardeners must work out their own plant marriages according to their own regions and, indeed, the microclimates in their own gardens.

But suppose we would like to avoid going down to the wire with color clashes in our own garden. One way might be for us to plant *Astilbe* 'Rheinland' with other astilbes having slightly different tints of pink. In another part of our garden, in fact, we alternate the mid-pink 'Rheinland' with another cultivar, 'Peach Blossom,' which has pale pink flowers. Usually, colors close to each other combine quite well. (The summer phloxes, which some gardeners are apt to dismiss with the epithet magenta, are a good example.) One exception is red; if one tint is orange-red, as in the Maltese-cross (*Lychnis chalcedonica*), and the other is pinkish-red, as in the rose campion (*Lychnis coronaria*), the combination can be like squeaky chalk on a blackboard.

An increasing number of gardeners are beginning to appreciate silver foliage for its value as a straight man that can bring out the best flower color in other plants. These days, probably the most widely sold perennial in the Northeast is a plant called silver mound, *Artemisia schmidtiana* 'Nana' of the trade. In one section of our garden, it is used as an edging for a drift of *Astilbe* 'Peach Blossom.' It provides early summer elegance, but then silver mound would complement anything except a giant sequoia. Even brassy yellows and oranges look dignified in its presence.

Silver mound performs best in the cooler parts of the country, but even there it has a tendency to flop open halfway through the season, resembling a silver cloud—sometimes a cirrus one at that. If you like tight little mounds, grow it in very sandy soil in full sun. I don't mind the former effect as long as the cloud has a silver lining, but there are situations where this plant should be pruned sharply in mid-summer if it is to look well the rest of the growing season.

If summers in your area are very hot, consider substituting lavender cotton, *Santolina chamaecyparissus*, for the same silvery effect, but be aware that this delightful subshrub has yellow flowers in summer that will clash with pinks. Some gardeners routinely remove these flowers, as they do the flowering stalks of another useful silver-leaved plant, lamb's-ears (*Stachys byzantina*), but the discord that results from leaving them on is not serious.

Let us return for a moment to rose campion, *Lychnis coronaria*. There is precious little that is "rose" about it. It is a color that, because of its vulgar loudness, appeals mainly to people with "tin eyes." We evicted this old-time, free-seeding, short-lived perennial from our garden with a vengeance after discovering young plants cavorting with 'Enchantment' lilies. The first-year foliage rosette is a wonderfully seductive, satiny gray, but we can have that in a white-flowered form with *L. coronaria* 'Alba,' which comes true from seed if kept away from the loud type.

No flower color is intrinsically bad, but I have the highest regard for any gardener who uses rose campion well. Such a person is Mildred Van Vlack. Mrs. Van Vlack's Connecticut garden is at its peak in the latter part of June, when old roses and the first wave of delphiniums are in fine fettle. The rose campion has a backdrop of good, pink old roses, and there are several perennials nearby with good green foliage, as well as a smattering of plants with white flowers. It is a winning combination, and I often think of it, though I have never actually tried it. Mrs. Van Vlack is a bolder person than I am.

Floral combinations with perennials are transient, because most plants bloom for just three weeks or so. Perhaps that is just as well, because we can have a succession of combinations through the season, with something new to look forward to as the months go by. Lately, I have had a special interest in extending the period in which the garden is attractive further into autumn. Normal people admire sugar maples or watch football games in fall. My taste runs more toward combating seasonal senescence in the garden, delaying the inevitable, and more positively, preserving beauty. Summer in the North is too short, and I don't see any reason to throw in the trowel on Labor Day, particularly when some of the year's best weather is yet to come.

Of course, there is always the chrysanthemum, which seems to be a tyrant of fall gardens. When I visit a garden center in September, I get the uneasy feeling that every flower in the world has a rounded form. Chrysanthemums have become events rather than garden plants. In recent years, they have evolved apart from the garden and are now to many people just an extension of a florist crop. It is hard to classify the autumn chrysanthemum taxonomically and even seasonally; it is not quite a perennial, it is not an annual, and many of the cultivars start to flower by late July. Of course, if we want such flowers programmed into bloom, we can go to a florist even in March.

I do not really care to see a chrysanthemum in March nor in July, and I do not think that poodle-ization has made the plant prettier. Do not mistake me: I am fond of the chrysanthemum— single-flowered and pompom sorts that will bloom in September and October and maybe even November in the severe land where I live, and ones that will survive winter in good shape and not need yearly division or staking. A dream, you say? No, I see these in older gardens from time to time, and ask for cuttings. Unfortunately, they do not seem to be in the trade anymore.

How much richer our gardens would be if we thought of the chrysanthemum as *one* of autumn's plants rather than its *exclusive* one. That time of year may be top-heavy with daisy flower forms, but there are other plants that can relieve the possible monotony. Foremost are the spikes of the late-blooming snakeroot, *Cimicifuga simplex*, whose pure white bottlebrushes on three- to six-foot-tall stems rise from the sea of chrysanthemums, each complementing the other. The spikes of a September-flowering false dragonhead, *Physostegia virginiana* 'Bouquet Rose,' are useful with white chrysanthemums, since the latter are apt to fade to a purplish-pink and need some visual support so as not to appear tatty. Chrysanthemums, like most plants, should have their spent flowers removed. In this case, removing the flowers can extend the season of effective bloom considerably. Pink turtlehead, *Chelone lyonii*, can serve much the same function as false dragonhead, though its individual flowers are hunchbacked.

My favorite combination for autumn doesn't include a chrysanthemum, and the blooms last a long time. This is a *ménage à trois* combining *Sedum* 'Autumn Joy,' with flat clusters of Indian-red flowers on two-foot-tall stalks; Canadian burnet, *Sanguisorba canadensis*, whose five-foot-tall stalks topped by white bottlebrushes are less showy but more frost-resistant than those of *Cimicifuga simplex*; and the fall monkshood, *Aconitum carmichaelii* (sometimes listed as *A. fischeri*), with clear blue flowers on stalks that usually attain three feet. A fourth partner is evident in the background if it is a cool summer and flowering is delayed. This is *Helenium* 'Copper Spray,' which is four to five feet tall, yellow, orange and showy. Off to another side is *Rudbeckia nitida* 'Goldquelle,' with yellow flowers that are fully double. This plant resembles a scaled-down version of golden-glow, *R. laciniata* 'Hortensia,' the dowdy, turn-of-the-century matron one still encounters near old farmhouses. A few New England asters, the white-flowered *Boltonia asteroides* 'Snowbank,' and a tall ornamental grass or two (for example, *Miscanthus sinensis* 'Silver Feather,' or zebra grass, *M. sinensis* 'Zebrinus,' with its horizontal yellow bands) would provide a quite tolerable autumn border—enough to wean all but die-hard machos away from the television set on a Saturday afternoon in October. They probably wouldn't even notice that chrysanthemums were missing.

To the innovative gardener, shade is an opportunity, not a problem, and in warmer parts of the country it is a blessing for plants as well as for people. Approximately 40 percent of the best-known perennials demand shade or are shade-tolerant (there is a difference between the two). This gives the gardener who is looking for aesthetically pleasing combinations plenty of plants with which to experiment. The warmer the area, the greater the number of plants that welcome some shade, especially in the afternoon.

Plant partnerships are not forever, but one I like very much is the European wild ginger, *Asarum europaeum*, planted in front of maidenhair fern, *Adiantum pedatum*. The deep green, leathery, chunky foliage of the former is enhanced by the light-textured, delicate green of the latter. In time, the fern grows too tall, and the combination must be reworked periodically. If you can obtain the more compact-growing Aleutian form of maidenhair fern

(*A. pedatum* var. *aleuticum*) from a rock garden nursery, you might use it as a substitute. Another variation of the theme is to substitute one of the southern wild gingers—either *Asarum shuttleworthii* or *A. virginicum*, with their attractively marbled foliage—for the European species.

Foliage combinations are more durable than floral ones because the leaves are present throughout the growing season. In the case of the three wild gingers I have mentioned, the leaves are, in fact, evergreen. Should you want to add an attractive floral partner, Korean goatsbeard (*Aruncus aethusifolius*), with feathery, astilbe-like foliage and eight-inch-tall stalks of white flowers, is a fitting companion. The foliage itself is winning, and the plant makes a fine ground cover in a small area.

Another low-growing foliage combination for the shade is *Hosta venusta* and a dwarf meadow rue, *Thalictrum minus*, which grows only one foot tall in its better forms and has small, lacy foliage that looks best after a rain, when beads of water cling to it. *H. venusta* is the smallest true species of hosta (only a couple of inches high), but with a blocky effect. One variant even smaller than that, *H. venusta* 'Minus,' is useful for rock garden troughs. Both the thalictrum and hosta bloom, but the flowers are irrelevant, except perhaps to the plants and to the sort of gardener who judges plants only by blossoms.

The above combinations are satisfactory in fairly deep shade, but the number of choices increases in light shade. The focal point in July and August in our main border, in a section that receives less than five hours of sun each day, is a grouping of five plants of a largely neglected American woodlander, the black snakeroot (*Cimicifuga racemosa*). These were planted in a woodsy, moisture-retentive soil in 1964 and have not been divided since, nor have they been fertilized more than two or three times over the years.

The actual flowering period of the black snakeroot in our garden is no longer than a month, but the six- or seven-foot-tall stalks are prominent for two weeks before the pearl-shaped white buds open, and the stalks have architectural merit for several more weeks after flowering. I was not much of a gardener in 1964, and my immediate aim then was to hide a statue of a little girl my mother left me. The snakeroot did not perform its task very well, though it did soften the statue, and the main beneficiaries have been the surrounding

plants that were selected for summer bloom: *Heliopsis* 'Gold Green-
heart'; magnificently scented regal lilies; and clear pink summer
phlox 'Sir John Falstaff,' which will linger in bloom until September
if the old flower heads are removed and if we have been consci-
entious in applying the fungicide Benomyl to control mildew.

There is a rustle of interest in ornamental grasses these days—
an interest that, to my way of thinking, is long overdue. Fine public
displays are evident around some of the federal buildings in Washington, D.C., where the grasses are used particularly in conjunction
with *Sedum* 'Autumn Joy' and *Rudbeckia fulgida*, the perennial
black-eyed Susan. My own initial acquaintance with these grasses
was at the Brooklyn Botanic Garden, where a substantial border
was given over largely to them, with a sprinkling of hemerocallis,
yuccas and bulbs. In November this "monocot" border was striking
in the morning sun, which provided a brilliant backlighting effect.
It was, in a sense, "a garden of a golden morning"; the foliage of
the seven- or eight-foot-tall grasses took on wonderful tints of yellow,
and gossamer seed heads of *Miscanthus* and ravenna grass (*Erian-
thus ravennae*) waved in a soft wind. Many of these ornamental
grasses can actually be attractive until late in the winter even in the
colder reaches, turning the color of parchment by mid-winter. Combined with evergreens, birches and winterberry holly (*Ilex verti-
cillata*), they add interest to what is all too often a desolate landscape.

[*American Horticulturist* (1985)]

Pamela J. Harper
It Began with Butterfly Weed

Our gardens would be dull indeed if there were universal consensus about what went best with what, but many people would agree that orange creates disharmony more often than any other color, and some shun it for that reason. I have done so myself in the past, but discussions with friends whose gardens, and in one instance paintings, I admire have caused me to reconsider.

Orange looks superb alone. To my mind's eye comes a conflagration of poppies on a California hillside and the gorgeous daisy-like flowers of devil's paintbrush (*Hieracium aurantiacum*) decorating what might otherwise have been a squalid wasteland. Orange also looks wonderful with blue; I recall Indian paintbrush (*Castilleja*) with wild lupine on Mt. Rainier and, in a California garden, orange geums over a carpet of blue forget-me-nots. Nature often masses color, but a single clump of orange has considerable impact: now I am remembering a solitary plant of butterfly weed (*Asclepias tuberosa*) in a New England meadow. Orange seems to advance toward you, and it has great garden value for spotlighting areas that otherwise might go unnoticed, either because they are distant or because the colors used are cool, receding blues and greens. For a single spot of attention-getting orange I know no better plant than the lily 'Enchantment,' a splash of vivid color undiluted by green leaves.

Orange mixes well with the palest tones of purple if leavened with plenty of green. A patch of orange marigolds struck just the right note in the corner of a partly shaded kitchen garden filled with parsley, mint, and pale pinkish-purple *Allium senescens*. It is when we see orange in close proximity to bright purple or bright pink that most of us recoil. Loath as I am to discard a healthy plant, *Rhododendron* 'P.J.M.' may have to go because the long, warm autumns of the Southeast induce a second burst of purplish bloom to coincide with the orange autumnal hues of the older leaves. And striking as are the tomato-shaped, tomato-red hips of *Rosa rugosa*, I wish it didn't combine these with magenta flowers. We can, fortunately, have the beauty and fragrance without the color clash by choosing a white-flowered cultivar rather than others.

At Sissinghurst, one of England's finest gardens, the orange bottle-shaped hips of *Rosa moyesii* are poised on arched canes over a perennial border in which pinks and purples predominate. Testing my own ambivalent reaction, I planted an orange-berried pyracantha next to a group of *Callicarpa americana* with berries of vibrant— almost virulent—violet-purple; I then stood back and flinched. Some gardeners combine purple and orange with deliberate intent to startle, contending that a garden should exhilarate. Most of us pass by with averted eyes. I am reminded of the old lady who thought her granddaughter's suitor unsatisfactory as a potential husband because his temperament was so different from hers. "Opposites attract," said the girl, drawing the tart retort that just being man and woman was opposite enough. Just being orange is exhilarating enough; it doesn't need purple from which to strike sparks. Scale makes a difference though; one each of two colors seems unintended, while five of each may be acceptable.

It is often suggested that adding white will meld two inharmonious colors, but I don't think this is so. Gray might do the trick, but white takes on the character of its companions. Put it with soft blue, gray, pale yellow, or pale pink and the mood is restful. With crimson each becomes more exuberant by contrast with the other. Putting white between purple and orange seems to add restlessness to disharmony—one's eye hops back and forth seeking unity in vain.

Why does a combination of colors usually thought to clash occasionally bring delight? One memorable herbaceous border struck no jarring note despite its apparently unplanned assortment of colors. On closer inspection it was clear that the colors were not mixed indiscriminately. The orange spires of red-hot poker (*Kniphofia*) reared up behind red dahlias, flanked by coppery heleniums and yellow achilleas. The eye absorbed this group as a unit before moving on to bright pink *Sedum spectabile* with paler pink Japanese anemones, white cosmos, and pale lavender perovskia. Sometimes a medley of bright colors is unified by similarity of shape and texture: a mixed planting of Persian ranunculus, for example, or chrysanthemums, or the mixed color strains of such annuals as portulaca.

Exhilaration without clash is most easily achieved by grouping together yellows, oranges, and reds in a part of the garden well separated from the pinks and purples. Such a bed in my garden began with butterfly weed. In the Northeast this flowers in July, but in Virginia it flowers in early June, as did, a yard away, my bright pink Satsuki azaleas. So furiously did these two colors wage war that the combatants had to be separated. The butterfly weed survived the move to settle down in what is now evolving into a bed of sunny colors—scarlet (but not crimson), orange, and golden (not lemony) yellows.

When I looked for perennials to go with the butterfly weed I found yellows galore, but none too many oranges and rather few reds. In the course of the search I became aware that while most yellow and orange flowers do best in sun and well-drained soil, several of the best reds need moist soil, among them *Schizostylis coccinea*, *Lobelia cardinalis*, *Monarda didyma*, *Astilbe* 'Fire', and *Lychnis chalcedonica*. In hot-summer regions the last four also do best with a bit of afternoon shade.

The soil in this bed is sandy and beyond the reach of the hose, which limits what can be grown. The best I have found is gaillardia; mine are the Monarch strain, long-lived and self-seeding true to type with scarlet, yellow-rimmed wheels of flowers. These produce at least a few flowers every day through the summer, even if not deadheaded, and the heads themselves are attractive.

The low, spreading, prickly pear, *Opuntia humifusa*, thrives on neglect—insofar as its spines allow one to ignore it. Coinciding in bloom with the butterfly weed, its yellow flowers are as opulent as water lilies and the ripening pink fruits are also decorative. I have on trial a spineless form, but cactus experts tell me that in a different climate spines may develop.

As spectacular, though different in every way, is *Ipomopsis* (*Gilia rubra*), a biennial native to eastern Texas, South Carolina, and Florida. Scatter seed where it is to grow and that year (or the next if sown in autumn) it will make tuffets of thread-like leaves. The following summer the upper half of five-foot, bright green, leafy plumes will be ablaze with brilliant scarlet flowers. By holding over some seed for a year I hope to establish a colony of plants, half flowering one year, half the next, maintained thereafter by self-sowing.

Most montbretias (*Crocosmia*) and the taller, similar *Curtonus* and *Chasmanthe* are easy-going tuberous-rooted perennials with orange flowers. Those with yellow flowers seem less robust. *Crocosmia* 'Lucifer,' readily available, is a good red. So is a selection of *Crocosmia masoniorum* called 'Dixter,' but this is scarce as yet in the United States.

Blackberry-lilies (*Belamcanda*) do well if the soil is first enriched. *B. chinensis* makes handsome two-foot fans (taller in rich soil) of iris-like leaves topped by sprays of orange-speckled flowers; these are followed by clusters of glossy black fruits for autumn and winter interest. *B.* 'Freckle Face' is similar but shorter, and the smaller *B. flabellata* (sold as 'Hello Yellow') has unspeckled yellow flowers and grayish leaves. For autumn flower there is *Chrysopsis mariana*, native here and a very garden-worthy perennial. From basal rosettes of gray-green leaves come two- to three-foot stems massed with bright yellow daisies. I think this is a better plant than *Chrysopsis villosa*, which is sold by nurseries as *Aster* 'Golden Sunshine,' a taller plant that usually needs staking. There are also some excellent, drought-resistant, sun-loving, yellow-flowered perennials among the sundrops, a muddled group known variously as *Oenothera fruticosa*, *O. tetragona*, and *O. pilosella*. Most grow twelve to eighteen inches high and spread quite rapidly. For winter interest I have added the gold-leaved *Abelia* 'Francis Mason,' an orange-berried, low-growing pyracantha, and a yellow-striped yucca.

There are plenty of annuals in the red, yellow, and orange range for filling in gaps: zinnias, marigolds, scarlet sage, poppies, nasturtiums, and the compact plumed celosia called 'Apricot Brandy,' to name just a few. Cosmos 'Diablo' and 'Sunset' are also good; they self-seed and reappear each spring.

Pinks and purples need not clash with orange, but they do so more often than not. Combining them successfully takes greater artistry than most of us can manage, and timid experiments invariably fail. For those of us lacking the courage to attempt such riotous color schemes, the red, yellow, and orange bed or border gives stimulating effect without risking disastrous confrontation.

[*Pacific Horticulture* (1986)]

FRAGRANCE

Celia Thaxter
The Breath of Flowers

Says the wise Lord Bacon again: "And because the Breath of Flowers is far sweeter in the Aire (when it comes and goes, like the Warbling of Music) than in the hand, therefore nothing is more fit for that delight than to know what be the Flowers and Plants that doe best perfume the Aire."

The most exquisite perfume known to my garden is that of the Wallflowers; there is nothing equal to it. They blossom early, and generally before June has passed they are gone, and have left me mourning their too swift departure. I wonder they are not more generally cultivated, but I fancy the fact that they do not blossom till the second year has much to do with their rarity. It requires so much more faith and patience to wait a whole year, and meanwhile carefully watch and tend the plants, excepting during the time when winter covers them with a blanket of snow; but when at last spring comes and the tardy flowers appear, then one is a thousand times repaid for all the tedious months of waiting. They return such wealth of bloom and fragrance for the care and thought bestowed on them! Their thick spikes of velvet blossoms are in all shades of rich red, from scarlet to the darkest brown, from light gold to orange; some are purple; and their odor,—who shall describe it! Violets, Roses, Lilies, Sweet Peas, Mignonette, and Heliotrope, with a dash of Honeysuckle, all mingled in a heavenly whole. There is no perfume which I know that can equal it. And they are so lavish of their scent; it is borne off the garden and wafted everywhere, into the house and here and there in all directions, in viewless clouds on the gentle air. To make a perfect success of Wallflowers they must be given

lime in some form about the roots. They thrive marvelously if fed
with a mixture of old plastering in the soil, or bone meal, or, if that
is not at hand, the meat bones from the kitchen, calcined in the
oven and pounded into bits, stirred in around the roots is fine for
them. This treatment makes all the difference in the world in their
strength and beauty. After the Wallflowers, Roses and Lilies, Mignonette, Pinks, Gillyflowers, Sweet Peas, and the Honeysuckles
for fragrance, and of these last, the monthly Honeysuckle is the
most divine. Such vigor of growth I have never seen in any other
plant, and it is hardy even without the least protection in our northern climate. It climbs the trellis on my piazza and spreads its superb
clusters of flowers from time to time all summer. Each cluster is a
triumph of beauty, flat in the centre and curving out to the blossoming edge in joyous lines of loveliness, most like a wreath of
heavenly trumpets breathing melodies of perfume to the air. Each
trumpet of lustrous white deepens to a yellower tint in the centre
where the small ends meet; each blossom where it opens at the lip
is tipped with fresh pink; each sends out a group of long stamens
from its slender throat like rays of light; and the whole circle of
radiant flowers has an effect of gladness and glory indescribable:
the very sight of it lifts and refreshes the human heart. And for its
odor, it is like the spirit of romance, sweet as youth's tender dreams.
It is summer's very soul.

This beautiful vine will grow anywhere, for anybody, only give
it half a chance, such is its matchless vigor. I wonder why it is not
found in every garden; nothing so well repays the slightest care.

Next in power come the Sweet Peas, blossoming the livelong
summer in all lovely tints save only yellow, and even that the kind
called Primrose approaches, with its faint gold suffusion of both
inner and outer petals. I plant them by myriads in my tiny garden—
all it will hold. Transplant, I should say, because of my friends the
birds, who never leave me one if I dare plant them out of doors.
but this transplanting is most delightful. I thoroughly enjoy digging
with the hoe a long trench six inches deep for the strong young
seedlings, lifting them from the boxes, carefully disentangling their
long white roots each from the other as I take them out, and placing
them in a close row the whole length of the deep furrow, letting
the roots drop their whole length, with no curling or crowding, then
half filling the hollow with water, drawing the earth about the roots

and firming the whole with strong and gentle touch. They do not droop a single leaf so transplanted; they go on growing as if nothing had happened, if only they are given all the water they need. Already they stretch out their delicate tendrils to climb, and I love to give them for support the sticks with which the farmers supply their pea vines for the market; but on my island are no woods, so I am thankful for humble bayberry and elder branches for the purpose. It is another pleasure to go afar among the rocks for these and wheel them to the flower beds in a light wheelbarrow, which is one of the most useful things one can possess for work about the garden. At once the vines lay hold of the slender sticks and climb to the very top, fain are they to go much farther. But I cut the tops so that they may branch from the sides and keep within bounds, and they soon make a solid hedge of healthy green. Oh, when the blossoms break from these green hedges like heavenly winged angels, and their pure, cool perfume fills the air, what joy is mine!

I find Sweet Peas can hardly have too rich a soil, provided always that they are kept sufficiently wet. They *must* have moisture, their roots must be kept cool and damp,—a mulch of leaves or straw is a very good thing to keep the roots from drying,—and they must always be planted as deep as possible. Wood ashes give them a stronger growth. Their colors, the great variety of them, and their vivid delicacy are wonderful; they are most beautiful against the background of the sea; they are a continual source of delight, and never cease to bloom, with me, if gathered every day and watered abundantly, the whole summer long, even through the autumn till November. But they must never be suffered to go to seed; that would check their blossoming at once. I revel in their beauty week after week, bringing them into the house and arranging them in masses every other day.

[*An Island Garden* (1894)]

Mrs. Dana
The Leafy Month of June

When Coleridge called this

the leafy month of June,

it seems to me that he struck the note of the first summer month more distinctly than our own Bryant, who wrote of "flowery June." June is, above all things, "leafy," seeming chiefly to concentrate her energies on her foliage; for although she really is not lacking in flowers, they are almost swamped in the great green flood which has swept silently but irresistibly across the land. At times one loses sight of them altogether, and fancies that a sort of reaction has set in after that

festival
Of breaking bud and scented breath

which enchained our senses a few weeks since.

But the sight of a clover-field alone suffices to dispel the thought. There is no suggestion of exhaustion in the close, sweet-scented, wholesome heads which are nodding over whole acres of land.

South winds jostle them,
Bumble-bees come,
Hover, hesitate,
Drink, and are gone,

sings Emily Dickinson, who elsewhere calls the clover the

> *flower that bees prefer*
> *And butterflies desire.*

Indeed, although this is not a native blossom, it seems to have taken a special hold on the imagination of our poets. Mr. James Whitcomb Riley asks,

> *What is the lily and all of the rest*
> *Of the flowers to a man with a heart in his breast,*
> *That was dipped brimmin' full of the honey and dew*
> *Of the sweet clover-blossoms his babyhood knew?*

It is generally acknowledged that our sense of smell is so intimately connected with our powers of memory that odors serve to recall, with peculiar vividness, the particular scenes with which they are associated. Many of us have been startled by some swiftly borne, perhaps unrecognized fragrance, which, for a brief instant, has forcibly projected us into the past; and I can imagine that a sensitively organized individual—and surely the poet is the outcome of a peculiarly sensitive and highly developed organization—might be carried back, with the strong scent of the clover-field, to the days when its breath was a sufficient joy and its limits barred out all possibility of disaster.

If we pluck from the rounded heads one tiny flower and examine it with a magnifying-glass we see that it has somewhat the butterfly shape of its kinsman, the sweet-pea of the garden. We remember that as children we followed the bee's example and sucked from its slender tube the nectar; and we conclude that the combined presence of irregularity of form, nectar, vivid coloring, and fragrance indicates a need of insect visitors for the exchange of pollen and consequent setting of seed, as Nature never expends so much effort without some clear end in view.

As an instance of the strange "web of complex relations," to quote Darwin, which binds together the various forms of life, I recall a statement, which created some amusement at a meeting of the English Royal Agricultural Society, to the effect that the growth of pink clover depended largely on the proximity of old women. The speaker argued that old women kept cats; cats killed mice; mice were prone to destroy the nests of the bumble-bees, which alone were fitted, owing to the length of their probosces, to fertilize the blossoms of the clover. Consequently, a good supply of clover depended on an abundance of old women.

[*According to Season* (1894)]

Alice Morse Earle
The Bitter Fragrance of Box

*They walked over the crackling leaves in
the garden, between the lines of Box,
breathing its fragrance of eternity; for this
is one of the odors which carry us out of
time into the abysses of the unbeginning
past; if we ever lived on another ball of
stone than this, it must be that there was
Box growing on it.*

—Elsie Venner,

OLIVER WENDELL HOLMES,

1861

To many of us, besides Dr. Holmes, the unique aroma of the Box,
cleanly bitter in scent as in taste, is redolent of the eternal past; it
is almost hypnotic in its effect. This strange power is not felt by all,
nor is it a present sensitory influence; it is an hereditary memory,
half-known by many, but fixed in its intensity in those of New
England birth and descent, true children of the Puritans; to such
ones the Box breathes out the very atmosphere of New England's
past. I cannot see in clear outline those prim gardens of centuries
ago, nor the faces of those who walked and worked therein; but I
know, as I stroll to-day between our old Box-edged borders, and
inhale the beloved bitterness of fragrance, and gather a stiff sprig
of the beautiful glossy leaves, that in truth the garden lovers and
garden workers of other days walk beside me, though unseen and
unheard.

About thirty years ago a bright young Yankee girl went to the
island of Cuba as a governess to the family of a sugar planter. It was

regarded as a somewhat perilous adventure by her home-staying folk, and their apprehensions of ill were realized in her death there five years later. This was not, however, all that happened to her. The planter's wife had died in this interval of time, and she had been married to the widower. A daughter had been born, who, after her mother's death, was reared in the Southern island, in Cuban ways, having scant and formal communication with her New England kin. When this girl was twenty years old, she came to the little Massachusetts town where her mother had been reared, and met there a group of widowed and maiden aunts, and great-aunts. After sitting for a time in her mother's room in the old home, the reserve which often exists between those of the same race who should be friends but whose lives have been widely apart, and who can never have more than a passing sight of each other, made them in semi-embarrassment and lack of resources of mutual interest walk out into the garden. As they passed down the path between high lines of Box, the girl suddenly stopped, looked in terror at the gate, and screamed out in fright, "The dog, the dog, save me, he will kill me!" *No dog was there*, but on that very spot, between those Box hedges, thirty years before, her mother had been attacked and bitten by an enraged dog, to the distress and apprehension of the aunts, who all recalled the occurrence, as they reassured the fainting and bewildered girl. She, of course, had never known aught of this till she was told it by the old Box.

Many other instances of the hypnotic effect of the Box are known, and also of its strong influence on the mind through memory. I know of a man who travelled a thousand miles to renew acquaintance and propose marriage to an old sweetheart, whom he had not seen and scarcely thought of for years, having been induced to this act wholly through memories of her, awakened by a chance stroll in an old Box-edged garden such as those of his youth; at the gate of one of which he had often lingered, after walking home with her from singing-school. I ought to be able to add that the twain were married as a result of this sentimental memory-awakening through the old Box; but, in truth, they never came very close to matrimony. For when he saw her he remained absolutely silent on the subject of marriage; the fickle creature forgot the Box scent and the singing-school, while she openly expressed to her friends her surprise at

Alice Morse Earle

his aged appearance, and her pity for his dulness. For the sense of sight is more powerful than that of smell, and the Box might prove a master hand at hinting, but it failed utterly in permanent influence.

[*Old-Time Gardens* (1901)]

Alice Lounsberry
Gardens of Sweet Scent

After many gardens have been considered, and their inhabitants have been located and scanned, it often seems that those in which the individuality of the owners had run riot were the ones to live longest in the memory. For the garden is not only a place in which to make things grow and to display the beautiful flowers of the earth, but a place that should accord with the various moods of its admirers. It should be a place in which to hold light banter, a place in which to laugh, and, besides, should have a hidden corner in which to weep. But above all, perhaps, it should be a place of sweet scent and sentiment.

A garden without the fragrance of flowers would be deprived of one of its true rights. Fortunately, those near the sea are unusually redolent of sweet scent, the soft moisture of the atmosphere that surrounds them causing their fragrance to be more readily perceived than if the atmosphere were harsh and dry. It is still an open question to what extent the memory and the imagination of people are stirred by scents recurring at intervals through their existence. To many the perfume of flowers has more meaning than their outward beauty. In it they feel the spirit and the eternity of the flowers.

Undoubtedly, a particular fragrance will bring back quickly to the mind, and with much vividness, scenes and associations which have apparently been forgotten and which might otherwise lie dormant for a lifetime. The odors of many flowers are very distinctive. The perfume of the strawberry shrub is like none other; fraxinella, lavender, lilacs, and an infinite number of flowers are as well known by their fragrance as by their appearance. And although we smell them a hundred times a season, under many and dissimilar circumstances, there is perhaps only the one association that they will definitely recall. It is the one that has affected us deeply and moved our sentiment.

The first strawberry shrub that I ever saw was given to me when a small child by a red-cheeked boy just as I went into church with my grandmother. I slipped it into the palm of my hand under my glove, and throughout the service I kept my nose closely to the opening of the glove, smelling the flower. I was reproved again and again, but I continually reverted to my new and exquisite diversion; for, in those days, the time spent in church seemed longer than the rest of the whole week. Even now, each spring, when the first of these strange little flowers gives its scent to the air, I am for an instant transplanted, as it were, back to that stiff church pew, aching to be out in the open, and smelling the strawberry shrub in my glove.

[*Gardens Near the Sea* (1910)]

Louise Beebe Wilder
Pleasures of the Nose

Man only doth smel and take delight
in the odours of flowers and sweet things.
—WILLIAM BULLEIN, 1562

A garden full of sweet odours is a garden full of charm, a most precious kind of charm not to be implanted by mere skill in horticulture or power of purse, and which is beyond explaining. It is born of sensitive and very personal preferences yet its appeal is almost universal. Fragrance speaks to many to whom colour and form say little, and it "can bring as irresistibly as music emotions of all sorts to the mind." Besides the plants visible to the eye there will be in such a garden other comely growths, plain to that "other sense," such as "faith, romance, the lore of old unhurried times." These are infinitely well worth cultivating among the rest. They are an added joy in happy times and gently remedial when life seems warped and tired.

Nor is the fragrant garden ever wholly our own. It is, whether we will or no, common property. Over hedge or wall, and often far down the highway, it sends a greeting, not alone to us who have toiled for it, but to the passing stranger, the blind beggar, the child skipping to school, the tired woman on her way to work, the rich man, the careless youth. And who shall say that the gentle sweet airs for a moment enveloping them do not send each on his way touched in some manner, cheered, softened, filled with hope or renewed in vigour, arrested, perhaps, in some devious course?

In mediaeval times there was a widespread belief in the efficacy of flower and leaf scents as cures or alleviations for all sorts of ills of the flesh, but more especially of the spirit, and as a protection against infection. This belief is testified to again and again in early horticultural and medical works. "If odours may worke satisfaction," wrote Gerard, "they are so sovereign in plants and so comfortable that no confection of apothecaries can equall their excellent virtue." In the *Grete Herball* it is written, "Against weyknesse of the brayne smel to Musk." The scent of Basil was thought stimulating to the heart and "it taketh away melancholy and maketh a man merry and glad." The fragrance of Sweet Marjoram was deemed remedial for those "given to over much sighing." The smell of Violets was thought an aid to digestion, and of Rosemary it was written, "Smell of it and it shall keep thee youngly." "As for the garden of Mint," wrote Pliny, "the very smell of it alone recovers and refreshes our spirits, as the taste stirs up our appetite for meat." To smell of Wild Thyme was believed to raise the spirits (and does it not?) and the vital energies, while the odour of Garlic preserved those who partook of it or carried it about with them from infection.

Nor need we peer back into the dim past for corroboration. We all know persons who are affected for better or for worse by certain odours. A woman once told me that the smell of white Lilac revived her no matter how low she might feel in mind or body. My father was made actively ill by the scent of blossoming Ailanthus trees and he carried on a small but animated feud with a neighbour who had two in her garden and refused to part with them—quite unreasonably, thought my father. To me the smell of Clove Pinks is instantly invigorating, while that of Roses (the true old Rose scent such as is possessed by the lovely dark red Rose Étoile de Hollande) is invariably calming. Over and over again I have experienced the quieting influence of Rose scent upon a disturbed state of mind, feeling the troubled condition smoothing out before I realized that Roses were in the room, or near at hand. The soothing effects of Lavender preparations are well known, and certain flower odours have an opposite effect, causing headache or nausea, even to the point of catastrophe, especially in a close room. [. . .]

But the subject is full of indistinctness, for a perfume that is a delight to one individual may be a horror to another. Memory, imagination, sentiment, a weak or strong stomach, are inextricably involved in our reactions. But do not many of us know from experience that a chance whiff from a hayfield, a Pine grove, the wayside bramble, the sea, often changes the mood of a whole day? A very old man once told me that whenever he smelled freshly sawed wood he felt instantly young and vigorous for a time. His youth had been passed in a New England village where there was a large saw mill and the acrid odour of fresh-cut wood was so strongly associated in his mind with youth and its abounding energy that it affected him physically.

Of course some persons are far more sensitive to such influences than others. Some there are, sadly enough, who are partially, or totally, anosmic, or nose blind, and to these a whole world of sensation and experience is closed. But there is undoubtedly a close and intimate connection between the sense of smell and the nerve centers and it is probably not fully understood how far reaching and profound is the influence of odour upon our mental state and physical makeup. Montaigne wrote:

Physicians might in mine opinion draw more use and good from odours than they doe. For myself have often perceived that according unto their strength and qualitie, they change and alter and move my spirits and worke strange effects in me which make approve the common saying that the invention of insense and perfumes in churches, so ancient and so far dispersed throughout all nations and religions, had a special regard to rejoyce, to comfort, to quicken, to rouse, and to purify the senses, so that we might be the apter and readier unto contemplation.

Ancient books teach that the smell of many plants, Rosemary among them, strengthens the memory, but none that I have come across calls attention to the trick that perfume sometimes plays us of suddenly calling up out of the past a scene, an episode, a state of mind, long buried beneath an accumulation of years and experience. How often the scent of some flower—Honeysuckle, Jasmine, Lilac—stealing upon our sense in the night, causes the darkness to flower in visions of hallucinatory vividness. "Smell," wrote E. F. Benson, "is the most memoristic of the senses."

Fragrance, perhaps, speaks more clearly, however, to age than to youth. With the young it may not pass much beyond the olfactory nerve, but with those who have started down the far side of the hill it reaches into the heart. [. . .] More than once I have seen eyes suddenly clouded with tears at the scent of some flower whose like may have grown in the dooryard of the old home, or about which cluster precious memories of a country-spent childhood. In the delightful letters of Robert Southey, one of whose own books, John Rea's *Flora*, with his name inscribed in faded brown ink upon the fly leaf, is in my library, one reads that the poet was constantly reminded of his early childhood by the peculiar fragrance of decaying Walnut leaves, while the scent of Barberry brought to his mind the memory of a certain bush that grew in a garden where many of his happiest days had been spent.

The gardens of my youth were fragrant gardens and it is their sweetness rather than their patterns or their furnishings that I now most clearly recall. My mother's Rose garden in Maryland was famous in that countryside and in the nearby city, for many shared its bounty. In it grew the most fragrant Roses, not only great bushes of Provence, Damask and Gallica Roses, but a collection of the finest Teas and Noisettes of the day. Maréchal Niel, Lamarque and Gloire de Dijon climbed high on trellises against the stone of the old house and looked in at the second-story windows. I remember that some sort of much coveted distinction was conferred upon the child finding the first long golden bud of Maréchal Niel. [. . .]

Why do garden makers of to-day so seldom deliberately plan for fragrance? Undoubtedly gardens of early times were sweeter than ours. The green enclosures of Elizabethan days evidently overflowed with fragrant flowers and the little beds in which they were confined were neatly edged with some sweet-leaved plant—Thyme, Germander, Lavender, Rosemary, cut to a formal line. The yellowed pages of ancient works on gardening seem to give off the scents of the beloved old favourites—Gilliflower, Stock, Sweet Rocket, Wallflower, white Violet. Fragrance, by the wise old gardeners of those days, was valued as much as if not more than other attributes. Bacon said immortal things about sweet scented flowers in his essay, "Of Gardens," as well as in his less known curious old *Naturall Historie*. Theophrastus devoted a portion of his *Inquiry into Plants* to odours, chiefly floral and leaf odours. Our books of to-day make sadly little of the subject.

Our great-grandmothers prized more highly than any others what they called their posy flowers, Moss Rose, Southernwood, Bergamot, Marigold, and the like. Indeed it would seem that save in that strangely tasteless period of the nineteenth century, when all grace departed from gardens and hard hued flowers were laid down upon the patient earth in lines and circles of crude colour like

Berlin wool-work, Geranium, Calceolaria, Lobelia, and again Geranium, Calceolaria, Lobelia, no period has been so unmindful of fragrance in the garden as this in which we are now living. We have juggled the Sweet Pea into the last word in hues and furbelows, and all but lost its sweetness; we have been careless of the Rose's scent, and have made of the wistful Mignonette a stolid and inodorous smudge of vulgarity. We plan meticulously for colour harmony and a sequence of bloom, but who goes deliberately about planning for a succession of sweet scents during every week of the growing year?

[The Fragrant Path (1932)]

Louise Beebe Wilder
Fragrant Annuals

Through the open door
A drowsy smell of flowers—gray heliotrope
And white sweet clover, and shy mignonette
Comes faintly in, and silent chorus leads
To the pervading symphony of Peace.

—WHITTIER

Annuals labour under the disadvantage of being annuals. They blossom, seed and die and next year we must begin all over again with them. But if they are fragrant they amply pay their way and the trouble we are put to in their behalf seems as nothing in comparison with the pleasure we have derived from them. Annual flowers with a sweet scent are not so many but that most of them might be included in a fair sized garden; some of them are indispensable to any garden. Who would be without the spicy scent of Stocks, of Mignonette, or the cool sweetness of the Sweet Pea?

But let us begin at the beginning of the catalog and take them alphabetically: The first is *Ambronia umbellata*, the Sand Verbena, a little trailing plant from California, with bright rose-colored flowers, a little sticky, that are honey-scented especially towards evening. It likes sandy places and flourishes near the sea. It is sometimes used in hanging baskets.

And then we have *Alyssum*, Sweet Alyssum, it is called with good reason (*Alyssum maritimum*), its little bunches of tiny white flowers smell exactly like new mown hay, particularly when the sun shines hot upon them or after a shower. It is good, as every gardener knows, as an edger or as a carpeter; and how the bees love it! Once let this little hardy annual into the garden and it is there for good; always there will be drifts of sweetness in odd corners and it blooms

long and late. Last December I found a small wave of it beating
against the base of the rock garden—where it had never been sown
by hand—and scenting the winter air. In parts of England it has
escaped from gardens and wanders about the countryside. The ordinary kinds grow about six inches high, but there have recently
been introduced some very dwarf and compact forms. They should
all be sown where they are to flower. [. . .]

Dianthus comes next but the annual Pinks have little to recommend them in the way of fragrance. They try to make up for this
serious defect by the gorgeousness of their raiment, but one has
rather a grudge against them, notwithstanding. A Pink should be
sweet if anything. But there are some so-called annual Carnations,
hybrids between the scentless Chinese Pinks and *Dianthus cary-
ophyllus* that smell with the best. They are called Marguerite Carnations, and they come in soft colours—white, pale yellow, pink,
rose, crimson, with fringy petals and a fine spicy scent. A fair proportion of them comes double. I once had a lovely border edge of
these Marguerite Carnations that flowered within six months of
sowing (seed having been sown in a box indoors in February) and
bloomed until frost, furnishing innumerable bouquets the while.

There are many charming California annuals that are little known.
One of these is *Limnanthes Douglasii*, one of the many plants named
for the young Scotch plant hunter, Douglas, who lost his life so
tragically while in pursuit of his calling in the Sandwich Islands.
Behind many a simple plant lies a brave tale of derring-do. Douglas
was a Scotch botanist who explored our Northwest in the early part
of the last century, introducing the Douglas Fir to the gardening
world and leaving his name to a genus of plants, *Douglasia*, as well
as supplying the specific name to a great many, *Phlox Douglasii*,
and *Limnanthes Douglasii*, among them. The last named little plant
sprays about in a delicate pretty way, the six-inch stems bearing
yellow blossoms, pale at the edges, which gives them a rather faded
or fainting look. They are pleasantly fragrant and attract the bees
in great numbers. Limnanthes should be sown where it is to flower
and in succession, for it is soon over.

Annual Lupines have the fresh scent of Cowslips and are very
delightful plants besides, possessing the beauty of leaf and flower-
spike that is characteristic of the fine perennial garden varieties.
Sutton of Reading, England, offers a dwarf yellow-flowered kind

which is particularly rich in fragrance. The annual Lupines transplant with ill grace. It is best to raise them in paper pots indoors, or to plant them in the garden where they are to flower. But be sure to thin them out to breathing distance—they want space and air.

Marigolds, with their rough, pungent scent, have their place in another chapter among the Nose-twisters, but Martynia comes in here—if you like it. I do not. Once I grew a great bed of it lured by the ingratiating description of its charms in a catalog, but I rooted them up before the season was over. Their odour was sweet beyond all bearing, and the plant (American born) a great coarse thing with heavy-lipped flowers, purplish and freckled. *Martynia fragrans* has a delightful sound, but heed it not. Much pleasanter is *Mirabilis*, that the French call Belle-de-nuit. It is our old Marvel of Peru, or Four O'Clock, not often seen now-a-days in fine gardens but still cherished in old fashioned neighbourhoods. It is a plant that will take you back to your country-spent childhood—if you are so lucky as to have had one. The little bushes are trigly symmetrical and gaily set forth with bright yellow, or crimson, or pure white flowers, round as pennies and smelling of Oranges. On cloudy days the flowers open early and remain open all day, but under a warm sun they justify their name and remain tightly closed until four of the clock, or thereabouts.

Mirabilis is one of the flowers that grew in old Gerard's garden in Fetter Lane. The great Elizabethan gardener wrote of it with excitement and inaccuracy, for it was but lately introduced from the New World, whence so many wonderful plants were finding their way into England at that time. Gerard states that it remains open all day and closes at night, "and so perishes." He continues, "This marvelous variety doth not without cause bring admiration to all that observe it; for if the flowers be gathered and reserved in several papers, and compared with those flowers that will spring and flourish the next day, you will easily perceive that one is not like another in colour, though you shall compare one hundred which flower one day, and another which flower the next day, and so on during the whole time of their flowering." By the time Parkinson wrote his *Paradisus* the excitement over the new plant had a little subsided and he is able to give a less imaginative account of it, though he is obviously greatly captivated by it. He calls it "Maruaile (Marvel) of

the World" and devotes nearly two pages to a minute description
of it. Parkinson notes the diversity of the colours, saying that you
will hardly see two alike as long as they blow, "which is until the
winters, or rather autumns cold blastes do stay their willing prone-
nesse to flower: And I haue often also observed that one side of a
plant will giue fairer varieties than another, which is most commonly
the Easterne, as more temperate and shadowie side."

Shirley Hibberd wrote, "A plant may have no history, and yet
be full of fame. It is so with the Mignonette, which was unknown
to the authors of the best of our old English gardening books, and
the history of which may be written on the thumb nail." Its story
began but yesterday, but few flowers have attained to greater fame
or been more beloved by high and low. Some one has said that as
much has been written about Mignonette as about Shakespeare. Its
scent was its fortune for there was little to attract in the small grey
and brown blossoms. Indeed, had it not been for its exquisite fragrance it would never have emerged from obscure weedhood. But
how prophetic was the nose of the man who first sniffed its possibilities and brought it out of Egypt to its promised land. France
received it with delight, calling it Little Darling—Mignonette, and
immediately it had a great and universal vogue. It was grown in
fine gardens for the pleasure of the illustrious, and the grisette
inhaled its sweetness from a box on her narrow window ledge. Soon
the rumour of its fragrance carried it across the Channel to London
where it was so much used in window boxes that a writer of the
time said, "We have frequently found the perfume of Mignonette
so powerful in some of the better streets that we have considered
it sufficient to protect the inhabitants from those effluvia which bring
disorders with them in the air." The scent of Mignonette seems
somehow as appropriate to the grey old London streets as does that
of Lavender to an old lady's lace cap.

Many years ago when I came as a girl in the early spring on a
visit to New York, I remember that I was made homesick for my
Maryland woods by the scent of the Trailing Arbutus that was for
sale on nearly every corner. To-day even the most pervasive flower
scent could not rise above the stench of gasoline that is the characteristic city odour.

The true scent of Mignonette has never been caught by the
skill of the perfumer; numerous perfumes have been called by its

name but the keen sweet odour of this little flower remains for the enjoyment of those who would rather smell a flower than a handkerchief or a bottle. Some have compared the scent of Mignonette to that of the Vine flower, others to Raspberries, but it is to my nose like no other flower scent. It is ethereal yet definite, with a cool, clean quality and a fine sweetness. No nosegay is so delicious as one made of Mignonette and Sweet Peas, unless it be that other of my favourites—a bitter-sweet combination—Moss Rose and Southernwood.

It is interesting to read that Cowper, that flower-loving poet, came to his majority in the same year that Mignonette arrived in London to shower its perfume from window ledge and balcony. He could not but celebrate it:

> *the sashes fronted with a range*
> *Of orange, myrtle, or the fragrant weed,*
> *The Frenchman's darling.*

There are many who will have it that the so-called improved varieties of Mignonette are far less sweet than the earlier kinds, and indeed many of the stout trusses one meets with in florists' shops do not seem to carry the wild sweet fragrance that was their birthright. But some are certainly still very delightful, among them New York Market, Barr's Covent Garden Favorite, Parson's White, and Sutton's Giant, which grows eighteen inches tall, so requires plenty of space in which to develop. It may not generally be known that Mignonette is more fragrant when grown in a poor soil. It flourishes in rich soil but its sweetness fails. Also it is a lover of lime. Where it does not prove a success and makes a sickly, poor-coloured growth, a generous application of lime will generally mend matters speedily. Its scent is strongest when the sun shines hottest.

The present day Ten-week Stock in its fine opulent beauty is little reminiscent of its humble forebear, the little plant with dusty leaves and single blossoms that clings to rocky declivities above the Mediterranean. But the sweetness is the same. Only with the doubling of the petals that has made the modern Stocks like spikes of little Roses the perfume also has been doubled. The development of the Stock from wild-flowerhood to its present state we owe, according to Mrs. Louden, to the patience and skill of the weavers of

The American Gardener

Saxony. Whole villages were once devoted to this industry and it is said that but one colour was permitted to be grown in each village in order that the strains be kept pure. Once the weavers of Lancashire, England, had a like interest in growing Carnations and Pinks, and it is pleasant to think of men turning from the labours of the day to such fragrant tasks. Our industrial workers to-day are too intent upon getting to the movies or speeding in their new Ford cars from one hot-dog stand to another to concern themselves with such matters as Stocks and Carnations. But to every age its preoccupations.

Stocks like Pinks have spices in their throats. Few flowers have a better scent and their colours reproduce those of old and worn chintzes—old rose, dim purple, delicate buff, cream, and so on. Raise them indoors or in a hotbed and plant them out when settled weather comes—and enjoy them for the rest of the summer.

Complaints are being registered against the modern Sweet Pea. It has lost, say the complainers, its original exquisite fragrance. To-day growers talk of "poise" and "brilliance" in connection with this once simple flower, of "waves" and "frills," and there are those who claim that with every wave and frill some of the old sweetness took wing and that there are now many almost scentless varieties. I do not know. I think I never put any Sweet Pea to the test that disappointed me, though it may be true that the old grandiflora types are sweetest. At any rate let us insist that the name shall not become a misnomer and buy only those which we are sure have the old fragrance. [. . .]

Do I imagine it or is it a fact that lavender and mauve and purple Sweet Peas have the sweetest fragrance? There is an old variety called Lady Grisel Hamilton that is delightful. White and very pale pink varieties have a delicate "transparent" scent, the purest and most innocent of all perfumes, seemingly. How delightful it is to walk along the rows of Sweet Peas in the early morning when the dew is still upon them. It is then that they are the sweetest and most refreshing to inhale. It is then also that they should be gathered for the house. If not gathered before ten o'clock they should be left until evening.

The Sweet Pea is a Sicilian and was discovered in that sunny isle by an Italian monk, Father Francis Cupani, not much more than a hundred years ago, a little catching, clutching plant, with a dull purplish flower. One can imagine perhaps, as the good monk went his way, it caught at the sleeve of his cassock, and freeing himself from its frail clutch its ineffable fragrance caught his nose. And so history was made. The first Sweet Pea bloomed in England in the garden of Dr. Uvedale at Enfield in 1813. In 1860 Carter of England offered nine varieties. But it was not until the latter part of the nineteenth century when Mr. Henry Eckford in England, and Mr. Atlee Burpee in America, gave their minds to the development of the Sweet Pea, that it became the delight of the flower-growing world.

[*The Fragrant Path* (1932)]

Rosetta E. Clarkson
Old-Time Fragrant Favorites

Mignonette, heliotrope, lemon verbena, Bible leaf, lavender, marjoram, rosemary. These collected fragrances wafted to us out of the past recall to our hearts half forgotten memories, imagined scenes. Perhaps a whiff of mignonette as our little grandmother in billowy skirts passed near us as she went through the room. Perhaps we held the garden basket as she cut the tips of lavender, or the delicate sprays of lemon verbena, both to be laid between piles of linen. Or perhaps our lovely young aunt with blushing cheeks and starry eyes clasped a tight little nosegay, a tussie-mussie prim and neat with its frilly border. To us the fragrance of the heliotrope in the center was the appeal; to our aunt it was the sentiment expressed by her suitor in the language of the flowers—devotion.

In an old town along the New England coast is one of the loveliest, most restful little walled herb gardens to which I have ever been fortunate enough to be a frequent visitor. This was not planted and looked after by a paid gardener, but loved and cared for by an active little lady. On each side of the central path are rectangular beds, faithful to the tradition of ancient herb gardens. My friend first points out on one side the beds of basil, burnet, chives, but as she turns to the other side her eyes sparkle with a happy light. For this is her tussie-mussie garden, mignonette, rosemary, lemon verbena . . . all of the old-time favorites. Each plant is a personality, each kind of herb a fragrant memory for any visitor to the garden. [. . .]

The odor of heliotrope, more than any other plant, can surround me with memories of other days, other times; can stir my imagi-

Rosetta E. Clarkson

nation to scenes of dainty ladies receiving courtly gentlemen to afternoon tea, of an opera party in the 'nineties with the guests in full regalia assembling in the box overlooking the stage. There is something intoxicating about the odor and as I bury my nose again and again in the fragrant cluster, more memories, more scenes crowd around me. To some people, heliotrope has a disagreeable, close, musty odor. Some define the odor as that of vanilla. The old-time, colloquial name for the plant was cherry-pie, because of the almond-like odor found in cherry pits which was thought similar to that of heliotrope. Unfortunately, little essential oil can be obtained from the flowers themselves, so that practically all heliotrope perfume is synthetic.

Again we find an old favorite of our grandmother's garden not in the ancient line of English garden tradition, for heliotrope was introduced from Peru to Europe about 1757 and from its source comes the botanical name *Heliotropium peruvianum*. There are some 90 species of the genus to be found in tropical and subtropical regions. In warm climates the plants become bushes rising to a height of 8 or 10 feet and heliotrope hedges are often made.

As we read the old English herbals we find many mentions of heliotrope or "turnsole," the literal translation of the word "heliotrope." But the name was applied to sunflowers and marigolds, which each day followed the course of the sun from east to west, so we must not be misled by our own conception of heliotrope when we come upon the word in the old books.

The fragrant South American plant with hue so distinctive as to give its name to a color was also named from its habit of following the sun from dawn to dark and obtained for itself, in the language of the flowers, the symbolism of devotion. The plant loves warm, light, rich soil and may be propagated by cuttings and by layering. It makes a lovely border, although it is tender.

Mignonette is another plant of our grandmother's garden that spells romance. Bret Harte wrote,

> *The delicate odour of Mignonette,*
> *The remains of a dead and gone bouquet,*
> *Is all that tells of a story; yet*
> *Could we think of it in a sweeter way?*

[157]

It, too, is a plant of comparatively recent importation to England. It was originally a weed in Egypt but was considered an herb of magic by the Romans. Pliny said that it possessed the power to take away disorders. Near an Italian city, now called Rimini, the plant was used to reduce swellings, and when applying it as a remedy the natives repeated the following charm, spitting on the ground three times at each repetition:

> *Reseda, cause these maladies to cease;*
> *Knowest thou, knowest thou, who has driven pullets here?*
> *Let the roots have neither head nor foot.*

Botanically, mignonette is *Reseda odorata*, "reseda" coming indirectly from a Latin verb meaning to assuage. Sentimentally the plant has been called "Herbe d'Amour," a love flower. A spray of mignonette has led the way to many a romance and once to the coat of arms of a noble family in Saxony. This is the story. The Count of Walstheim was in love with the spoilt and coquettish Amelia of Nordburg, while her companion, Charlotte, of humble family, was gentle and modest. At a party one evening, each lady chose a flower and the gentlemen were to write verses for each one. Amelia had flirted disgracefully all evening and the count wrote for her rose, "She lives but for a day and pleases but for a moment." For the gentle Charlotte's mignonette he wrote, "Your qualities surpass your charms." The count became deeply attached to Charlotte, finally married her, and to the ancient arms of his family he added a spray of mignonette with the line he had written to her that evening.

[*Green Enchantment* (1940)]

Henry Beetle Hough
Now the Sweet Pepperbush

August rises to its greatest triumph, perhaps, in the scent of the sweet pepperbush. Open your window and you will feel yourself invited by this fragrance borne from roadsides and marshes so far away that you have forgotten them. The moist air of a humid summer carries into vapor such fragrances and delivers them to you as an elixir, an inhalant extraordinary.

Sweet pepperbush is much prized by the keepers of bees because of the fine honey the bees make from the blossoms of this native shrub. We do not feel this is any particular credit to the bees, for if they could not make a superb article of honey out of the sweet pepperbush they should go out of business. Doubtless it requires great skill and diligence to wrest honey from some flowers, but the blossoms of the sweet pepperbush offer a heaven-sent opportunity. They are practically honey in themselves.

Some have invited this native shrub into their gardens. In catalogues the name is *Clethra alnifolia*. The pepper in the popular name comes from the small brownish dots carried by the spikes of creamy flowers—a matter of appearance only, for there is nothing peppery in the nature of shrub or flower. Not all flower books list the appellation familiar to us, but all note the term "alder," a species this resembles but to which it does not belong, for it is really a member of the heath family.

Sweet pepperbush helps August in its role of lazy month, contributes to its boon for the idle of spirit and souls fond of dallying.

[*Singing in the Morning* (1951)]

[159]

Katharine S. White
March 5, 1960

In this cold winter of 1960—cold, that is, in the Maine coastal town from which I write—I have been thinking about the fragrance of flowers, a subject that has occupied my mind and nose all year, but one that the garden-catalogue writers, except for the rose growers, tend to neglect. Even the rose men, because they are stuck with a great many scentless varieties, do not give it the emphasis they might. My own nose is not a very good organ, because I am a heavy smoker, but nevertheless I value fragrance and find it one of the charms of a garden, whether indoors or out. The flowers I enjoy most that are in bloom indoors just now are my two big pots of freesias, a white and a yellow; their delicate scent is there for the sniffing, but it does not overwhelm the room, as some lilies do. Colette once wrote that the ideal place for the lily is the kitchen garden, and remembers that in the garden of her childhood "it was lord of all it surveyed by virtue of its scent and its striking appearance," but she goes on to say that her mother would sometimes call from her chair, "Close the garden gate a little, the lilies are making the drawing room uninhabitable!" The young Colette was allowed to pick these lilies by the armful and

. . . bear them away to place on the altar for the Hail Mary celebration. The church was hot and stuffy and the children burdened with flowers. The uncompromising scent of the lilies made the air dense and disconcerted the hymn singing. Some of the congregation hurriedly left the building, while others let their heads droop and slumbered, transported by a strange drowsiness.

We all know this phenomenon—the somnolent Easter Day service in a lily-laden church. Outdoors, for my taste, lilies cannot be too sweet, and I especially love the strong Oriental scent of the auratums.

Fragrance, whether strong or delicate, is a highly subjective matter, and one gardener's perfume is another gardener's stink. My tastes are catholic. I very much like the pungent late-summer flowers—the marigolds, calendulas, and chrysanthemums, even the old-fashioned single nasturtiums that have not been prettied up by the hybridizers. These ranker autumn flowers, some of whose pungency comes from the foliage, are what Louise Beebe Wilder, in her book *The Fragrant Path* (1932), calls "nose twisters"; the very word "nasturtium" *means* "nose twister" in Latin. It is my habit to keep two little vases filled with small flowers on our living-room mantelpiece all summer; by September, these are often filled with nose twisters—French marigolds, miniature Persian Carpet zinnias, calendulas, and a few short sprays from the tall heleniums, all in the tawny and gold shades of autumn. But to some people the aromatic scents of these flowers and their leaves are unbearable. In fact, one friend of mine cannot tolerate them at all, and her pretty nose will wrinkle with disgust when she is in the room with them. If I know she is coming to the house in September, I hastily change my bouquets to the softer tones and sweeter scents of the late-blooming verbenas, annual phlox, and petunias.

I know next to nothing about fragrance. A year of trying to learn about it has left me as ignorant as ever, beyond a few simple facts that everybody knows, such as that a moist, warm day with a touch of sun will bring out fragrance, that hot sun and drought can destroy it, that frost sometimes releases it, and that rain will draw out the good chlorophyll scents of grass and foliage. The commonest complaint one hears today from the amateur gardener is that modern flowers, particularly roses, are losing their fragrance, thanks to the hybridizers' emphasis on form and color, and it had seemed to me, too, that many flowers smell less sweet than they used to. Sweet peas: The ones I grow are sweet, of course, but I remember them as sweeter still in my aunts' flower garden of long ago. Iris: It is rare to find a fragrant flower among the hybrids we now grow on our terrace, but a gardening friend with a particularly alert nose remembers the old-fashioned "flag lilies" of his childhood as very fragrant. Lilacs: The common single farmyard lilac for me has the headiest spring scent of all, and some of the double modern French hybrids are said to be as fragrant, yet the double lilacs we grow here are distinctly less sweet than our common lilacs (*Syringa vulgaris*), probably because one of their ancestors was the only wild lilac that has no scent at all. Pansies: Oh, the list of lost sweet smells could go on and on.

These vexing doubts have given me courage to write around, asking questions of the scientists and horticulturists and commercial growers whom I dared to bother with my inquiries. A few of them have answered helpfully, a few evasively, but most of them mysteriously. The only consensus I can gather is that fragrance is not now a strong incentive among the growers and breeders. Color and form and hardiness are the thing, because that is what the public demands. This may be so, but it seems to me that the least the seedsmen and nurserymen can do for those of us who value fragrance is to tell us in their catalogues more often than they now do when a flower is particularly sweet-scented.

[Onward and Upward in the Garden (1979)]

Thalassa Cruso
I Remember, I Remember

For many people the scent of certain plants can revive memories
with a vividness that nothing else can equal, for the sense of smell
can be extraordinarily evocative, bringing back pictures as sharp as
photographs of scenes that had left the conscious mind. Whenever
I come in contact with flowering ivy, I find I have almost total recall
of a very early ground plan of my parents' first country garden. That
particular garden was later entirely redesigned as my parents developed new tastes, and when I think back consciously about how
and where they managed their plants, I always visualize the details
of the later stage, which I knew far longer and also when I was
getting interested in plants. But the instant some dormant lobe in
my mind is retriggered by the pungent, heavy, almost unpleasant
smell of flowering ivy, I suddenly see with great clarity the first
garden including minute details—with which I sometimes confound
my brother, who does not possess this visual sense of total recall.
Above all, I remember the source of the ivy memory jogger: a small
peat shed, my special hiding place during the early years of our
occupation of that house, which had to be taken down around about
the time I was nine years old. It was so weighted down with luxuriant
ivy that it was judged unsafe.

In New England, except for the Baltic variety, ivy rarely flowers; the harsh winters kill it back too hard. For ivy must scramble
to a certain height above the ground and reach a fixed stage of leaf
maturity before it will set a bud. And it was not until I recently
brushed against a flowering spray, in a warmer section of the country
where ivy flourishes all too happily, that I again realized that the

old nerve still existed and was only waiting to be plucked. Tree ivies, by which I do not mean the modern hybrid of ivy and a fatsia, called fatshedera, but true ivy grown into a standard form, are no longer popular. They used to be very fashionable and were used as what then were called "dot," or to us "accent," plants to give height to an area planted entirely in low annuals. True ivy standards are now hard to come by partly because they take time and patience and a good deal of room for winter storage, but also because they can be made only from cuttings of ivy that are mature enough to flower, and rooted cuttings of old wood are always hard to strike. I have no passionate wish to possess a tree or standard ivy; I suspect I would have just the same trouble with it as I have with the juvenile trailing form we all grow. But I had almost forgotten their very existence until that pungent smell also reawakened the visual memory of my grandfather's long parterre beds with the ivies standing like sentinels at regular intervals along it.

Unlike many people, I am not all that enthusiastic about roses. I love climbing roses and grow a lot of them as well as old-fashioned rambler roses, but in a very simple style scrambling among the trees or flinging themselves over stone walls where they give no trouble except to require an occasional thorny cutting out. But I am not much interested in rose gardens, and I dislike the heavy scent of roses indoors. I can rationalize this by saying that roses in this country take too much care and are prone to too many diseases, while roses indoors shatter irritatingly fast, all of which is perfectly true. But I think the truth of my indifference has deeper roots. The family rose garden, which was my father's delight, was always at its superlative best in June, the time of year when vital examinations were held in English schools. I was rather a ten o'clock scholar and used to leave a great deal undone until the last possible moment. Then I used to pace around and around the circular rose garden, which was a little set off to one side and therefore a quiet place, feverishly cramming for the upcoming examinations. The scent and sight of roses have therefore an association of tension in the back of my mind, and this is probably the real reason for my lack of interest in them.

And I find this childhood association syndrome exists in all sorts of gardening matters. Our country garden is surrounded by tall hedges in which we battle the twin plagues of bittersweet and Japanese honeysuckle. In spite of our counterattacks both plants are going to outlast us, and where the bittersweet is concerned I find I have ambivalent feelings about cutting out the fruiting strands even though they are doing their best to strangle us. As a child I used to hunt for bittersweet berries in the hedges along the chalk downs. Those two-tone sprays that I now cut out were there a trophy to be proudly carried home, for bittersweet is not the nuisance in England that it has become in some areas here. I am sure it is a relic of this feeling that leads me to emphasize the importance of the berries for the bird population and turn my fiercest efforts against the unberried strands.

I deplore the pythonlike grip with which the Japanese honeysuckle strangles everything within reach, but I love the elusive fragrance with which it envelops the country garden at this season. To me that epitomizes everything we enjoy about this slightly ramshackle but deeply loved garden, and that same scent, it seems, is apparently going to affect my children just as ivy keeps its hold over me. For recently standing on the porch in the evening with honeysuckle perfuming the air, a visiting daughter who now lives where this vine does not grow suddenly remarked that to her the smell of honeysuckle would always mean that school was out and the endless sunny summer had begun. She had forgotten the sensation until that very moment.

Scents bring memories, and many memories bring nostalgic pleasure. We would be wise to plan for this when we plant a garden.

[*To Everything There Is a Season* (1973)]

NATIVE PLANTS

Thomas Jefferson
To Madame de Tessé

Washington, Oct. 26. 05

The blockade of Havre still continuing and being likely to be of
equal duration with the war, I had despaired almost of being able
to send you any seeds this year. but it was lately suggested to me
that a package sent to Nantes may go through the canal de Briare
to Paris, and thus avoid a land carriage which would cost you more
than the object is worth. I have therefore hastily made up a box
of seeds, of such articles as those I propose to furnish you annually
as the present season admits of being gathered. they are as follows. 1. Juglans nigra. 2. Liriodendron tulipifera. 3. Quercus alba.
4. Prinus. 5. Q. Phellos. 6. Q. Palustris. 7. Juniperus Virginica.
8. Cornus Florida. 9. Rosa sylvestris elatior foliis inodoris Clayton. 10. Bignonia Catalpa. 11. Magnolia acuminata. the preceding
were in your catalogue, to which in order to fill vacant spaces I
have added 12. Diospyros Virginiana. 13. Platanus occidentalis.
14. Cucurbita verrucosa Miller. 15. Arachis hypogaea. the season
would have admitted procuring some other articles from a distance,
but I was yesterday informed that the brig *Lucy* sails three days
hence from Baltimore to Nantes. I therefore close the box to-day
and send it off by stage tomorrow, the only means of getting to
Baltimore in time. it is a box 4 feet long, and 1 foot wide and deep;
will be addressed to you to the care of William Patterson, commercial agent of the U.S. at Nantes, with instructions first to ask
your orders how to have them conveyed and to follow those orders.
I shall make some observations on some of these articles. of the oaks
I have selected the alba, because it is the finest of the whole family,
it is the only tree with us which disputes for pre-eminence with

the Liriodendron. it may be called the Jupiter while the latter is the Juno of our groves. the Prinos, or chestnut oak is also one of the fine and handsome species. the Phellos, or willow oak combines great irregularity with beauty, the Palustris of Michaux, which is the Quercus rubra dissecta R of La Marck Encyclop. Method. Botan. 1. 721. is nearly as singular by the deep indenture of it's leaves and their very narrow lobes, as the Phellos, and very handsome. it has also been called by some Quercus montanus, just as improperly as Palustris. it grows well in dry as well as moist lands. the acorns of the Q. Phellos are the smaller, we know. they fall early in the season, and I send you every individual acorn which multiplied researches could now procure. probably some of the minutest may not come up, but I trust a sufficient number will be found good. in each of the cells of the box are some leaves of the identical trees from which the acorns were gathered. Juniperus virgin. I presume some method is known and practiced with you to make the seeds come up. I have never known but one person succeed with them here. he crammed them down the throats of his poultry confined in the hen-yard and then sowed their dung, which has been completely effectual. Cornus Florida. we have a variety of this with a flesh coloured blossom, but it is so rare that I have seen it in but one place on my road from hence to Monticello, and could only be known at this season by marking the tree when in blossom. this research must be reserved for a situation more favorable than my present one. Magnolia acuminata. this plant is not of Virginia, except it's South Western angle, 250 miles from hence. I send you the only cone of it I ever saw, and which came to me accidentally not long since. the tree I have never seen. Platanus occidentalis, a most noble tree for shade, of fine form, its bark of a paper-white when old, and of very quick growth. cucurbita verrucosa, cymling. I recommend this merely for your garden. we consider it one of our finest and most innocent vegetables. I found the chicorée as dressed by your cooks in a pulpy form to resemble our cymling. Arachis hypogaea, a very sweet ground-nut. it grows well at this place where we can have neither figs nor artechokes without protection through the winter. it is hardier therefore than they are, and cannot be a mere-green house plant with you as Miller and Dumont Courset suppose. I write to you almost in despair that you will get either my letter or the box of seeds. such are the irregularities committed on the ocean by the armed vessels of all the belligerent powers that nothing is safe committed to that element. were it not for this, I would ask you to send me by some occasion some acorns of the Quercus rubre, some seeds of the Cedrus Lebani which you have in the Jardin des plantes, and perhaps some nuts of your Marronier: but I should only expose myself to the mortification of losing them. . . .

P. S. since writing the above I have been able to get some of the Pyrus coronaria, or malus sylvestris virginiana floribus odoratis of Clayton. both the blossom and apple are of the finest perfume, and the apple is the best of all possible burnishers for brass and steel furniture which has contracted rust.

[*Thomas Jefferson's Garden Book* (1944)]

Bernard McMahon
Beautiful Ornaments
from Woods and Fields

I cannot avoid remarking that many flower gardens, &c., are almost destitute of bloom during a great part of the season; which could be easily avoided, and a blaze of flowers kept up, both in this department and in the borders of the pleasure-ground, from March to November, by introducing from our woods and fields the various beautiful ornaments with which nature has so profusely decorated them. Is it because they are indigenous that we should reject them? Ought we not rather to cultivate and improve them? What can be more beautiful than our Lobelias, Orchises, Asclepiases, and Asters; Dracocephalums, Gerardias, Monardas and Ipomœas; Liliums, Podalyrias, Rhexias, Solidagos and Hibiscuses; Phloxes, Gentianas, Spigelias, Chironias, and Sisyrinchiums, Cassias, Ophryses, Coreopsises and Cypripediums; Fumarias, Violas, Rudbeckias and Liatrises; with our charming Limodorum, fragrant Arethusa, and a thousand other lovely plants which, if introduced, would grace our plantations and delight our senses?

In Europe, plants are not rejected because they are indigenous; on the contrary, they are cultivated with due care; and yet here we cultivate many foreign trifles, and neglect the profusion of beauties so bountifully bestowed upon us by the hand of nature.

[*The American Gardener's Calendar* (1806)]

Andrew Jackson Downing
The Neglected American Plants

May, 1851

It is an old and familiar saying that a prophet is not without honor, except in his own country, and as we were making our way this spring through a dense forest in the State of New Jersey, we were tempted to apply this saying to things as well as people. How many grand and stately trees there are in our woodlands, that are never heeded by the arboriculturist in planting his lawns and pleasure-grounds; how many rich and beautiful shrubs, that might embellish our walks and add variety to our shrubberies, that are left to wave on the mountain crag, or overhang the steep side of some forest valley; how many rare and curious flowers that bloom unseen amid the depths of silent woods, or along the margin of wild water-courses. Yes, our hot-houses are full of the heaths of New Holland and the Cape, our parterres are gay with the verbenas and fuchsias of South America, our pleasure-grounds are studded with the trees of Europe and Northern Asia, while the rarest spectacle in an American country place, is to see above three or four native trees, rarer still to find any but foreign shrubs, and rarest of all, to find any of our native wild flowers.

Nothing strikes foreign horticulturists and amateurs so much, as this apathy and indifference of Americans, to the beautiful sylvan and floral products of their own country. An enthusiastic collector in Belgium first made us keenly sensible of this condition of our countrymen, but Summer, in describing the difficulty he had in procuring from any of his correspondents, here, American seeds or plants—even of well known and tolerably abundant species, by telling us that amateurs and nurserymen who annually import from him every new and rare exotic that the richest collections of Europe possessed, could scarcely be prevailed upon to make a search for native American plants, far more beautiful, which grow in the woods not ten miles from their own doors. Some of them were wholly ignorant of such plants, except so far as a familiarity with their names in the books may be called an acquaintance. Others knew them, but considered them "wild plants," and therefore, too little deserving of attention to be worth the trouble of collecting, even for curious foreigners. "And so," he continued, "in a country of azaleas, kalmias, rhododendrons, cypripediums, magnolias and nysas,—the loveliest flowers, shrubs, and trees of temperate climates,—you never put them in your gardens, but send over the water every year for thousands of dollars worth of English larches and Dutch hyacinths. *Voilà le goût Republicain!*"

In truth, we felt that we quite deserved the sweeping sarcasm of our Belgian friend. We had always, indeed, excused ourselves for the well known neglect of the riches of our native Flora, by saying that what we can see any day in the woods, is not the thing by which to make a garden distinguished—and that since all mankind have a passion for novelty, where, as in a fine foreign tree or shrub, both beauty and novelty are combined, so much the greater is the pleasure experienced. But, indeed, one has only to go to England, where "American plants" are the fashion, (not undeservedly, too,) to learn that he knows very little about the beauty of American plants. The difference between a grand oak or magnolia, or tulip-tree, grown with all its graceful and majestic development of head, in a park where it has nothing to interfere with its expansion but sky and air, and the same tree shut up in a forest, a quarter of a mile high, with only a tall gigantic mast of a stem, and a tuft of foliage at the top, is the difference between the best bred and highly cultivated man of the day, and the best buffalo hunter of the Rocky Mountains, with his sinewy body tattooed and tanned till you scarcely know what is the natural color of the skin. A person accustomed to the wild Indian only, might think he knew perfectly well what a man is—and so indeed he does, if you mean a red man. But the "civilizee" is not more different from the aboriginal man of the forest, than the cultivated and perfect garden-tree or shrub (granting always that it *takes* to civilization—which some trees, like Indians, do not), than a tree of the pleasure-grounds differs from a tree of the woods.

Andrew Jackson Downing

Perhaps the finest revelation of this sort in England, is the clumps and masses of our mountain laurel, *Kalmia latifolia*, and our azaleas and rhododendrons, which embellish the English pleasure-grounds. In some of the great country-seats, whole acres of lawn, kept like velvet, are made the ground-work upon which these masses of the richest foliaged and the gayest flowering shrubs are embroidered. Each mass is planted in a round or oval bed of deep, rich, sandy mould, in which it attains a luxuriance and perfection of form and foliage, almost as new to an American as to a Sandwich Islander. The Germans make avenues of our tulip-trees, and in the South of France, one finds more planted magnolias in the gardens, than there are, out of the woods, in all the United States. It is thus, by seeing them away from home, where their merits are better appreciated, and more highly developed, that one learns for the first time what our gardens have lost, by our having none of these "American plants" in them. [. . .]

[*Rural Essays* (1854)]

Amanda B. Morris
Poison Ivy

The Poison Ivy is a vine entirely too common from Canada to Florida, and from the Atlantic coast to Utah. It is made up of a tough woody stem thickly bearded with hairy air-roots by which it climbs over rocks, fences and to the tops of high trees, with leaves composed of *three leaflets only*, and wears in June loose clusters of dull greenish flowers growing from the leaf-axils, soon replaced by glassy, opaque berries of a similar hue. Thus equipped, it pursues its career of mingled beauty and vice. Being myself as yet immune to its poisoned breath and touch, I cannot but dwell upon its beauty, for it rivals the five-leaved Virginia Creeper in being one of the two most truly decorative vines of New England, making up what it lacks in grace of growth by an abrupt vigor. It covers stone heaps and tumble-down walls, lends new foliage to half-dead trees, and turns fence-posts into grotesque plant forms; for when it reaches the top of a support and can climb no further, it promptly abandons its trailing habits and turns into a shrub, sticking out short arms in every direction until, in some places, one may find miles of rail fences with every post decorated by this bushy crown. The berries, though not sufficiently attractive to be dangerous to humanity, are eaten by many winter birds, and the seeds so scattered establish the vine more firmly each year, for the only method taken by townships to eradicate the plague is to cut it annually with a stub scythe where it grows on the highways, a proceeding that merely increases its strength of root.

When Autumn comes, Poison Ivy chooses its colors of mellow yellows, salmon-pink, bronze and crimson with discretion, individual vines often keeping distinct tones, some always turning plain yellow, and others varying from pink to crimson without a single yellow tinge. Alack, how we shall miss this vine in the landscape when twentieth century magic perhaps shall have taught us to outwit it!

So much for beauty. Now for the bad side of its character. Poison Ivy is full of an acrid oil, which does not easily evaporate upon the drying of the plant that generates it, and which, like other oils, does not dissolve in water. Consequently when it is liberated from the leaf tissue,—and the merest touch will do it—this oil at once permeates the skin of its victim and spreads its irritation on the surface, and not through the blood as was once supposed. To the susceptible a tingling of the skin may be the first warning that they have even been in the vicinity of the plant; for to absolutely bruise the leaf is unnecessary with those easily affected, a mere whiff of the oil, slightly volatile as it is, being sufficient to transmit the poison. The tingling sensation is soon succeeded by watery blisters set deep in the toughened cuticle. These blisters are often thickest between the fingers, behind the ears, or in folds of skin where the oil remains undisturbed.

Of course it is best to avoid Poison Ivy, but it is hardly possible so to do if one desires to learn more of nature than can be seen from a piazza or from a neatly graveled garden walk. In fact, even there this vine may be found sneaking its way along an arbor, where a myrtle warbler, seeking shelter on a wintry day, has dropped the seed. So, after having done your best to shun the vine with a *hairy, woody stem, three leaflets and greenish white berries,* try to rid the skin as quickly as possible of the oil when once it has touched you. If you are by a roadside or in a field, take a handful of dust or fresh earth and rub the spot of contact thoroughly. Water will avail little in removing such a persistent oil. This is an invention of my own for absorbing the oil, that I use with great success [. . .] Then, when you can reach a drugshop, have prepared a saturate solution of sugar of lead in seventy-five parts alcohol (alcohol cuts oil) to twenty-five parts water. Be sure that this prescription is marked *poison* and ornamented with a red skull and cross-bones, before you take a clean bit of cotton, sop your afflicted spots with the solution and put the rest away for future use. Sugar of lead is deadly when taken internally, but as an unfailing remedy for the horrible irritation of

Ivy poison it is a clear but exceptional case of two wrongs making a right.

The double qualities of beauty and evil possessed by this plant were truly if sentimentally summed up in a poem written by a North countryman, who once worked for us, his mind being more ready to immortalize weeds in legends than his fingers to eradicate them from the paths. Not being familiar with the language of the Sagas, in which the verses were given me, I asked for an interpretation. The Poet willingly dropped his hoe, clasped his hands, and, choking with the emotional memory of his recent and first experience in poisoning by a gorgeous and deceitful vine that he had plucked and brought home over his shoulder, he began in a whisper, which rapidly arose to a shriek:

"Once there was a woman, very beautiful, tall, slender and bending. She had a lovely color in her face and wild eyes that shot fire and were gray and green and golden at one time. Her robes wreathed about her and were more beautifully garnished than the Spring fields. *But she was false!* Then for her punishment she was turned into a vine, wearing in its season the colors that her eyes had flashed,—a vine so beautiful that all men desire to possess it, but deadly to the touch. Though some are of such strength and good blood that they at first may handle it, *yet they know not when their hour of trouble may come!*"

[*Wildflowers and Where They Grow* (1882)]

Mrs. Dana
Golden-rod and Aster

In an interesting article on "American Wildflowers" which appeared in *The Fortnightly Review* some years ago, the English naturalist, Mr. Alfred Wallace, commented upon the fact, or what seemed to him the fact, that nowhere in our country could be seen any such brilliant masses of flowers as are yearly displayed by the moors and meadows of Great Britain.

I have not the article with me and do not recall certainly whether Mr. Wallace saw our fields and hill-sides in their September dress, but I do remember that he dwelt chiefly upon our earlier flowers, and while, of course, he alluded to the many species of golden-rods and asters to be found in the United States, it seems to me quite impossible that he could have seen our country at this season and yet have remained unconvinced of the unusual brilliancy of its flora.

Despite the beauty of our woods and meadows when starred with the white of bloodroot and anemone, and with the purple-red of the wake-robin, they are perhaps less radiant than those of England "in primrose-time." And although our summer landscape glows with deep-hued lilies and milkweeds, and glitters with black-eyed Susans, yet in actual brilliancy it must yield the palm to an English field of scarlet poppies. But when September lines the road-sides of New England with the purple of the aster, and flings its mantle of golden-rod over her hills, and fills her hollows with the pink drifts of the Joe-Pye-weed or with the intense red-purple of the iron-weed, and guards her brooks with tall ranks of yellow sunflowers, then I think that any moor or meadow of Great Britain might be set in her midst and yet fail to pale her glory.

Of the hundred or so classified species of golden-rod, about eighty belong to the United States. Of these some forty can be found in our Northern States. The scientific name of the genus, *Solidago*, signifying "to make whole," refers to the faith which formerly prevailed in its healing powers. It belongs to the composite family, which now predominates so generally. Its small heads are composed of both ray and disk flowers, which are of the same golden hue, except in one species. These flower-heads are usually clustered in one-sided racemes, which spring from the upper part of a leafy stem.

One of the commonest species, and one of the earliest to blossom, is the rough golden-rod, a plant with hairy stem, thick, rough, oblong leaves, and small heads, each one of which is made up of from seven to nine ray-flowers and from four to seven disk-flowers. Occasionally it will be found growing to a height of five or six feet, but ordinarily it is one of the lowest of the genus. The elm-leaved species is a somewhat similar-looking plant, with thinner, larger leaves, a smooth stem, and with only about four ray-flowers to each little head. The so-called Canadian golden-rod, with its tall, stout stem, pointed, sharply toothed leaves and short ray-flowers, is one of the commonest varieties.

The lance-leaved species is seldom recognized as a member of the tribe, because of its flat-topped clusters, which form a striking contrast to the slender, wand-like racemes which usually characterize the genus. It is often mistaken for the tansy, which is also a yellow composite, but which is quite dissimilar in detail, having deeply divided leaves, the segments of which are cut and toothed, and sometimes much crisped and curled, and button-like, deep-hued flower-heads, which appear to be devoid of ray-flowers. Strictly speaking, the tansy is not a wild flower with us. It was brought from Europe to the gardens of New England, where it was raised as a valuable weed. Now it dyes yellow the hollows of the abandoned homestead and strays lawlessly to the borders of the highway.

The tribe of asters is even larger than that of golden-rods, numbering some two hundred species. Italy, Switzerland, and Great Britain each yields but one native variety, I believe, although others are largely cultivated, the Christmas and Michaelmas daisies of English gardens being American asters. One species, *Aster glacialis* of the botanies, is found growing 12,000 feet above the sea. The blue and purple varieties, those having blue and purple ray-flowers, that is, are much commoner than those with white ray-flowers. Over fifty of the former are found in the Northeastern States to about a dozen of the latter.

Of the white species, the earliest to blossom is the corymbed aster, which can be identified by its slender, somewhat zigzag stems, its thin, heart-shaped leaves, and its loosely clustered flower-heads. It grows plentifully in the open woods, especially somewhat north-ward. In swamps and moist thickets we find the umbelled aster, with its long, tapering leaves, and flat clusters, which it lifts at times to a height of seven feet. A beautiful variety which is abundant along the coast is the many-flowered aster. This is a bushy, spreading plant, somewhat suggestive of an evergreen, with little, narrow, rigid leaves, and small, crowded flower-heads.

The tall, stout stems and large violet heads of the New England aster mark one of the most striking of the purple species. It floods with color the low meadows and moist hollows along the road-side, while the wood-borders are lightened by the pale blue rays of the heart-leaved variety.

There are many other species without English titles which can hardly be described without the aid of technical terms. Even the trained botanist finds himself daunted at times in his efforts to identify the various species, while the beginner is sure to be sorely tried if he set himself this task. Yet if he persevere he will be rewarded, as every road-side will supply an absorbing problem; for there is a decided fascination in detecting the individual traits of plants that to the untrained eye have nothing to distinguish them from one another. The significance of the scientific title of the genus *Aster* is easily appreciated, for the effect of its flowers is peculiarly star-like.

[*According to Season* (1894)]

Neltje Blanchan
Our Golden Daisies

So very many weeds having come to our Eastern shores from Europe, and marched farther and farther west year by year, it is but fair that black-eyed Susan (*Rudbeckia hirta*), a native of Western clover fields, should travel toward the Atlantic in bundles of hay whenever she gets the chance, to repay Eastern farmers in their own coin. Do these gorgeous heads know that all our showy rudbeckias—some with orange red at the base of their ray florets—have become prime favorites of late years in European gardens, so offering them still another chance to overrun the Old World, to which so much American hay is shipped? Thrifty farmers may decry the importation into their mowing lots, but there is a glory to the cone-flower beside which the glitter of a gold coin fades into paltry nothingness. Having been instructed in the decorative usefulness of all this genus by European landscape gardeners, we Americans now importune the Department of Agriculture for seeds through members of Congress, even Representatives of States that have passed stringent laws against the dissemination of "weeds." Inasmuch as each black-eyed Susan puts into daily operation the business methods of the white daisy, methods which have become a sort of creed for the entire composite horde to live by, it is plain that she may defy both farmers and legislators. Bees, wasps, flies, butterflies, and beetles could not be kept away from an entertainer so generous; for while the nectar in the deep, tubular brown florets may be drained only by long, slender tongues, pollen is accessible to all. Anyone who has had a jar of these yellow daisies standing on a polished table indoors, and tried to keep its surface free from a ring of golden dust around the flowers, knows how abundant their pollen is. There are those who vainly imagine that the slaughter of dozens of English sparrows occasionally is going to save this land of liberty from being overrun with millions of the hardy little gamins that have proved themselves so fit in the struggle for survival. As vainly may farmers try to exterminate a composite that has once taken possession of their fields. [. . .]

To how many sun-shaped golden disks with outflashing rays might not the generic name of the helianthus clan (*helios* = the sun, *anthos* = a flower) be as fittingly applied: from midsummer till frost the earth seems given up to floral counterparts of his worshipful majesty. If, as we are told, one-ninth of all flowering plants in the world belong to the composite order, of which over sixteen hundred species are found in North America north of Mexico, surely over half this number are made up after the daisy pattern, the most successful arrangement known, and the majority of these are wholly or partly yellow. Most conspicuous of the horde are the sunflowers, albeit they never reach in the wild state the gigantic dimensions and weight that cultivated, dark brown centred varieties produced from the common sunflower (*H. annuus*) have attained. For many years the origin of the latter flower, which suddenly shone forth in European gardens with unwonted splendor, was in doubt. Only lately it was learned that when Champlain and Segur visited the Indians on Lake Huron's eastern shores about three centuries ago, they saw them cultivating this plant, which must have been brought by them from its native prairies beyond the Mississippi—a plant whose stalks furnished them with a textile fibre, its leaves fodder, its flowers a yellow dye, and its seeds, most valuable of all, food and hair-oil! Early settlers in Canada were not slow in sending home to Europe so decorative and useful an acquisition. Swine, poultry, and parrots were fed on its rich seeds. Its flowers, even under Indian cultivation, had already reached abnormal size. Of the sixty varied and interesting species of wild sunflowers known to scientists, all are North American.

Moore's pretty statement,

> As the sunflower turns on her god when he sets
> The same look which she turn'd when he rose,

lacks only truth to make it fact. The flower does not travel daily on its stalk from east to west. Often the top of the stem turns sharply toward the light to give the leaves better exposure, but the presence or absence of a terminal flower affects its action not at all.

Formerly the garden species was thought to be a native, not of our prairies, but of Mexico and Peru, because the Spanish conquerors found it employed there as a mystic and sacred symbol, much as the Egyptians employed the lotus in their sculpture. In the temples the handmaidens wore upon their breasts plates of gold beaten into the likeness of the sunflower. But none of the eighteen species of helianthus found south of our borders produces under cultivation the great plants that stand like a golden-helmeted phalanx in every old-fashioned garden of the North. Many birds, especially those of the sparrow and finch tribe, come to feast on the oily seeds; and where is there a more charming sight than when a family of goldfinches settle upon the huge, top-heavy heads, unconsciously forming a study in sepia and gold? [. . .]

Glorious masses of *Coreopsis lanceolata*, a prolific bloomer, persistently outshine all rivals in the garden beds throughout the summer. Cut as many slender-stalked flowers and buds as you will for vases indoors, cut them by armfuls, and two more soon appear for every one taken. From seeds scattered by the wind over a dry, sandy field adjoining a Long Island garden one autumn, myriads of these flowers swarmed like yellow butterflies the next season. Very slight encouragement induces this coreopsis to run wild in the East. *Grandiflora*, with pinnately parted narrow leaves and similar flowers, a Southwestern species, is frequently a runaway. Bees and flies, attracted by the showy neutral rays which are borne solely for advertising purposes, unwittingly cross-fertilize the heads as they crawl over the tiny, tubular, perfect florets massed together in the central disk; for some of these florets having the pollen pushed upward by hair brushes and exposed for the visitor's benefit, while others have their sticky style branches spread to receive any vitalizing dust brought to them, it follows that quantities of vigorous seed must be set.

"There is a natural rotation of crops, as yet little understood," says Miss Going. "Where a pine forest has been cleared away, oaks come up; and a botanist can tell beforehand just what flowers will appear in the clearings of pine woods. In northern Ohio, when a piece of forest-land is cleared, a particular sort of grass appears. When that is ploughed under, a growth of the golden coreopsis comes up, and the pretty yellow blossoms are followed in their turn by the plebeian rag-weed which takes possession of the entire field." [. . .]

Jerusalem Artichoke, Earth Apple, Canada Potato, Girasole (*Helianthus tuberosus*), often called Wild Sunflower, too, has an interesting history similar to the dark-centred, common garden sunflower's. In a musty old tome printed in 1649, and entitled "A Perfect Description of Virginia," we read that the English planters had "rootes of several kindes, Potatoes, Sparagus, Carrets and Hartichokes"—not the first mention of the artichoke by Anglo-Americans. Long before their day the Indians, who taught them its uses, had cultivated it; and wherever we see the bright yellow flowers gleaming like miniature suns above roadside thickets and fence rows in the East, we may safely infer the spot was once an aboriginal or colonial farm. White men planted it extensively for its edible tubers, which taste not unlike celery root or salsify. As early as 1617 the artichoke was introduced into Europe, and only twleve years later Parkinson records that the roots had become very plentiful and cheap in London. The Italians also cultivated it under the name *Girasole Articocco* (sunflower artichoke), but it did not take long for the *girasole* to become corrupted into Jerusalem, hence the name Jerusalem Artichoke common to this day. When the greater value of the potato came to be generally recognized, the use of artichoke roots gradually diminished. Quite different from this sunflower is the true artichoke (*Cynara Scolymus*), a native of Southern Europe, whose large, unopened flower-heads offer a tiny edible morsel at the base of each petal-like part.

The Jerusalem artichoke sends up from its thickened, fleshy, tuber-bearing rootstock, hairy, branching stems six to twelve feet high. Especially are the flower-stalks rough, partly to discourage pilfering crawlers. The firm, oblong leaves, taper pointed at the apex and saw-edged, are rough above, the lower leaves opposite each other on petioles, the upper alternate. The brilliant flower-heads, which are produced freely in September and October, defying frost, are about two or three inches across, and consist of from twelve to twenty lively yellow rays around a dull yellow disk. The towering prolific plant prefers moist but not wet soil from Georgia and Arkansas northward to New Brunswick and the Northwest Territory. Omnivorous small boys are not always particular about boiling, not to say washing, the roots before eating them.

[*Nature's Garden* (1900)]

Neltje Blanchan
Witch-Hazel

To find a stray apple blossom among the fruit in autumn, or an occasional violet deceived by caressing Indian Summer into thinking another spring has come, surprises no one; but when the witch-hazel bursts into bloom for the first time in November, as if it were April, its leafless twigs conspicuous in the gray woods with their clusters of spidery pale yellow flowers, we cannot but wonder with Edward Rowland Sill:

> *Has time grown sleepy at his post*
> *And let the exiled Summer back?*
> *Or is it her regretful ghost,*
> *Or witchcraft of the almanac?*

Not to the blue gentian but to the witch-hazel should Bryant have addressed at least the first stanza of his familiar lines:

> *Thou waitest late, and com'st alone*
> *When woods are bare and birds have flown,*
> *And frosts and shortening days portend*
> *The aged year is near his end.*

The shrub doubtless gives the small bees and flies their last feast of the season in consideration of their services in transferring pollen from the staminate to the fertile flowers. Very slowly through the succeeding year the seeds within the woody capsules mature until, by the following autumn, when fresh flowers appear, they are ready to bombard the neighborhood after the violets' method, in the hope of landing in moist yielding soil far from the parent shrub to found a new colony. Just as a water-melon seed shoots from between the thumb and forefinger pinching it, so the large, bony, shining black, white-tipped witch-hazel seeds are discharged through the elastic rupture of their capsule whose walls pinch them out. To be suddenly hit in the face by such a missile brings no smile while the sting lasts. Witch-hazel twigs ripening indoors transform a peaceful living room into a defenceless target for light artillery practice.

Nowhere more than in the naming of wild flowers can we trace the home-sickness of the early English colonists in America. Any plant even remotely resembling one they had known at home was given the dear familiar name. Now our witch-hazel, named for an English hazel tree of elm lineage, has similar leaves it is true, but likeness stops there; nevertheless, all the folk-lore clustered about that mystic tree has been imported here with the title. By the help of the hazel's divining-rod the location of hidden springs of water, precious ore, treasure, and thieves may be revealed, according to old superstition. Cornish miners, who live in a land so plentifully stored with tin and copper lodes they can have had little difficulty in locating seams of ore with or without a hazel rod, scarcely ever sink a shaft except by its direction. The literature of Europe is filled with allusions to it. Swift wrote:

> *They tell us something strange and odd*
> *About a certain magic rod*
> *That, bending down its top divines*
> *Where'er the soil has hidden mines;*
> *Where there are none, it stands erect*
> *Scorning to show the least respect.*

A good story is told on Linnaeus in Baring-Gould's *Curious Myths of the Middle Ages*: "When the great botanist was on one of his voyages, hearing his secretary highly extol the virtues of his divining-wand, he was willing to convince him of its insufficiency, and for that purpose concealed a purse of one hundred ducats under a ranunculus, which grew by itself in a meadow, and bid the secretary find it if he could. The wand discovered nothing, and Linnaeus's mark was soon trampled down by the company present, so that when he went to finish the experiment by fetching the gold himself, he was utterly at a loss where to find it. The man with the wand assisted him, and informed him that it could not lie in the way they were going, but quite the contrary; so they pursued the direction of the wand, and actually dug out the gold. Linnaeus said that another such experiment would be sufficient to make a proselyte of him."

Many a well has been dug even in this land of liberty where our witch-hazel indicated; but here its kindly magic is directed chiefly through the soothing extract distilled from its juices.

[*Nature's Garden* (1900)]

Neltje Blanchan
The Trailing Arbutus

Can words describe the fragrance of the very breath of spring—that delicious commingling of the perfume of arbutus, the odor of pines, and the snow-soaked soil just warming into life? Those who know the flower only as it is sold in the city streets, tied with wet, dirty string into tight bunches, withered and forlorn, can have little idea of the joy of finding the pink, pearly blossoms freshly opened among the withered leaves of oak and chestnut, moss, and pine needles in which they nestle close to the cold earth in the leafless, windy northern forest. Even in Florida, where broad patches carpet the woods in February, one misses something of the arbutus's accustomed charm simply because there are no slushy remnants of snow drifts, no reminders of winter hardships in the vicinity. There can be no glad surprise at finding dainty spring flowers in a land of perpetual summer. Little wonder that the Pilgrim Fathers, after the first awful winter on the "stern New England coast," loved this early messenger of hope and gladness above the frozen ground at Plymouth. In an introductory note to his poem "The Mayflowers," Whittier states that the name was familiar in England, as the application of it to the historic vessel shows; but it was applied by the English, and still is, to the hawthorn. Its use in New England in connection with the trailing arbutus dates from a very early day, some claiming that the first Pilgrims so used it in affectionate memory of the vessel and its English flower association.

> *Sad Mayflower! watched by winter stars,*
> *And nursed by winter gales,*

> *With petals of the sleeted spars,*
> *And leaves of frozen sails!*

> *But warmer suns ere long shall bring*
> *To life the frozen sod,*
> *And through dead leaves of hope shall spring*
> *Afresh the flowers of God!*

Some have attempted to show that the Pilgrims did not find the flowers until the last month of spring, and that, therefore, they were named Mayflowers. Certainly the arbutus is not a typical May blossom even in New England. Bryant associates it with the hepatica, our earliest spring flower, in his poem, "The Twenty-seventh of March":

> *Within the woods*
> *Tufts of ground laurel, creeping underneath*
> *The leaves of the last summer, send their sweets*
> *Upon the chilly air, and by the oak,*
> *The squirrel cups, a graceful company*
> *Hide in their bells a soft aërial blue.*

There is little use trying to coax this shyest of sylvan flowers into our gardens where other members of its family, rhododendrons, laurels, and azaleas make themselves delightfully at home. It is wild as a hawk, an untamable creature that slowly pines to death when brought into contact with civilization. Greedy street venders, who ruthlessly tear up the plant by the yard, and others without even the excuse of eking out a paltry income by its sale, have already exterminated it within a wide radius of our Eastern cities. How curious that the majority of people show their appreciation of a flower's beauty only by selfishly, ignorantly picking every specimen they can find!

[*Nature's Garden* (1900)]

Alice Lounsberry
Shortia Galicifolia

About the sprightly form of shortia there clings a strange story. It is the plant that has interested great men who searched for it until its haunts were revealed and its beauty universally acknowledged. It was the much desired of Dr. Asa Gray, and is as indelibly associated with his memory as is the Catawba rhododendron with that of Michaux.

When Dr. Gray was in Paris in 1839 he observed in the herbarium of the elder Michaux an unnamed specimen of a plant. The leaves and a single fruit were all that was preserved of it, and its label stated simply that it had been collected in "les hautes montagnes de Carolinie." Its power to arouse Dr. Gray's curiosity was so great that on his return to America he hunted assiduously for the plant in the mountains of North Carolina, but wholly without success. In fact, in an account he gave after his return from these mountains, he said: "We were likewise unsuccessful in our search for a remarkable undescribed plant with the habit of pyrola and the foliage of galax which was obtained by Michaux in the high mountains of Carolina. The only specimen extant is among the Plantæ incognitæ of the Michauxian herbarium, in fruit; and we were anxious to obtain flowering specimens that we might complete its history: as I have long wished to dedicate the plant to Professor Short of Kentucky whose attainments and eminent services in North American botany are well known and appreciated both at home and abroad."

Two years after this, however, Dr. Gray ventured to describe the plant and dedicated it, as he had wished, to Dr. C. W. Short.

In this way it received its first public recognition. Henceforth no botanist ever visited the region without searching for shortia. It was courted almost as faithfully as was the philosopher's stone. In the meantime, Dr. Gray had found among a collection of Japanese plants a specimen almost identical with the well-remembered one of Michaux, a coincidence which strengthened his faith in the existence of the American species. It was not, however, until 1877 that it was found, and then quite accidentally, by G. M. Hyams, a boy who knew little about the good luck that had befallen him. He had picked it up on the banks of the Catawba River near the town of Marion in McDowell County, North Carolina. Fortunately the father of this boy was a professed herbalist and through a correspondent finally learned the true nature of the plant. It had been collected when in flower. With its aid, therefore, Dr. Gray was enabled to substantiate his original ideas of the genus and to perfect its description. But as for its natural habitat he still maintained that Michaux could not have been so mistaken; that the true home of shortia must be in "les hautes montagnes de Carolinie." It was quite possible, he argued, that the point on the Catawba where it had been found was an outlying haven to which it might have been washed. So with renewed energy it was searched for through the mountains until discouragement lagged the footsteps of the seekers.

In the autumn of the year 1886 Professor Sargent visited the mountainous region of North Carolina about the head waters of the Keowee River, the great eastern fork of the Savannah, with the object in view of rediscovering Magnolia cordata. At Hog Back, a place now called Sapphire, he was met by Mr. Frank Boynton. One evening after dark Professor Sargent came in with his portfolio and took from it, among other things that he had gathered, a leaf. "What is it?" he asked. Mr. Boynton was about to answer, "It is galax"; but on looking at the leaf more closely, he said he didn't know. During that evening the Professor's mail was brought in, among the letters being one from Dr. Gray, which read as follows:

September 17, 1886

My dear Sargent:

Would I were with you! I can only say crown yourself with glory by discovering a habitat—the original habitat of shortia—which we will believe

Michaux found near where the Magnolia cordata came from—or in that first expedition.

Yours ever,
Asa Gray

Mr. Stiles the editor of *Garden and Forest* who also was present on this eventful evening then said, in a joking way: "That's shortia you have in your hand." This proved to be true. The leaf was shortia. Professor Sargent had found it, just ninety-eighty years after Michaux's discovery, probably near the same spot.

About two weeks later, when this astonishing fact had been fully ascertained by Professor Sargent, he sent word to Mr. Boynton who, with his brother, then went back definitely to locate the plant. They found it growing near Bear Camp Creek in a rather limited quantity, but still enough for them to carry away a bag full of specimens for distribution.

In the following spring Mr. Harbison started out in quest of it. He went beyond Bear Creek to the forks of the rivers. There he saw it growing in great masses, acres, in fact, which were as thickly covered as clover fields. Wagon-loads of it were eventually taken away and still there appeared to be no diminution of its abundance.

So ended the search for shortia, once deemed so rare. Through the further efforts of Mr. Harbison the plant is now well known, and a common one in nursery catalogues. In its wild state it grows best under the shade of kalmias and rhododendrons.

[*Southern Wildflowers and Trees* (1901)]

Mabel Osgood Wright
Children Gathering Wildflowers— and Their Names

The farmers who saw us "forever lugging home a lot of stuff" used
to look at us admiringly, on account of our indefatigable perseverance; and they thought we were of the "right sort," though what
was it "good for," they'd like to know. One man used to call out
"*Weeds! weeds!* And you are all burnt up!"

Another would come out of his house, and, stooping down over
our baskets to see what the contents were, ask, his face brimming
over with curiosity and kindliness, "What ye got NOW?"

Some of the people thought we must be getting things "to make
beer of," or were gathering "greens." And one old man stopped us
and told us what everything we had was "good for." We should
never have rheumatism if we ate this. That was good for fever. If
we followed his directions we should be saved from all ills. He was
as wise as the "Indian doctors" whom the country places used to
know. He talked about the flower called "high pride," and the
smaller which was "low pride," and showed us what "cohosh" was,
and "wickabee"—Indian names.

If we heard of a new plant (that is, new to us), we set out in
search of it. And, depend upon it, if you are determined to find a
thing, you will. It was often our chief perplexity to ascertain what
the name was. Sometimes, in our inquiries, we would stumble upon
some vernacular that was curious or pretty. For instance, sarsaparilla
was pettimorrel; clintonia was "heal-all"; lady's-slipper was "Noah's
ark."

Usually, however, we received for answer, "Oh, that is some

kind of a river weed." *"That,* that is *brook greens."* One man scru-
tinized a flower we showed him, and then answered, as one having
authority, "That is a plant which has no name"; and we feigned
satisfaction.

"The name! the name!" was what we harped upon, as Shylock
did upon "the bond." We partly analyzed and partly guessed; groped
in the dark, made many blunders, and often were very, very wide
of the truth; eventually coming slowly to that little, absurdly "little
learning" which is such an unsatisfying thing.

But guessing is not knowing. Resemblance does not necessarily
prove anything in botany. How good and how comfortable *certainty*
is!

We had at last a helper in a born botanist. True, he was sixty
miles off; but the "weeds" went in the mail-bag, with an interro-
gation point after the name if we were slightly in doubt, an exclamation point if we were very much so. And they came back labelled
aright. And those were days of mutual congratulation, when we
could put our fingers on something and say we had learned a fact.
It was not much, but yet a great deal to us, that the little we knew—
we *knew,* or trusted we did.

It was an event when we found the tall anemone, and ascertained which was the bulbous crowfoot; and that the thinly rayed
flower as common as dandelions was the daisy flea-bane. A little
creeper by the wayside, which has so fine a stem and leaf, and tiny
lavender-red cup, was the spurry sandwort. We had fondly believed
in it as a pimpernel. We had so declared it; for did it not open at
seven o'clock in the morning, and close by half-past two? And on
cloudy days did it not stay shut? And if that did not answer to the
description of "poor man's weather-glass," then what did?

No doubt these details seem absurd, and quite too personal;
but they were red-letter days to us, illuminated days on which they
happened.

[*Flowers and Ferns in Their Native Haunts* (1907)]

Thalassa Cruso
Where Have All the Flowers Gone

When we bought our house in the country, we found that along with a rather heterogeneous collection of furniture we had inherited a bookcase of garden books that had belonged to the previous owner. Our predecessor at the house had been a distinguished horticulturist, and her books covered a wide range that dealt with every aspect of gardening, and involvement with the land, as it was practiced about seventy years ago.

Since they came into my hands, I have read and reread these books many times, partly to see how gardening knowledge and practices have changed, but also for sheer pleasure. Almost everyone who grows things enjoys gardening books no matter how old-fashioned, for over and above the specific information they contain, they provide glimpses into a way of life that is not only gone forever but already in danger of being forgotten. Sentences that start, "My superintendent informed me that . . ." or "I instructed the men always to . . ." belong to a world that has very little to do with ours. For the sociologically minded they provide an unparalleled chance, not provided so clearly in any other domestic context, to read of the relationship between the talented amateur instructor and the skilled professionals who did the actual labor. Like Mrs. Beeton's book of *Household Management*, old gardening books should be read for their human interest values as well as for any useful instructions they may contain.

But there is one book in this inherited collection that I do not read in such a scholarly or impersonal manner, for I still find it completely practical. It is called *How to Know the Wild Flowers* and was published in 1893. The author was Mrs. William Starr Dana. In these days of increased sensitivity to female identity, I wonder who this highly talented lady actually was—other than the wife of Mr. William Starr Dana—but there is nothing in my old edition that gives any clue in this matter.

In this excellent handbook are recorded, together with many fine line drawings, the wild flowers of the eastern seaboard of the United States, and I have yet to find a more useful handbook.

The book clearly was an immediate success: my copy is an enlarged revised edition published in 1897, and final proof of its enduring excellence is the fact that there is now a modern paperback edition.

It is not hard to see why it was and is still so popular and why I cherish it. Unlike innumerable other excellent books on wild flowers, this was written with the uninformed reader in mind and arranged so that even without any previous knowledge of wild flowers it is simple to use. The plants are grouped according to the colors of the flowers, and the average flowering time of each specimen is included. This means that someone like myself who was not familiar with American wild flowers could see a small pink something in bloom in June and identify it by looking up the color and the time of year, and then checking the possibilities against the description and the drawings. This admirable book also spans the tricky gulf between the ignorant and the highly sophisticated reader by providing both groups with sufficient satisfying information. For the novice mere identification of an unknown plant is often all that is wanted; for the better-informed there are included long plant lists with the Latin as well as the common name and accurate botanical descriptions.

Almost everything I know about our local wild flowers I have learned from Mrs. Dana's book, and I still carry it into the woods with me when I am in doubt. But the process of educating myself about the native flora (as well as the intrusive foreign plants) of this area has brought with it some severe frustrations.

The original owner of my book used to take her children on plant-hunting expeditions, and she and they made it a practice to write in the margin of Mrs. Dana's book the date and place where they found some of the rarer specimens. The record begins in 1898, and one of the attractions of the entries is that they are not all in the same hand. A large family grew up in what is now our house, and apparently there was fierce competition to be the first to spot a rare plant and it was a privilege to be allowed to make the penciled entry. One wavering sentence flows with triumph: the handwriting is unsteady and extremely youthful, but the words leap out, "Rochester Road, 1912 MAYFLOWERS!!!"

I know from correspondence with the youngest of these same children, now herself a great-grandmother, that it was a family custom to pack a picnic lunch and set off on an all-day plant-hunting excursion in a horse and buggy. They used to start very early in the morning and come back in the cool of the evening twilight with the children curled up asleep in the bottom of the buggy. I could reach Rochester in ten minutes by car today, but I shouldn't find those Mayflowers: the place where they used to grow is now a development. But although I have to search rather farther afield, I have been able to keep the book fairly well up to date and record almost all the same flowers those excursionists found with one exception—and the exception is unfortunately a sad one. I have been able to track down almost none of the wild orchids that apparently once grew in this area in profusion. Where the book records seven or eight unusual specimens from "Mary Allen's bog," I have found only one orchid in the swampy land adjoining the now vanished bog, and that stand is decreasing. The book itself records fewer and fewer sightings of these orchids during the later years in which the record was kept, and their decline appears to coincide with the "discovery" of this neighborhood by summer people and the consequent filling in of swamps and marshland for building.

It's no good lamenting what has gone; what lies before us now is to prevent wanton destruction, through carelessness or greed, of what remains. Anyone who knows where rare wild flowers grow would be wise these days to keep this information to himself. This sounds selfish, but very luckily for us there are reservations where we can go and see the missing flowers reestablished and preserved. A natural stand of a rarity is such a fragile matter that the less general knowledge there is of it the better. For, unfortunately, the immediate uninformed reaction to any such discovery is either to pick the flowers or, in more sophisticated circumstances, to return later to try to gather ripe seed. And either action deprives the plants of one of their most important methods of self-perpetuation. There are also those who feel rare plants should be dug up and taken to the so-called safety of a garden. This again is the road to despoliation. Wild plants do not transplant easily; they need special soil bacteria which garden soil usually cannot provide. Digging up orchids, for example, and setting them out in your own yard is just as certain a route to death as if the plant had been thrown away.

The only occasion in which transplanting wild flowers can ever be justified is when the area in which they grow is threatened with a development or road building, and then the work should be left to professionals. Almost every state has a society devoted to the preservation of wild flowers, and it is to them that you should apply if you happen to stumble upon something unusual and fear that it will soon be destroyed.

And there is another action we can take to help the preservation of our lovelier and rarer flowers, and that is to visit and support the reservations where they are protected. We should take our children to let them learn by seeing, just as the children from this house did so long ago. We should give them a chance to appreciate a threatened heritage before it is too late. Family excursions of this sort can be made every bit as exciting as a visit to the beach and almost more worthwhile. For the memory of flowers that will stay with interested children can remain a very happy thing over a lifetime. I know this from my own experience and from a letter from the onetime child who wrote about Mayflowers in my book:

"This must have been when I was quite little and I well remember the joy of uncovering a mayflower and seeing a wild lupin and lovely tasting checkerberries . . . I have so many happy memories of getting wild flowers with mother and daddy."

[*To Everything There Is a Season* (1973)]

William Lanier Hunt
Wild Flowers of June and July

While June gardens are full of the masses of gaudy roses and daylilies we love so much, a more subtle show is going on in southern woods and fields. Millions of tiny white umbrellas make up the big white parasols of Queen Anne's lace, in bloom now for nearly a month. Blackberries are ripening in fence corners. Trumpet vines hang out their brassy instruments in a shower from old trees and fences, and several wild flowers in a lower key are blooming in the edges of woods and fields.

Green-and-gold (*Chrysogonum virginianum*) is still in bloom in the woods. The small, orange coreopsis is gone, but one of our longest-flowering wild flowers is putting on a show with its airy blossoms. This one is *Coreopsis major*. The bright golden blossoms seem to float over the plants around them. If you look very hard, you will see that there really are nearly invisible wiry stems supporting the flowers above rosettes of narrow leaves. The stems seem to grow right through their own leaves. Where patches of it are growing with other plants, you will have to strain to see anything but the flowers themselves.

This little coreopsis has been telling me for years how important it is in the summer landscape. I am willing now to give it a high rating for length of bloom and the ability to grow almost anywhere. It will grow, too, in competition with more robust wild flowers. So you may hope that it will take up its abode in your garden or woods. Seeds are ripening right now and will produce a batch of seedlings. Once you have it, it will multiply by the little rhizomes. In the woods, it makes patches of plants—all hooked together under-ground.

Another of our fascinating wild flowers is called wild quinine in some books, but I cannot find any record of its having been used as medicine. The plant is *Parthenium integrifolium*. Its heads of white flowers look like small asters with no petals, and you can see them along almost any roadside now. The root is a big tuber, and this must have been the source of "quinine." The driest, poorest soil seems to be what it likes.

Also in the driest places the little white-topped or silky asters (*Aster paternus*) are in bloom right now. How they can live in the dry places they inhabit is hard to see. They make neat, small plants that never fail to bloom no matter how high the temperature goes. Perhaps the hairy stems and leaves hold in what moisture there is.

I am always amazed at the number of American wild flowers in the famous perennial border at Hampton Court, up the Thames from London. The border was some six or eight feet wide when I first saw it in 1927. Today, it is fourteen feet deep and should inspire us to cultivate our own wild flowers.

[*Southern Gardens, Southern Gardening* (1982)]

Jeanne Goode
In Praise of Virginia Creeper

With their muted tones of gold and azure, the early goldenrods and asters hint at approaching autumn. Yet it is the brilliant scarlet of another native, Virginia creeper, that proclaims fall's actual presence. Once Virginia creeper has reached its climax of color, soon the trees and shrubs that support the gentle vine make their own addition to the brief splendor of October in North America.

Although it is the glory of woodlands from Newfoundland to Florida and westward to Ohio, Illinois, and Missouri, *Parthenocissus quinquefolia*, the true, five-leaved Virginia creeper, is seldom seen in gardens. Yet it was as an embellishment to gardens that its early champions welcomed it. John Tradescant, the 17th-century plant collector, is credited with being the first to grow the vine in England from plants he received as a subscriber to the Virginia Companie, around 1617. By 1629 the "Virginian Ivie" had become a great favorite and was widely planted on the Continent as well as in England. "This slender, but tall climbing Virginia Vine," observed John Parkinson, "riseth out of the ground with divers stems, none much bigger than a man's thumb, many less, whence shoote forth many long weake branches, not able to stand upright."

As Parkinson noted, the stems and branches of Virginia creeper are too weak to support themselves, but given a suitable support such as a rough wall or a tree, the plant manages to climb as well as creep. It travels by sending out numerous tendrils that form small adhesive disks, or cushions, when they reach a rough surface, permitting the plant to attain heights of up to 50 feet. Anywhere from two to five inches long, the five leaflets of each compound leaf are purplish in spring, bright green in summer, and scarlet in fall, adding beauty and grace to any support. No wonder that for many years it was the vine of choice for decorating the walls of castles and cottages, porches and pergolas. Even Americans, who often scorn native plants in favor of more exotic species, were persuaded by no less an arbiter of taste than Andrew Jackson Downing to introduce it into their gardens as a drapery and a screen. Downing was also instrumental in popularizing the vine as an adornment for otherwise dreary public buildings.

The discovery of *P. tricuspidata* in China and its introduction in the West in 1862 by James Veitch put an end to the dominance of *P. quinquefolia*, and today it is this three-lobed Asian species, sometimes miscalled Virginia creeper in England and known as Boston ivy in America, that supplies the drapery for many ivy-covered walls. Because the leaves of *P. tricuspidata* are broader and thicker and the cover it provides somewhat denser, the Asian species came to be preferred, even though it is somewhat less hardy (to USDA Zone 4, compared to Zone 3 for *P. quinquefolia*). True Virginia creeper can still be found in Britain and Europe, however, gracing the ruins of ancient manors, crumbling palazzos, and very old gardens.

One famous garden furnished with the vine was Charles Darwin's. He spent many hours studying the specimen that still covers the walls of his house in Kent and wrote a detailed description of it in a book published in 1888, *The Movements and Habits of Climbing Plants*. Here is his observation of the disk-forming process:

In the course of about two days after a tendril has arranged its branches so as to press on any surface, the curved tips swell, become bright red, and form on their undersides the well-known discs or cushions with which they adhere firmly. In one case the tips were slightly swollen in 38 hours after coming in contact with a brick, in another case they were considerably swollen in 48 hours and in an additional 24 hours were firmly attached to a smooth board.

The disks, which secrete a resinous cement, enable the vine to climb trees as well as walls, and in another famous garden, Kew, it grows triumphantly on tall pines, its lacy, bright leaves contrasting dramatically with the dark mass of the evergreens.

In this country, many state highway departments have begun using Virginia creeper. In Iowa and Maryland it softens harsh concrete walls, and in Washington it serves as an attractive groundcover in median areas. Rather than welcome it when it appears in their gardens, however, many people ruthlessly uproot the vine. It seems a pity to deprive ourselves of so rewarding a plant just because it grows wild in the woods. I, for one, prefer it to *P. tricuspidata*: it is less dense, more graceful, and its leaves form more pleasing patterns. It is as easy to grow today as it was when Downing first praised its "rich and beautiful festoons of verdure. It will grow anywhere," he wrote, "in the coldest situations, and only asks to be planted, to work out its own problems of beauty without further attention."

The deep, rich, moist, and well-drained soil that is a necessity for so many other ornamentals is ideal for Virginia creeper too, but it will succeed handsomely in a variety of soils, including heavy clay, and will tolerate both sun and shade. Although any soil from pH 4 to 7 will do, a specially prepared bed at planting time will help Virginia creeper establish itself more rapidly. An area two feet deep and two to three feet wide for each vine can be improved by the addition of garden loam and well-rotted manure, leaf mold, or compost.

Virginia creeper is particularly good for seaside gardens, since salt spray does not damage it. A member of the grape family, Vitaceae, the vine has only inconspicuous flowers, but its small, pea-sized fruits are lovely against the scarlet foliage in autumn. Newly planted vines set out in early spring usually take two or three years to become established, but after that they grow vigorously and can be increased easily by cuttings or layering. Because its roots are slender and deep, Virginia creeper can be planted close to buildings without fear of damage to their foundations. The small adhesive disks do not penetrate the mortar between bricks and can be pulled away from windows. The vines should be pruned when necessary, of course, so as not to obscure architectural features.

Virginia creeper is best used on rough stone, brick, or stucco walls and is not recommended for wood or shingle because these require regular painting or staining. However, if you already have Virginia creeper growing on a wall that needs painting and you do not wish to lose the plants, you can cut them to five or six inches above ground level the spring before a fall paint or staining job is scheduled. New growth the following spring will be rapid, and the drapery will quickly be restored.

Besides beautifying buildings, Virginia creeper can be an invaluable decoration on boundary and retaining walls, giving these necessary but often unattractive structures a surprising charm. Two or three well-grown plants can also provide welcome shade for a patio. And it makes an attractive groundcover in naturalistic, woodland gardens and on slopes, where it gives a dramatic, cascading effect. Frequent pruning when the vines are young will induce branching, and the creeper will soon spread over a wide area, rooting at the joints.

One of the happiest ways to enjoy woodbine, as it is sometimes called, is to allow it the freedom to climb up evergreens, as it does at Kew. Downing often recommended this use, remarking that "its greatest beauty is seen when it runs up in the centre of a dark cedar or other evergreen, exhibiting in October the richest contrast between the two colors." Some gardeners may be unwilling to attempt this, having been conditioned to be suspicious of vines and consider them dangerous. It is true that many vines *should* be looked upon with suspicion. A few are parasitic, feeding on the plants that form their supports and depriving them of nourishment. Others, because of their twining habit of growth, can strangle their host plants, quickly destroying young trees and shrubs and causing severe damage to older ones. And, of course, in the competition for sunlight, vines shade out portions of their host trees. Unfortunately, many people now believe that all vines are harmful to their hosts and should be removed.

At one time even the blameless Virginia creeper was accused of endangering the woodlands and was threatened with eradication. Luckily, a study done by Joseph T. Bridges in 1976, "The Ecological Impact of Virginia Creeper on Other Plant Species in the West Pond Area of Jamaica Bay," saved the specimens that flourish in that valuable wildlife refuge in New York and has been instrumental in preventing the summary removal of Virginia creeper from other wooded areas. Gardeners, too, can be reassured by Bridges's findings and should feel free to welcome this lovely native plant, letting it festoon not only pergolas, porches, and walls but deciduous trees and evergreens as well. Bridges demonstrated that Virginia creeper's linear manner of climbing in no way harms the host, that the adhesive disks "do not penetrate, draw nutrients from or in any way parasitize the plants to which they are attached," and that the occasional tendril that does manage to wrap itself around a stem is "too short and delicate to girdle or impede." The removal of Virginia creeper from Jamaica Bay, he argued, would seriously harm the area as a refuge for wildlife—not only because it provides a safe cover for many small birds and mammals but also because it provides a food source for more than 39 species of wildlife that feed on the fruit and seeds. Even the flowers, he noted, are used by honeybees for nectar.

Among the birds that rely on Virginia creeper as their preferred food are the pileated woodpecker, the eastern kingbird, the great crested flycatcher, the brown thrasher, the American robin, the wood thrush, and the white-eyed vireo. Scarlet tanagers, chickadees, nuthatches, and vereys are also drawn to it for cover and food, so bird lovers will need little encouragement to plant the vine wherever possible.

But its beauty is reason enough, for Virginia creeper is still more than fit to furnish any garden. It may be difficult to find, since most nurseries limit their offerings to Boston ivy, but it is worth seeking out. Two cultivars of note are 'Engelmannii,' whose smaller leaves give a more refined texture suitable for smaller-scale use, and 'Saint-Paulii,' whose more highly branched tendrils allow it to cling well to masonry walls. If you live near a woodland, of course, there will be no problem. Cuttings taken in the spring will root readily in moist peat moss. Plant them in a cold frame in the fall and transplant to their permanent locations the following spring. Before too long your garden should rival the woods in autumn glory.

[*Horticulture* (1986)]

Elizabeth Lawrence
Rosa Hicks

In our North Carolina mountains, the greatest number of native wild flowers are advertised by people who have lived for generations on Route 3, fourteen miles from Banner Elk, a town in Avery County near the Tennessee border. The one regular advertiser I've come to know best is Mrs. Ray Hicks.

Some time back, Mrs. Hicks sent me a handwritten list of more than sixty native species that she grows on her place. More were available, she said, but she couldn't always remember to put down everything. At her request, I sent her my first order early in the year, as she needed to know what I wanted before the time came to dig. We began to correspond, and since Mrs. Hicks always wrote "Dear Elizabeth," a mountain custom, I asked to call her Rosa. Her full name is Rosa Violet, which is most fitting. "Dear Elizabeth," she wrote me on the last day of February, 1975.

I have been a while answering your letter, as we are getting over the flu. Granny is in the hospital real bad. I just expect to hear anything. We are having our winter now. Today has been a wonderful day, but it can change so fast. We have had plenty of water. Our roads have gone down in places, and our mail doesn't run too good when the roads are bad, but I think I can get you some of what you want of what I have. I haven't been out since I got sick, but I hope to get things off in April.

One sunny morning early that July, while I was staying with my friends the Hechenbleikners on Grandfather Mountain, Martha Hechenbleikner drove me to Banner Elk. There we stopped at a service station to ask our way to Rosa's and had no trouble getting directions: everyone knew Ray Hicks. We drove along Shawneehaw Creek to Blueberry Farm with its trim cornfields and orchards and the mountains blue in the distance, and turned onto Gwaltney Road, which runs into Wautaga County and on through Pisgah National Forest. All along the roadside, daisies, chicory, black-eyed susans, butterfly weed, and sunflowers were in bloom, and on shady banks scarlet bergamot, the tall, white spires of black cohosh, and *Viburnum cassinoides*, which the mountain people call shawneehaw, withe-rod, and wild raisin for its edible dark blue fruit.

After crossing the northern boundary line of Pisgah Forest, we came to the last turn. There beside the mail box we found Mr. Ray Hicks himself and his two sons. I had written to say we were coming but hadn't said when, and I don't know how long he had been standing there, watching for us to pull up in the car. The Hicks's house is on a narrow, dead-end road on the side of Rocky Knob, at an altitude of 4,200 feet. Behind it, there is a sheer drop of 2,000 feet to the Wautaga River. Beyond the river lies a chain of distant mountains on the line between North Carolina and Tennessee.

As we entered the house, Mr. Hicks called, "Here's your friend!" Rosa and Granny—who was cheerful, loving, and wheezing like a kettle about to boil, but hale and hearty except for asthma—came into the living room to greet us, and we sat down to talk like old friends, which Rosa's letters made me feel we were. After meeting those three stalwart mountain men, waiting so patiently on the hot and dusty roadside by the mailbox, Rosa was a surprise: so slight and slender, so dainty in her fresh cotton print, it was hard to believe that she was the mother of those two strapping young men or that she scrubbed on the scrubbing board all of those mudstained overalls. But her fragile appearance was deceptive. Rosa Hicks has the strength of her mountain heritage and a vitality of her own. Quick to sorrow, quick to mirth, she has a light in her dark eyes.

Granny is Ray Hicks's mother, Mrs. Nathan Hicks. The two grown sons and the youngest daughter, Juanita, made up the household. Two older daughters had married and gone to live in Tennessee.

Mr. Hicks had spent his life in the woods and fields gathering herbs and roots and barks to sell to the wholesale drug companies. His family has lived on Rocky Knob for generations, and he has a great store of mountain lore. His father, he says, was an orphan child who lived with his grandfather, who built the house. His father's great-grandfather, who is buried down by the Wautaga River, lived in a log cabin.

Rosa calls her flowers by their mountain names, but she uses *Wild Flowers of North Carolina*, by Justice and Bell, to identify them. By referring to Dr. Justice's photographs, when we wrote to one another, we could match the local names with the Latin ones.

Rosa's flower garden is a bank between the road and the lawn, with no paths between the plants. "You can travel there," she said, "without hurting anything." But the slope was so steep that I couldn't penetrate the upper reaches even with the aid of my cane. Summer flowers were in full bloom on that July day when Martha and I were there, and the colorful bank looked like an English herbaceous border. I saw the musk mallow, *Malva moschata*, for the first time. It is a European and North African perennial that has escaped from old gardens and become naturalized in meadows and along roadsides from North Carolina to Canada. The plants are bushy, about two feet tall, and covered with fragrant flowers of a clear and glowing but delicate pink with faint lines of a deeper rose, like those of *Malva sylvestris* in size and shape, but more effective in the garden. There is scant reference to this lovely plant in garden literature, except by Miss Jekyll, who liked to plant pink mallows with steel-blue sea holly, *Eryngium maritimum*. Also in bloom in Rosa's garden was *Linaria vulgaris*, commonly called butter-and-eggs. This little European toadflax (because someone thought that the flowers look like toads, or perhaps that the plants attracted toads), seldom found in nurseries, has escaped to our roadsides from the gardens where few Americans now grow it, thinking it too invasive, but in England it has always been appreciated. In Rosa's garden I also admired her wild raspberry, *Rubus odoratus*. It used to bloom in deep shade in my Raleigh garden, from May into July, but never freely. In the South, it thrives only in the mountains. The magenta flowers are like wild roses, the leaves three- to five-lobed, like maples. It is unarmed, only the fruits being like those of brambles, and the berries, which may ripen as late as September and can appear simultaneously with flowers, are delicious.

It was a good day, the day I finally met Rosa Hicks, and I wrote her right away to say so and to send her some sedum and to ask about some of the other sedums on her list, as well as hedyotis, saxifrages, and meadow rues.

"Been slow in answering your letter," she wrote on the twelfth of August. "We are in the canning rush. Good to see the jars fill up, but having trouble getting lids. I decided to take time now to answer. The white sedum is like the one on the top of page eighty-one."

This white sedum is *Sedum ternatum*, a native of rich woods in the mountains and piedmont of the Carolinas. I first saw it on a mountainside in Buncombe County, along the rocky banks of Reems Creek. It flourished in my Raleigh garden under the oak trees, but I could never get it established under the pines in Charlotte. Now Rosa has sent me a nice clump, and I hope this time it will take hold. It blooms in April, with the white flower heads and also the little round leaves in threes. I had sent Rosa *S. sarmentosum*, a yellow-flowered Chinese species and also *S. acre*, which the early herbalists called wall-pepper because of the sharp taste of its leaves and which English cottagers, for reasons I can't quite fathom, call welcome-home-husband-though-never-so-drunk.

The hedyotis, Rosa says, is not the familiar bluet (once *Houstonia caerulea*, now *Hedyotis caerulea*) that stars the spring woods, but the mountain bluet (*H. purpurea*), whose blossoms are not at all blue, but delicate pink. In the garden it is apt to be weedy, but as I saw it one April at the foot of Morrow Mountain, growing along a small, clear stream with *Oxalis violacea* and *Hieracium venosum*, it was dainty enough for an Alpine garden. A southern species, it ranges from Maryland to Georgia and Alabama.

Rosa's saxifrage is mountain lettuce, the *Saxifraga micranthidifolia* of Justice and Bell's *Wild Flowers of North Carolina*. It has large, thin, light green leaves up to a foot long and panicles of small, white flowers in early summer. And Rosa says two species of meadow rue grow on the mountain, but she doesn't know which they are. One is probably *Thalictrum revolutum*, one of several tall ones that occur in the mountains. I grow another of the tall sorts in my garden, *T. polygamum*, which has narrow leaflets with pointed lobes and produces myriads of tiny, white flowers, like a spray of water, in July. The plant grows to eight feet and flops unless staked.

When I sent another list of questions to Rosa in mid-August, she wrote, "See if I can answer you earlier than I did your last letter.

If I don't I'll probably be in another canning round. About the waterleaf, the leaves are like those of the one on page 158 of the Justice book, *Hydrophyllum virginianum*. I just went to check mine, but it had died back or the menfolk had cut it down." Waterleaf is often called Shawnee salad, for its tender, young shoots were eaten by various tribes of American Indians.

In November, Granny died, and Juanita Hicks went to Tennessee to visit her sister and look for a job. "Now I have more to do," Rosa wrote, "and will have to get used to doing things by myself again. Maybe my work will be so I don't have to be on the trot all the time. Maybe when you write again, I will have more time to answer. Well, I have more letters to write so I better get a move on me. Some people are easier to write to than others."

Early in the new year, when it was too cold to work outside and too cold inside to do anything but sit by the fire, Rosa made a list of all the plants in the Justice and Bell book that grow on her mountainside. There were seventy-three—and she listed many others that were not in the book. "Sitting inside looking out today, it's lovely outside," she wrote on the twelfth of February. "It has been cold and windy and a little snowy. We had up to six inches of snow, and there's still some of it around. A while back I took a peep at the flowers and noticed crocuses and snowdrops peeping up; was thinking of taking a peep today, but haven't got that far. Might be something else today, but I don't think so, because we have had too cold weather, and the ground has been frozen deep."

On the seventh of April, she wrote about the first wildflowers, "A pretty day—well, has been all week, but nights are frosty. Maybe that will help things and keep them tough and not so easy to get killed. I haven't noticed anything hurt by the freezing nights we had a while back. I haven't been in the woods to see what may be in bloom, but near the house the spring beauties, bloodroot, hepatica, and the round-leafed yellow violet are out. When I can find the halberd-leafed violet I will send you one—might be next week if nothing happens."

Spring-beauty (*Claytonia virginica*) has another charming name, good-morning-spring. I thought of that when I found it one St. Valentine's day blooming under oak trees on the campus of the University of Mississippi, covering the ground like grass, although it doesn't take the place of turf, since the leaves disappear when the flowers fade. In Mrs. Dana's day there were great patches of spring-beauty along the carriage drive in Central Park. "One is always glad to discover these country children within our city limits," she wrote, "where they can be known and loved by those other children who are not so fortunate." My earliest date for this plant is the first week in March, and that year it went on blooming until mid-April. The petals are white or flesh-colored, with hairline veins that vary from the palest pink to the deepest rose. But the claytonia that Rosa grows is not *C. virginica*. It is *C. caroliniana*, an endemic of the southern Alleghanies from Virginia to Georgia, occurring in North Carolina only in the mountains along the Tennessee line. It differs from *C. virginica* only in having wider leaves and fewer flowers and blooming a little later.

My earliest date for bloodroot (*Sanguinaria canadensis*) is the twenty-second of February, and its bloom was as brief as it was beautiful. I have a splendid form of it that came to me from a nursery in the roots of some other plant. The flowers have twelve gleaming white petals, and they are nearly three inches across. Each bud comes up wrapped in a gray-green leaf and rises above it as the flower opens. As the flowers fade, the leaves grow taller. In 1735, when John Custis of Williamsburg sent bloodroot to Peter Collinson in London, Collinson said he had "3 sorts of pecoone" in his garden, "one with a small flower, one with a large flower, one with a double flower," adding politely, "but I was glad of yours, perhaps it may prove a variety." Puccoon is an Indian name, shortened in Appalachia to coon root. Years ago I had the double variety, flore-pleno, praised in a catalog as "a rarity of unsurpassed beauty," and I ordered it. It was puny and did not persist. A pink form I sent for proved to be dingy white with a wine tinge on the reverse of the petals. Thomas Jefferson commented in his *Garden Book* on the ephemeral bloom of bloodroot at Shadwell in 1766: "April 6, Narcissus and Puckoon open; April 13, Puckoon flowers fallen." Looking over my own records I find that in some exceptional years I have had blood-roots last two or three weeks.

Rosa's hepatica is *H. acutiloba*, the only one found in the high mountains of North Carolina. Its habitat is the Appalachians from Maine to northern Georgia. The flowers are usually white, but they are sometimes tinted with blue-violet or pink. The ones I had in Raleigh had such numerous and such white sepals that they looked like bloodroot.

There are two species of yellow violets on Rocky Knob, the round-leaved and the halberd-leaved. *Viola rotundifolia* blooms the first of April, and its earliness led Mrs. Dana to believe this is the species Bryant had in mind when he wrote—

> When beechen buds begin to swell,
> And woods the blue-birds warble know,
> The yellow violet's modest bell
> Peeps from the last year's leaves below.

To call this flower a bell carries poetic license too far, even though to some people bell and blossom are synonymous. The halberd-leaved violet (*V. hastata*), a southern species belonging to the section called mock pansies, occurs in mixed woods from Pennsylvania to Florida and Alabama, and is available from We-Du Nurseries. When the long, tapered, spear-shaped leaves are variegated, as they often are, with patches of gray-green or reddish bronze, they are more decorative than the small yellow flowers.

Rosa also lists the white Canada violet (*V. canadensis*), another of the mock pansies. In North Carolina it is found only in a few mountain counties where it blooms from April to July. The buds are vinaceous, and there is a touch of yellow in the throats of the creamy flowers. Another mountain species, *V. striata*, has seeded itself all over my garden in Charlotte after I brought it from Raleigh, for sentimental reasons, leaving more valuable plants behind. It came from the cemetery in Marietta where several generations of our family are buried. Planting violets on graves is an ancient custom, but I have wondered how this species got there, as it is rare in Georgia, where it reaches its southern limit. When it blooms in mid-March or shortly thereafter, the clumps are tidy and covered with creamy flowers with violet stripes, but then it produces long and straggly stems which cover the basal leaves. Keeping them cut back is a terrible chore.

There is a tall, blue iris in the meadow below Rosa's house. Not knowing its Latin name, she calls it the orchid iris. When she sent it to me in bloom, it proved to be *Iris virginica*, the southern form of *I. versicolor*, a species ranging from Canada to Louisiana and Florida. As the specific name implies, it is variable as to color. The poorest forms, Dykes in *The Genus Iris* says, are small and pale, but the best have "large flowers of a good, deep blue-purple color, or even a velvety red-purple that borders on crimson." When Thoreau walked to White's Pond in June, 1853, he wrote in his Journal that blue flags were "growing thinly in the water about the shore," but when he went to Lupine Hill via Depot Field Brook in June of 1857, he described those he saw blooming in the meadows as having "variously streaked and colored petals." Another June day, he wrote that "some blue flags are quite a red purple, dark wine color." (The flags that I knew as a child were as blue as the waters of White's Pond. They grew in the ditches where the country road went through a shallow creek just beyond the last houses of Garysburg, North Carolina, the village we lived in when I was nine. I saw them there when I was riding my pony, one morning in May, and it was wonderful to me because they were the first wildflower I had found by myself and recognized by the picture in my flower book. Some sixty Mays later, when I drove over the same road, I found the creek running under it in a culvert—but the blue flags were still blooming.)

[*Gardening for Love* (1987)]

NAMING PLANTS

Thomas Jefferson
To Dr. John Manners

Monticello, February 22, 1814
The opinion which, in your letter of January 24, you are pleased to
ask of me, on the comparative merits of the different methods of
classification adopted by different writers on Natural History, is one
which I could not have given satisfactorily, even at the earlier period
at which the subject was more familiar; still less, after a life of
continued occupation in civil concerns has so much withdrawn me
from studies of that kind. I can, therefore, answer but in a very
general way. And the text of this answer will be found in an observation in your letter, where, speaking of nosological systems, you
say that disease has been found to be an unit. Nature has, in truth,
produced units only through all her works. Classes, orders, genera,
species, are not of her work. Her creation is of individuals. No two
animals are exactly alike; no two plants, nor even two leaves or
blades of grass; no two crystallizations. And if we may venture from
what is within the cognizance of such organs as ours, to conclude
on that beyond their powers, we must believe that no two particles
of matter are of exact resemblance. This infinitude of units or individuals being far beyond the capacity of our memory, we are
obliged, in aid of that, to distribute them into masses, throwing into
each of these all the individuals which have a certain degree of
resemblance; to subdivide these again into smaller groups, according
to certain points of dissimilitude observable in them, and so on until
we have formed what we call a system of classes, orders, genera
and species. In doing this, we fix arbitrarily on such characteristic
resemblances and differences as seem to us most prominent and
invariable in the several subjects, and most likely to take a strong

hold in our memories. Thus Ray formed one classification on such lines of division as struck him most favorably; Klein adopted another; Brisson a third, and other naturalists other designations, till Linnaeus appeared. Fortunately for science, he conceived in the three kingdoms of nature, modes of classification which obtained the approbation of the learned of all nations. His system was accordingly adopted by all, and united all in a general language. It offered the three great desiderata: First, of aiding the memory to retain a knowledge of the productions of nature. Secondly, of rallying all to the same names for the same objects, so that they could communicate understandingly on them. And thirdly, of enabling them, when a subject was first presented, to trace it by its character up to the conventional name by which it was agreed to be called. [. . .]

[*Thomas Jefferson's Garden Book* (1944)]

Alice Morse Earle
Plant Names

*The fascination of plant names is founded
on two instincts,—love of Nature and curiosity about Language.*
—English Plant Names,
REV. JOHN EARLE,
1880

Verbal magic is the subtle mysterious power of certain words. This
power may come from association with the senses; thus I have distinct sense of stimulation in the word scarlet, and pleasure in the
words lucid and liquid. The word garden is a never ceasing delight;
it seems to me Oriental; perhaps I have a transmitted sense from
my grandmother Eve of the Garden of Eden. I like the words, a
Garden of Olives, a Garden of Herbs, the Garden of the Gods, a
Garden enclosed, Philosophers of the Garden, the Garden of the
Lord. As I have written on gardens, and thought on gardens, and
walked in gardens, "the very music of the name has gone into my
being." How beautiful are Cardinal Newman's words:—

By a garden is meant mystically a place of spiritual repose, stillness, peace,
refreshment, delight.

There was, in Gerarde's day, no fixed botanical nomenclature
of any of the parts or attributes of a plant. Without using botanical
terms, try to describe a plant so as to give an exact notion of it to
a person who has never seen it, then try to find common words to
describe hundreds of plants; you will then admire the vocabulary
of the old herbalist, his "fresh English words," for you will find that
it needs the most dextrous use of words to convey accurately the

figure of a flower. That felicity and facility Gerarde had; "a bleak white color"—how clearly you see it! The Water Lily had "great round leaves like a buckler." The Cat-tail Flags "flower and bear their mace or torch in July and August." One plant had "deeply gashed leaves." The Marigold had "fat thick crumpled leaves set upon a gross and spongious stalke." Here is the Wake-robin, "a long hood in proportion like the ear of a hare, in middle of which hood cometh forth a pestle or clapper of a dark murry or pale purple color." The leaves of the Corn-marigold are "much hackt and cut into divers sections and placed confusedly." Another plant had leaves of "an overworne green," and Pansy leaves were "a bleak green." The leaves of Tansy are also vividly described as "infinitely jagged and nicked and curled with all like unto a plume of feathers."

The classification and naming of flowers was much thought and written upon from Gerarde's day, until the great work of Linnæus was finished. Some very original schemes were devised. *The Curious and Profitable Gardener*, printed in 1730, suggested this plan: That all plants should be named to indicate their color, and that the initials of their names should be the initials of their respective colors; thus if a plant were named William the Conqueror it would indicate that the name was of a white flower with crimson lines or shades. "Virtuous Oreada would indicate a violet and orange flower; Charming Phyllis or Curious Plotinus a crimson and purple blossom." S. was to indicate Black or Sable, and what letter was Scarlet to have? The "curious ingenious Gentleman" who published this plan urged also the giving of "pompous names" as more dignified; and he made the assertion that French and Flemish "Flowerists" had adopted his system.

These were all forerunners of Ruskin, with his poetical notions of plant nomenclature, such as this; that feminine forms of names ending in *a* (as Prunella, Campanula, Salvia, Kalmia) and *is* (Iris, Amaryllis) should be given only to plants "that are pretty and good"; and that real names, Lucia, Clarissa, etc., be also given. Masculine names in *us* should be given to plants of masculine qualities,—strength, force, stubbornness; neuter endings in *um*, given to plants indicative of evil or death.

I have a fancy anent many old-time flower names that they are also the names of persons. I think of them as persons bearing various traits and characteristics. On the other hand, many old English

Christian names seem so suited for flowers, that they might as well stand for flowers as for persons. Here are a few of these quaint old names, Collet, Colin, Emmot, Issot, Doucet, Dobinet, Cicely, Audrey, Amice, Hilary, Bryde, Morrice, Tyffany, Amery, Nowell, Ellice, Digory, Avery, Audley, Jacomin, Gillian, Petronille, Gresel, Joyce, Lettice, Cibell, Avice, Cesselot, Parnell, Renelsha. Do they not "smell sweet to the ear"? The names of flowers are often given as Christian names. Children have been christened by the names Dahlia, Clover, Hyacinth, Asphodel, Verbena, Mignonette, Pansy, Heartsease, Daisy, Zinnia, Fraxinella, Poppy, Daffodil, Hawthorn.

What power have the old English names of garden flowers, to unlock old memories, as have the flowers themselves! Dr. Earle writes, "The fascination of plant names is founded on two instincts; love of Nature, and curiosity about Language." To these I should add an equally strong instinct in many persons—their sensitiveness to associations.

I am never more filled with a sense of the delight of old English plant-names than when I read the liquid verse of Spenser:—

> *Bring hether the pincke and purple Cullembine*
> *   . . . with Gellifloures,*
> *Bring hether Coronations and Sops-in-wine*
> *   Worne of paramours.*
> *Sow me the ground with Daffadowndillies*
> *And Cowslips and Kingcups and loved Lilies,*
> *   The pretty Pawnce*
> *   The Chevisaunce*
> *Shall match with the fayre Flour Delice.*

Why, the names are a pleasure, though you know not what the Sops-in-wine or the Chevisaunce were. Gilliflowers were in the verses of every poet. One of scant fame, named Plat, thus sings:—

> *Here spring the goodly Gelofors,*
> *   Some white, some red in showe;*
> *Here pretie Pinks with jagged leaves*
> *   On rugged rootes do growe;*
> *The Johns so sweete in showe and smell,*

Distinct by colours twaine,
About the borders of their beds
In seemlie sight remaine.

If there ever existed any difference between Sweet-johns and Sweet-williams, it is forgotten now. They have not shared a revival of popularity with other old-time favorites. They were one of the "garland flowers" of Gerarde's day, and were "esteemed for beauty, to deck up the bosoms of the beautiful, and for garlands and crowns of pleasure." In the gardens of Hampton Court in the days of King Henry VIII, were Sweet-williams, for the plants had been bought by the bushel. Sweet-williams are little sung by the poets, and I never knew any one to call the Sweet-william her favorite flower, save one person. Old residents of Worcester will recall the tiny cottage that stood on the corner of Chestnut and Pleasant streets, since the remote years when the latter-named street was a post-road. It was occupied during my childhood by friends of my mother—a century-old mother, and her ancient unmarried daughter. Behind the house stretched one of the most cheerful gardens I have ever seen; ever, in my memory, bathed in glowing sunlight and color. Of its glories I recall specially the long spires of vivid Bee Larkspur, the varied Poppies of wonderful growth, and the rioting Sweet-williams. The latter flowers had some sentimental association to the older lady, who always asserted with emphasis to all visitors that they were her favorite flower. They over-ran the entire garden, crowding the grass plot where the washed garments were hung out to dry, even growing in the chinks of the stone steps and between the flat stone flagging of the little back yard, where stood the old well with its moss-covered bucket. They spread under the high board fence and appeared outside on Chestnut Street; and they extended under the dense Lilac bushes and Cedars and down the steep grass bank and narrow steps to Pleasant Street. The seed was carefully gathered, especially of one glowing crimson beauty, the color of the Mullein Pink, and a gift of it was highly esteemed by other garden owners. Old herbals say the Sweet-williams are "worthy the Respect of the Greatest Ladies who are Lovers of Flowers." They certainly had the respect and love of these two old ladies, who were truly Lovers of Flowers.

I recall an objection made to Sweet-williams, by some one years ago, that they were of no use or value save in the garden; that they could never be combined in bouquets, nor did they arrange well in vases. It is a place of honor, some of us believe, to be a garden flower as well as a vase flower. This garden was the only one I knew when a child which contained plants of Love-lies-bleeding—it had even then been deemed old-fashioned and out of date. And it also held a few Sunflowers, which had not then had a revival of attention, and seemed as obsolete as the Love-lies-bleeding. The last-named flower I always disliked, a shapeless, gawky creature, described in florists' catalogues and like publications as "an effective plant easily attaining to a splendid form bearing many plume-tufts of rich lustrous crimson." It is the "immortal amarant" chosen by Milton to crown the celestial beings in *Paradise Lost*. Poor angels! they have had many trying vagaries of attire assigned to them.

I can contribute to plant lore one fantastic notion in regard to Love-lies-bleeding—though I can find no one who can confirm this memory of my childhood. I recall distinctly expressions of surprise and regret that these two old people in Worcester should retain the Love-lies-bleeding in their garden, because "the house would surely be struck with lightning." Perhaps this fancy contributed to the exile of the flower from gardens.

There be those who write, and I suppose they believe, that a love of Nature and perception of her beauties and a knowledge of flowers, are the dower of those who are country born and bred; by which is meant reared upon a farm. I have not found this true. Farm children have little love for Nature and are surprisingly ignorant about wild flowers, save a very few varieties. The child who is garden bred has a happier start in life, a greater love and knowledge of Nature. It is a principle of Froebel that one must limit a child's view in order to coordinate his perceptions. That is precisely what is done in a child's regard of Nature by his life in a garden; his view is limited and he learns to know garden flowers and birds and insects thoroughly, when the vast and bewildering variety of field and forest would have remained unappreciated by him.

It is a distressing condition of the education of farmers, that they know so little about the country. The man knows about his crops, and his wife about the flowers, herbs, and vegetables of her garden; but no countrymen know the names of wild flowers—and few countrywomen, save of medicinal herbs. I asked one farmer the name of a brilliant autumnal flower whose intense purple was then unfamiliar to me—the Devil's-bit. He answered, "Them's Woilets." Violet is the only word in which the initial V is ever changed to W by native New Englanders. Every pink or crimson flower is a Pink. Spring blossoms are "Mayflowers." A frequent answer is, "Those ain't flowers, they're weeds." They are more knowing as to trees, though shaky about the evergreen trees, having little idea of varieties and inclined to call many Spruce. They know little about the reasons for names of localities, or of any historical traditions save those of the Revolution. One exclaims in despair, "No one in the country knows anything about the country."

This is no recent indifference and ignorance; Susan Cooper wrote in her *Rural Hours* in 1848:—

When we first made acquaintance with the flowers of the neighborhood we asked grown persons—learned perhaps in many matters—the common names of plants they must have seen all their lives, and we found they were no wiser than the children or ourselves. It is really surprising how little country people know on such subjects. Farmers and their wives can tell you nothing on these matters. The men are at fault even among the trees on their own farms, if they are at all out of the common way; and as for smaller native plants, they know less about them than Buck or Brindle, their own oxen.

In that delightful book, *The Rescue of an Old Place*, the author has a chapter on the love of flowers in America. It was written anent the ever-present statements seen in metropolitan print that Americans do not love flowers because they are used among the rich and fashionable in large cities for extravagant display rather than for enjoyment; and that we accept botanical names for our indigenous plants instead of calling them by homely ones such as familiar flowers are known by in older lands.

Two more foolish claims could scarcely be made. In the first place, the doings of fashionable folk in large cities are fortunately far from being a national index of habit. Secondly, in ancient lands the people named the flowers long before there were botanists, here the botanists found the flowers and named them for the people. Moreover, country folk in New England and even in the far West call flowers by pretty folk-names, if they call them at all, just as in Old England.

The fussing over the use of the scientific Latin names for plants apparently will never cease; many of these Latin names are very pleasant, have become so from constant usage, and scarcely seem Latin; thus Clematis, Tiarella, Rhodora, Arethusa, Campanula, Potentilla, Hepatica. When I know the folk-names of flowers I always speak thus of them—and *to them*; but I am grateful too for the scientific classification and naming, as a means of accurate distinction. For any flower student quickly learns that the same English folk-name is given in different localities to very different plants. For instance, the name Whiteweed is applied to ten different plants; there are in England ten or twelve Cuckoo-flowers, and twenty-one Bachelor's Buttons. Such names as Mayflower, Wild Pink, Wild Lily, Eyebright, Toad-flax, Ragged Robin, None-so-pretty, Lady's-fingers, Four-o'clocks, Redweed, Buttercups, Butter-flower, Cat's-tail, Rocket, Blue-Caps, Creeping-jenny, Bird's-eye, Bluebells, apply to half a dozen plants.

The old folk-names are not definite, but they are delightful; they tell of mythology and medicine, of superstitions and traditions; they show trains of relationship, and associations; in fact, they appeal more to the philologist and antiquarian than to the botanist. Among all the languages which contribute to the variety and picturesqueness of English plant names, Dr. Prio deems Maple the only one surviving from the Celtic language. Gromwell and Wormwood may possibly be added.

There are some Anglo-Saxon words; among them Hawthorn and Groundsel. French, Dutch, and Danish names are many, Arabic and Persian are more. Many plant names are dedicatory; they embody the names of the saints and a few the names of the Deity. Our Lady's Flowers are many and interesting; my daughter wrote a series of articles for the *New York Evening Post* on Our Lady's Flowers, and the list swelled to a surprising number. The devil and witches have their shares of flowers, as have the fairies.

I have always regretted deeply that our botanists neglected an opportunity of great enrichment in plant nomenclature when they ignored the Indian names of our native plants, shrubs, and trees. The first names given these plants were not always planned by botanists; they were more often invented in loving memory of English plants, or sometimes from a fancied resemblance to those plants. They did give the wonderfully descriptive name of Moccasin-flower to that creature of the wild-woods; and a far more appropriate title it is than Lady's-slipper, but it is not as well known. I have never found the Lady's-slipper as beautiful a flower as do nearly all my friends, as did my father and mother, and I was pleased at Ruskin's sharp comment that such a slipper was only fit for very gouty old toes.

Papoose-root utilizes another Indian word. Very few Indian plant names were adopted by the white men, fewer still have been adopted by the scientists. The *Catalpa speciosa* (Catalpa); the *Zea mays* (Maize); and *Yucca filamentosa* (Yucca), are the only ones I know. Chinkapin, Cohosh, Hackmatack, Kinnikinnik, Tamarack, Persimmon, Tupelo, Squash, Puccoon, Pipsissewa, Musquash, Pecan, the Scuppernong and Catawba grapes, are our only well-known Indian plant names that survive. Of these Maize, the distinctive product of the United States, will ever link us with the vanishing Indian. It will be noticed that only Puccoon, Cohosh, Pipsissewa, Hackmatack, and Yucca are names of flowering plants; of these Yucca is the only one generally known. I am glad our stately native trees, Tupelo, Hickory, Catalpa, bear Indian names.

A curious example of persistence, when so much else has perished, is found in the word "Kiskatomas," the shellbark nut. This Algonquin word was heard everywhere in the state of New York sixty years ago, and is not yet obsolete in families of Dutch descent who still care for the nut itself.

We could very well have preserved many Indian names, among them Hiawatha's

> *Beauty of the springtime,*
> *The Miskodeed in blossom.*

I think Miskodeed a better name than Claytonia or Spring Beauty. The Onondaga Indians had a suggestive name for the Marsh Marigold, "It-opens-the-swamps," which seems to show you the yellow stars "shining in swamps and hollows gray." The name Cowslip has been transferred to it in some localities in New England, which is not strange when we find that the flower has fifty-six English folknames; among them are Drunkards, Crazy Bet, Meadow-bright, Publicans and Sinners, Soldiers' Buttons, Gowans, Kingcups, and Buttercups. Our Italian street venders call them Buttercups. In erudite Boston, in sight of Boston Common, the beautiful Fringed Gentian is not only called, but labelled, French Gentian. To hear a lovely bunch of the Arethusa called Swamp Pink is not so strange. The Sabbatia grows in its greatest profusion in the vicinity of Plymouth, Massachusetts, and is called locally, "The Rose of Plymouth." It is sold during its season of bloom in the streets of that town and is used to dress the churches. Its name was given to honor an early botanist, Tiberatus Sabbatia, but in Plymouth there is an almost universal belief that it was named because the Pilgrims of 1620 first saw the flower on the Sabbath day. It thus is regarded as a religious emblem, and strong objection is made to mingling other flowers with it in church decoration.

[*Old-Time Gardens* (1901)]

Candace Wheeler
Plant Poetry

It is curious to note how much of love and appreciation certain flowers owe to certain poets. I have a friend who has made a "Shakespeare garden," in which nothing grows which the great magician has not noticed or praised. One may find there all of poor Ophelia's flowers and herbs,—things with beautiful names like rosemary and thyme and basil; but I am constrained to confess that they make far less show in the garden than is warranted by the impression they have made upon the mind.

There is surely many a daisy border which exists by virtue of the one "modest crimson-tippèd flower" which came to grief under the ploughshare of Robbie Burns. And how much of the love of succeeding generations do daffodils and primroses owe to the loving verse of Herrick,—to the tender likening of them to "children young, speaking with tears before ye have a tongue." As for roses and lilies and violets, it seems to me a library of poems could be made which name or praise or liken them to human roses or lilies or violets. Indeed, in certain rare collections there is a book filled from cover to cover with tributes in all languages and from all periods to the rose. It is not the least of the tokens of the royalty and dominion of the rose, that the choicest of the sensations which we call color is called by its name. We use it to describe a sunset sky or the tinting of a baby's finger-tips; and even the innumerable variations of shades and dyes of damasks and velvet and precious silken stuffs which commend their tints to human eyes, *rose-color* describes, and the flower mingles its remembrance with the loveliest of them all.

Rose-color leads the list of color names suggested by flowers in frequency of use; lavender, which comes next and covers as great a range of tints, is named from an herb which few know by sight, and of which, in fact, the most familiar association is a literary one. One knows it chiefly from English poets and writers—from lavender "strewings" and lavendered linen of English song and story. But it is in my garden, its tall, straight stalks grown out of dried and withered seeds which came to me in a letter from a woman whose face I have never seen. Violet and heliotrope are in the same range of tint that we call lavender, but we find their namesakes in every garden. We should have to invent new words for our color sensations, if we could not use the names of flowers and fruits. But, after all, how came their names? How came the word and the thing together ere they began their long travel down the ages? We may fancy that Eve—herself the first rose of womanhood—gave its name among the roses of Eden, and we like to think that as Adam "gave names to all cattle," Eve tried her syllables upon the flowers. Her joy in existence and love must have blossomed easily into words as she emphasized one after another of them.

Was it love or praise,
Speech half asleep, or song half awake?

But there were many outside flower-sisters, straggling afar from the closed limits of Eden, who awaited their names until the world was peopled, and then found them by virtue of the associations they touched and the sensations they evoked. We can almost trace the state and doings of mankind in their names. The sunflower suggests sun-worship, and the iris smacks of Pagan days, and the fleur-de-lis of banners and royal pageants; marigold and lady's-slipper and jewel-weed came into speech after the vanities were born and well grown among the daughters of men, but the lilies and roses and violets and daffodils of early English verse are inalienably ours, and belong to our race history, even although they might have begun in Eden, or at its very gates. Wake-robin, larkspur, and crowfoot, these smack of rustic observation and nature-love, of love of birds and living things. They have not been named from characteristics, but from form and likeness and faint suggestion. But it is not the same with herbs. Their names have grown from the needs and uses of men. Rue and sage, and summer savory! Human emotion and

[*231*]

human wisdom, and human satisfaction are behind them all; boneset is physical healing, caraway is mental philosophy, balm is for blessing, and pennyroyal is a lesson on the height possible to lowliness and poverty. And so through all the dear familiar names which come to us in long tradition, names given by rustic peoples who lived near the sod and whose experiences were of nature.

But among all names of all flowers, none ever appealed so surely to an experienced soul as heart's-ease. *Heart's-ease!* There is in it so profound a sense of world-sorrow, so tender an acceptance of comfort!

Some authoritative intelligence, whose elevation had not saved it from the common lot of suffering, found ministry in this small, cheerful, flowery demonstration of nature, and called it heart's-ease.

Or was it, perhaps, an inspiration of some botanist, prone to sentiment, who took the purple of its superior leaves for mourning, and its gay yellow ones, marked like the whiskers of a mask, for a sign of cheerfulness? Whichever it may have been, it appeals to us by sound, as other flowers do by sight.

No wonder Lowell chose "Heart's-ease and Rue" to make the title and foretell the sunshine and shadow of one of his latest books of verses, and it was like his gentle-heartedness to write in one which he gave to a girl friend,—

> *All heart's-ease be your days; no leaf of rue*
> *Darken the nosegay Time shall cull for you!*

The clear, delicate, pointed handwriting almost shines to the eyes of the woman who was a little while ago the girl for whom he wrote the inscription.

It is a high and awesome consciousness, that of holding in mortal hands the threads of a friendship which reach up to a soul set to shine in the mystery of heaven! But from flowers to stars, is the distance so great? If one stands beside them in the garden in the clear obscure of twilight, and watches the heavenly lights appearing faintly in the darkening sky, an inner feeling recognizes that they belong to the same world of influences, and that we are one with them both.

Dear Heart's-ease! one feels like exclaiming, beloved of heaven and of men for unseen ministry, growing freely wherever we invite and prepare for you, whether in hearts or gardens, give us of your humble joy and power of consolation!

The scientific names of flowers are a painful necessity; common names represent their relation to humanity, Latin names only scientific facts. When some clever friend gives me the Latin name of a favorite of my garden, and it immediately drops through and out of my consciousness, I comfort myself by remembering that Charlotte Cushman once said, she could "only remember two Latin words, and those were *delirium tremens*." Nevertheless I feel a lurking consciousness that it is hardly respectable not to know the Latin names and remote ancestry of things which you live with, just as it argues a certain culpable indifference to one's forebears—to those of our line who lived and loved and were responsible for our being—not to treasure their brief history and connection, and make a family catechism of their names for our children and our children's children.

[*Content in a Garden* (1902)]

Louise Beebe Wilder
Familiar Plant Names

The name that dwells on every tongue
No minstrell needs.

—DON JORGE MANRIQUE

Nowadays we are become so learned in the matter of Latin plant names that there is some danger that the familiar English names, their pet names, will disappear from our garden vocabulary and finally, perhaps, be altogether forgotten. More and more often do we hear the words Dianthus, Digitalis, Lychnis tripping easily from the tongues of young gardeners, and less and less the friendly, time-endeared appellations—Pink, Foxglove, Campion; and our garden conversations lose much of piquancy and agreeable intimacy in consequence. It is, of course, essential that we know the Latin names of our plants, for by no other means may we accurately designate them, but the passing of the old vernacular names would be a real loss. They are the connecting links between us and the flower lovers of all the ages—men, women, and children, a long line of them—stretching across the years through countless gardens, high and humble, through woods and meadows and marshes to the little gatherings of potent herbs and edible roots nestled against the protecting walls of ancient monasteries wherein were kept the first records of flowers and their names. Out of the simplicity and sweetness of each age these names were born and linger yet with the freshness and charm of the flowers themselves. [. . .]

How fascinating to trace out the beginnings of these old plant names! The origin of some is, of course, obvious enough, as for instance, Shepherd's Warning and Poorman's-weather-glass, for the Scarlet Pimpernell, that closes its tiny blossoms at the approach of a storm; Butter and Eggs for such flowers as display the fresh colours

[234]

of those good country products; Guinea-hen-flower and Checker Lily for the Little Fritillary whose bell is well checkered over with deeper colour; Hod-the-rake (hold-the-rake) and Rest Harrow (Arrest harrow) for meadow plants having such thickly growing roots that they impede the operation of rakes and harrows.

Many plants have received names indicatory of their habits; thus Four-o'clocks, Morning Glory, Evening Glory, John-go-to-bed-at-noon, Ten o'clock Lady, Flower-of-an-hour, Good-night-at-noon; and so also Turnesol (turning toward the sun), Catch-fly, Fly-trap, and so on.

Creeping plants with insistent colonizing proclivities usually receive some such name as Meg-many-feet, Gill-over-the-ground, Robin-run-in-the-hedge, Roaming Charlie, Creeping Jenny, Jack-jump-about, or Mother-of-thousands. Hundreds were named from some real or fancied resemblance to some object; thus Monkshood, Bluebell, Turtle-head, Ladies-tresses, Snow-in-summer, Adder's-tongue, Snowdrop, Quaker Bonnets, Dutchman's-breeches, Maltese Cross, Larkspur, Bird's-foot, Pussy-toes, and so on indefinitely. The words Bull or Horse used as a prefix to certain others, as Bull-rush and Horse-mint, simply indicate a coarser variety of rush or mint. Many twining plants were christened by sentimentalists Love-bind and Bind-with-love.

Several centuries ago John Parkinson wrote "I would not two things should be called by one name, for the mistaking and misusing of them." If there was this danger in Parkinson's day, it has increased a hundredfold in ours. Few of these old plant names are at all fixed in their application, many doing duty for numerous quite different and unrelated plants and others making part of a string of names of anywhere from two or three to fifty or sixty designating the same plant. Nearly all neat, rather small, round flowers have been called at some time or in some locality Bachelors Buttons; many flowers with soft whitish leaves Dusty Miller, and those having fringed petals were frequently called Ragged Robin or Ragged Sailor. There are countless Prince's Feathers, Bird's-eyes, Sweet Nancys, Cowslips, London Prides, Nonesuch, Cuckoo Flowers, Honeysuckles, Long-purples, Sweet Marys, Ladders-to-heaven, Forget-me-nots, Buttercups, Roses of Heaven, Butter and Eggs, Willow-herbs, Sweet Williams, and Ox-eyes—to name a few; and the number of Meadow Pinks, Indian Pinks, Squaw-roots, and May-flowers that flourish in our own floral kingdom would astonish the curious searcher into such matters. [. . .]

The flower that comes down the years without winning one or more pet names has somehow failed to draw close to the lives of the human beings beside whom it has grown. There are not many old-fashioned flowers of which this may be said, but it is a curious fact that a flower so appealing and distinctive as the Crocus should be one. Crocuses have been grown in gardens since the early part of the seventeenth century but none as far as I can ascertain has acquired a common name save Crocus sativus, which was called Saffron or Saff-flower. Its relative the Colchicum, on the other hand, boasts quite a number, the quaintness and intimate character of which seem to imply a special affection for the jaunty little autumn flower. [. . .]

It is not surprising that many plants acquired their names through a real or fancied power to alleviate certain human ills. The little Pansy was deemed a potent heart remedy or cordial and so received its name of Heartsease, and so also we have Lungwort, Throatwort, Consumption Root, Ague-weed, Palseywort, Pleurisy-root, Eye-bright and Woundwort. Some were believed to be so universal in their curative powers that they received the name of All-heal or Cure-all.

To the curious old cult called the Doctrine of Signatures, which at one time certainly won the credulity of suffering humanity, is traceable many plant names. This was a system for discovering the medical uses of a plant from something in its external appearance that resembled the disease it would cure or the portion of the body to be cured. In *The Art of Simpling* we read "Though Sin and Satan have plunged mankind into an Ocean of Infirmaties, yet the mercy of God, which is over all His works, maketh Grasse to grow upon the Mountains and Herbes, for the use of men, and hath not only stamped upon them a distinct form, but also give them particular signatures, whereby a man may read, even in legible characters the use of them." Imaginations must have run riot in the compilation of a pharmacopœia based upon this wild theory, and even after a lapse of several centuries one must feel pity for the poor creatures treated with Quaking Grass for chills, with Nettle tea for nettle rash, with Gromwell (on account of its hard seeds) for gall-stones, with

Scabiosa (by reason of its scaly pappus) for all affections of the skin, even unto leprosy. A heart-shaped leaf was good for the heart, a kidney-shaped leaf for the kidneys; a yellow flower cured jaundice, and a red one assuaged blood.

> *Thus lived our sires ere doctors learned to kill*
> *And multiply with theirs the monthly bill.*

And our heritage from these strange and seemingly terrible practices is a thousand flower names that serve to throw some light to-day upon the customs of those ancient times.

One might continue indefinitely to work out the origins of the old plant names; of many we are able to find the key for ourselves, and the old horticultural works teem with more or less plausible explanations. There are the many plants of a poisonous nature which bear testimony to the grim fact in such names as Death-come-quickly, Death-cup, Deadly Night-shade, Poison-berry; there are those associated with the ceremony of the bridal, as Bridal-wreath, Bridesweet, Bridewort, Wedding Posy; those named from some quality of fragrance as the Heliotrope, which is said to bear the name of Cherry Pie because of the resemblance of its perfume to that of the homely dainty; the many named in honour of the gods, as Jupiter's Beard, Flower of Jove, Juno's Rose, Venus' Looking Glass; those derived from natural history as Bird Cherry, Duck-weed, Cat-mint, Chickweed, Bee-nettle, and those which are corrupted or translated from a foreign word. Examples of these are Mallow from the Latin Malve, Fumatory from the French Fume-terre (Earth-smoke), Herb Bennet from Herba Benedicta (Blessed Herb).

Mr. Leonard Barron tells me of an interesting case that came within his experience of the manner in which a Latin name was most curiously changed. A nurseryman in a communicative mood told some children who were playing in a meadow near by the nursery that the name of the flower with which they were decorating themselves was Rudbeckia. The children received this unwieldy word, tossed it to and fro in their play until the harsh edges were softened and finally had it as Rosy Betty—a strange name indeed for the swarthy Black-eyed Susan—but one by which it is now generally known in that one locality. By some such incidents as this must we account for the many plant names to which we can find no clew; to such intriguing appellations as Jump-up-and-kiss-me, Impudent Lawyers, Meet-me-love, Blooming-down, Little-washer-women, Cast-me-down, Lad's Love, Kiss-me-behind-the-garden-gate, Cats and Keys, Seven-years-love, Sweet Mary Ann, Vettervoo, Stickadose, Suckie-sue, and innumerable others.

The familiar plant nomenclature of our own country is a sort of composite of that of many others; as widely various in origin as our population. Among the most poignant memories brought by the early settlers to our shores were doubtless those of the flowers that flourished in the gardens and along the familiar roadsides at home; so that it is small wonder that we find record not only of these flowers themselves early brought to the gardens and naturalized in the wild of the new land, but many cases where some homely flower name, the mere speaking of which must have eased the homesick hearts, had been fitted to an American flower bearing some resemblance to one that grew in the old country.

The names of such plants as are indigenous to this country may, with a fair amount of certainty, be labelled "made in America," and I dare say in a few cases we have bestowed titles upon the comers from over seas. Without doubt we have added Boston Pink to the many aliases by which pretty Bouncing Bet (Saponaria officinalis) is known in various localities, and it is safe to say, I think, that another of her names is of fairly recent American origin. This is Lady-by-the-gate, for it is only of recent years that Bet has chosen to toss aside her birthright as a garden child in exchange for the doubtful sociability of the open road. Now she is the Lady-by-the-gate—outside the gate and one may not travel through any rural neighbourhood where are the remains of old gardens and not appreciate the applicability of this name. Around my own white gate-posts and along the paling fence that encloses my dooryard this erst-while favourite crowds closely, dreaming wistfully, I believe, of the sheltered days when she grew in seemly rows with her sister Pinks and Campions and sweet-breathed Stocks and was hailed by all World's Wonder.

Another flower quaintly associated with gates, though perhaps we may not conclusively claim for this name American origin, is the Cypress Spurge, sometimes known as Welcome-to-our-home. In my neighborhood, where many old gardens have been left deserted or neglected by the ebbing tide of human interest or affection, this curious little plant crowds about the rotting gate-posts and straggles up the weed-claimed garden paths, providing still a green welcome where the human one is lacking to the searcher in old gardens and their precincts. [. . .]

Perhaps in my enthusiasm for the old-fashioned and familiar plant names I have not laid sufficient stress upon the importance of mastering the Latin names. I have not intended that this eulogy should in any way discount the necessity for exact knowledge along this line, and surely enough testimony has been offered to show what confusion would result were only the vernacular names made use of. My desire is simply that the friendly old names shall not be forgotten, that they shall be sometimes used in the bosom of our own gardens and in those of understanding friends that they and all they have stood for in past ages be not lost to the gardeners that shall come after us. Many of the Latin names, far from being simply difficult and uninteresting, repay a careful study and are quite charming in their meanings and derivations, and while some are truly terrible in their harshness and length, names "which no one can speak and no one can spell," others are quite pleasant-sounding enough to take their places by the side of the softest of the old "by-names."

[*Colour in My Garden* (1918)]

Julian R. Meade
Fine Flowers
with Atrocious Names

Today I was plowing faithfully through a horticultural tome when I came to a chapter which began thus, "If you would have a really successful garden, it behooves you—"

The hell it does. My garden is one place in the world where I am not behooved. I know it behooves me to dig up every clump of chrysanthemums I possess, because chrysanthemums like a fresh start each year if they are to be really fine. Yes, I know that—but a more slipshod method suits me better. I break a slip of every variety I like and give it a good send-off, pinch it back, water it and feed it. But a lot of the old clumps can be discarded or they can stay where they are and they won't be so insignificant at that.

The more I hear of Horticulture, the more I like plain gardening. There was an argument here today as to how we should pronounce Heuchera, a miserable cognomen for a good perennial whose racemes of pink, rose, white blossoms, airy little bell-shaped blooms on slender stems, look so cheerful with Dutch iris and sweet William and any of their many affinities. My dictionary says Heu'-ker-ah but why say anything like that about a flower with the respectable name of coral-bells? (Leave out the white variety, which isn't a heartbreaking act, and that name is accurate as well as pleasant.)

Another visitor—and this is no prevarication—insisted that I should know a beautiful new iris called "Cystitis." I felt sure the lady was wrong but she was impressively certain. I kept a straight face till she left and then rushed to Webster to see if I wasn't right in thinking she confused urology with horticulture. For once, Webster was with me! Poor lady! She was the very soul of propriety. I'd love to see her when she discovers her error.

Many fine flowers are cursed with atrocious names. I'd just as soon call an iris "Cystitis" as to call it a name inspired by some gasbag politician or some movie queen who wouldn't know her namesake's pistil from its stamens.

Flowers we like to grow should have names that please us and it's a joy to find them honoring men and women who have excelled in the world of gardens. Weeds, on the other hand, should have names we loathe, so we can go about their destruction with more zest and vim. The process of weeding is more sanative if you name the pests after your own special enemies and pet abominations. Don't bother to learn whether your new intruder is pig-weed or horse nettle. Just christen it in honor of some neighbor whom you find difficult to "love as thyself" and, while abolishing it, you also may vent your spleen.

[*Bouquets and Bitters* (1940)]

Louise Seymour Jones
Sedum Meaning to Sit

Spring flowers are long since gone. Summer's bloom hangs limp on every terrace. The gardener's feet drag a bit on the dusty path and the hinge in his back is full of creaks.

Even the winds are weary, resting in some cool mountain canyon, waiting the call of evening drafts that rise up out of the sea at sundown and coax them to play. Back and forth across our hillsides they tag each other, driving the heat away and making California's summer nights just about perfect.

Now is the time for all good gardeners to sit and enjoy their labors, and to catch up with some of the many fond intentions that lurk around every garden—not in the shape of paving stones however, but in little notes jotted down on margins of catalogues or garden diaries. "Better get acquainted with names" seems to have been suggested by the astonishing discovery that sedum comes from sedere meaning to sit; rather pat is it not, for the little occupants of our rock gardens who seem to be not the least particular how or where they fulfill their destiny.

Glancing through the nurserymen's literature with this thought in mind, it is apparent that words sprout just as miraculously as seeds. The Greeks disputed whether names were imposed on things by arbitrary arrangement or by nature. Bacon said by nature. Milton took the Bible as his authority; after he had created Earth in his *Paradise Lost*, according to precedent, clothed with verdant grass, yielding trees and the "humble shrub with frizzled hair," he brought Adam on the scene and then presented him with all the living things, saying: "I bring them to receive from thee their names."

Renan believed that man created his own language instinctively, just as a bird builds its nest or a bee constructs its cell; and as we constantly hear new words being coined before our very ears, we know they spring out of every day living. What might have gone down into garden nomenclature as Deadium stickium, we shall never know, because the poor things failed to come up. Walking one early spring day by a perennial border a young mother reeled off botanical names to her patient little son—aged six—as she poked under the winter litter of straw to see if the Lilium speciosum rubrum were alive or the Helenium autumnale superbum still thrived. Coming to a clump of dried branches cut close to the ground, she paused to catch her breath, really stumped to remember what had been planted in that place the preceding year. As she closed her eyes in an endeavor to capture the lost mouthful, the little boy came to her rescue, "Never mind, mother," he said, "don't rack your brains, call it Deadium stickium" and that is the way names are born.

Milton overlooked one Garden of Eden creation when he carried all the animals and plants to Adam to be named. It seems that later in the day as Adam and the Creator walked through the garden to check things over and see that the tags were on straight, a little voice came up out of the ferns asking: "By what name am I called, Adam?" Looking down the first gardener was quite humiliated to see what a perfectly exquisite little creature he had overlooked, and he answered, "Because I forgot you, you shall be called Forget-me-not." Myosotis (mouse-ear) was tacked on long after by some gardener who saw a likeness in the hairy leaves of this arvenis branch of the family.

Latin, being the language of science, provides most of the clues in satisfying our curiosity regarding flower names. Primulas come from primus, Ranunculaceae from a diminutive for frog, because the Grecian buttercups were wont to hide along the marshes; Delphinium is from dolphin and if we look, we shall see how the spur of the flower looks like a dolphin head. Honeysuckle is a grand illustration for its botanical name is Caprifoliaceae, from capra a goat and folium a leaf. The word capricious comes from this same root, a caprice being a movement of the mind as erratic as any hop, skip or jump of a goat. The honeysuckle, true to its name, is to be found in unexpected places all over the garden.

What would Pliny say to the double nasturtium, his little nasus-

tortus (meaning nose-twister) turned into what Mrs. Wilder terms
"an abomination" by hybridizers who can't leave nature alone. The
doubling process has improved few flowers; and could he speak,
there is no doubt the fiery old Roman would give a tongue lashing
to those meddlers, just as he did to the farmers of Ravenna who
ruined the flavor of asparagus by forcing it to monstrous size. To all
the gods of the garden we pray that the tulip may remain single,
for where else would the fairies put their babies to bed?

Vance Thompson says: "Every age must cull its own meta-
phors." Walking in the garden one realizes this at every turn; here
are the tiny pansykins called Johnny jump-ups by our grandmothers
and heartsease by Shakespeare, while a much older name, meet-
her-in-the-entry, Mrs. Earle tells us is comparable to the ancient
stonecrop, called welcome-home-husband-be-you-ever-so-drunk. Sara
Shafer calls baby pansies ladies delights and says, "They look up
into the face of their Heavenly Father as if they hadn't a thing to
be ashamed of."

[*Put a Feather in Your Hat* (1938)]

Anne Raver
Tendrils to the Heart

I was going back home for Father's Day and I didn't have a present, so I wandered around a mall, looking at ties and wallets and shirts. It all looked so anonymous, just the way I feel when I'm with my father. I never hit it off with him. He likes my oldest brother best, my sister next, my second brother after that. Then me.

I can't stand feeling anonymous. So I went into a boutique and tried on a white jump suit I'd seen in the window. It looked better on the mannequin, so I stuck my hip out and shot an arm up in the air. That was more like it, but I really couldn't walk around like that. I put my old clothes back on, pondering the father problem. Maybe a new recording of one of his favorite double concertos. (Thank you, he'd say. Let's compare it to my Shostakovich recording, the finest man in the world.) OK. How about some fine cheese? (Very good, he'd say. But remember that Stilton your brother used to bring down from Manhattan?) Have some more, Dad. Great for the arteries.

Could I knit a sweater vest overnight? My sister made a purple martin birdhouse one year. (I swear, he said, that girl can do anything she puts her mind to.)

I left the mall, sans present for Dad.

The problem is our minds do not run along the same lines. We are not kindred spirits. We do not sit for hours at the kitchen table—as do my mother and I—smoking forbidden cigarettes and allowing our mistakes in life to take a philosophical turn. So I'd probably end up with the usual shirt that said nothing and everything about our relationship. The thought almost sent me into a roadside deli for a bag of extra thick rippled potato chips, but I pulled into my favorite local nursery instead.

The wind was moving through the trees. No Muzak. A young man in old cutoffs and flip-flops was watering the vegetable seedlings and annuals with one of those rose attachments I wanted for my hose. We started talking about whether it was too hot to grow kale, and out of nowhere an image from the past floated up: a vigorous vine overflowing with big purple flowers, planted by my father to camouflage a telephone pole at the edge of our yard.

"Do you have any clematis?" I asked. We examined the ones he had: Comtesse de Bouchard, a rose pink with cream-colored stamens; Duchess of Edinburgh, with rosette-shaped double white blooms; *C. jackmanii*, a velvety purple. But I knew what I wanted: sweet autumn clematis (*C. paniculata*), a fragrant white flower that lasts through October. He had one tucked away in the greenhouse.

"Good choice," he said, with an appreciative look.

I left with my Father's Day present, feeling beautiful, and headed for Maryland the next day. Driving down the New Jersey Turnpike, I watered my clematis out of Burger King cups and kept an eye on its little leaves through the rearview mirror. *Don't worry, Clem*, I whispered. *If he doesn't like you, I'll take you back.* We crossed the Delaware Memorial Bridge and hit the sweet humid air of the mid-Atlantic states.

I grew up on a farm surrounded by other farms, fields of corn and soybeans, and a herd of fat black Angus fenced in with hedges of wild rose. My grandfather was one of thirteen; he built the farmhouse when his own family outgrew the wooden cabin down by the spring. Family legend tells how Granddad saved the farm during the Depression by selling produce to wealthy Baltimoreans from his horse cart. They couldn't get enough of Grandmother's fresh cottage cheese. But Dad got restless with the country life. He went to college, made money in the city, came home to carve the meat, and read the paper in the big chair that was saved for him.

It was Mother we talked to, pouring out our little childhood tragedies with the milk we drank ice cold from the fridge. When Dad appeared at the door, the weather changed. He laughed at our giant grape jokes—then corrected our grammar. He told us great stories—and expected us to do him one better. That air of competition always hung over the dinner table. Who could tell the funniest story. Who could really zing him one. Who won. It was never me. (That's *I*, Dad would say.)

Freshman year I tried to explain Henry James's sensibility to Dad. ("I never understood what he was talking about," he said. "Where's the plot?") I could have wedged Mom's homemade pie down his throat, but it was I who found it hard to swallow. He was choking *me*, but I just sat there, feeling that old familiar torpor sweep over me. It comes from being in a place where you'll never be known. Like Dorothy in the poppy field.

But this Sunday was different. I set the clematis on the front porch.

"Well, well," he said, stooping down to read the label. " 'Sweet autumn.' That's the one with the lovely fragrance." How strange to hear the word "lovely" from my father's lips. He straightened and took a deep breath. "Whoo," he said softly, waiting for his heart to slow. He's seventy-seven, with a heart problem. "Let's see, what's its Latin name? *Clematis* . . ."

"*Paniculata*," I said, feeling like a genius.

"That's it," he said, glancing at me through his bifocals.

We took a walk around the old grounds, proceeding slowly, in deference to his heart. "What's that?" I kept saying, but this time I really wanted to know.

"Spicebush. Or benzoin . . . we used to crush up the leaves and put it in the vaporizer when you couldn't breathe. It has those little yellow flowers in the early spring."

"Before the forsythia?" I asked.

"What about that, Mother?" he said.

"After," she said.

The old college prof paused. "By the way, for-SY-thia was named for a man named Forsythe, so it isn't pronounced for-SITH-ia, as everyone insists . . ."

I looked around for a heavy shovel . . . but he's so old now.

"Now fragrant viburnum's a good plant to put in up there," he said, switching the subject." We took a breather by the rose beds, where some of the old varieties Grandmother planted still bloom.

"What's that one called?" I asked about a little low bush with pink blooms.

"Oh heaven knows," he said companionably. "I *think* it's the original tea rose, from which the hybrid teas were grown, but I can't be sure. It's been moved so many times . . . and grown from slips, you know."

You know. The words of one kindred spirit to another. I just stood there, like a tender clematis, taking in the sun.

[*Newsday* (July 3, 1986)]

PESTS AND POISONS

Bernard McMahon
Destroy Insects on Fruit-Trees

Insects often do much damage to fruit-trees if not prevented. This is the time they begin to breed on the buds, leaves, and new advancing shoots of young trees, and also frequently on those of older growth. Proper means should be used to destroy them in time, before they spread over the general branches.

Where you perceive any of the leaves of these trees to have a crumpled, deformed, clammy appearance, &c., it is a sign of insects, notwithstanding it is sometimes produced by the extreme changes from warm, to wet and cold. Let the worst of these leaves be taken off as soon as they appear; and if the ends of any of the young shoots are also attacked, prune away such infected parts; and if furnished with a garden watering engine, it would be greatly serviceable therewith to dash the branches with water in dry weather, which, and the above precautions, if proceeded to in time will do a great deal in preventing the mischief from spreading considerably.

Or where wall-trees are much infested, first pull off all the curled or crumpled leaves, then get some tobacco-dust, or fine snuff, and scatter some of it over all the branches, but most on those places where the insects are troublesome. This should be strewed over the trees in the morning when the twigs and leaves are wet, and let it remain. It will greatly diminish the vermin, and not injure the leaves or fruit.

But fruit-trees are also sometimes attacked by insects of the caterpillar tribe, contained numerously in a minute embryo state in small webs deposited, on the branches, &c.; animated by the heat of the weather they soon overrun and devour the young leaves,

[251]

whereby neither the trees nor fruit prosper in growth, and which should be attended to, especially in young trees, by picking off the webs, &c., before the insects animate considerably; and, if accommodated with a watering engine, as above suggested, you might play the water strongly upon the trees, so as in the whole to diminish the increase and spreading depredations of the vermin as much as possible.

[*The American Gardener's Calendar* (1806)]

David Haggerston
To M. P. Wilder, Esq.,
President of the Massachusetts
Horticultural Society

Sir,—Having discovered a cheap and effectual mode of destroying the *Rose Slug*, I wish to become a competitor for the premium offered by the Massachusetts Horticultural Society. After very many satisfactory experiments with the following substance, I am convinced it will destroy the above insect, in either of the states in which it appears on the plant, as the fly, when it is laying its eggs, or as the slug, when it is committing its depredations on the foliage.

WHALE OIL SOAP, *dissolved at the rate of two pounds to fifteen gallons of water.* I have used it stronger, without injury to the plants, but find the above mixture effectual in the destruction of the insect. As I find, from experiments, there is a difference in the strength of the soap, it will be better for persons using it, to try it diluted as above, and if it does not kill the insect, add a little more soap, with caution. In corresponding with Messrs. Downer, Austin & Co., on the difference in its appearance, they say: "Whale Oil Soap varies much in its relative strength, the article not being made as soap, but being formed in our process of bleaching oil. When it is of very sharp taste, and dark appearance, the alkali predominates, and when light-colored and flat taste the grease predominates." The former I have generally used, but have tried the light-colored, and find it equally effectual, but requiring a little more soap,—say two pounds to thirteen gallons of water.

Mode of Preparation.—Take whatever quantity of soap you wish to prepare, and dissolve it in boiling water, about one quart to a pound; in this way strain it through a fine wire or hair sieve, which takes out the dirt, and prevents its stopping the valves of the engine, or the nose of the syringe, then add cold water, to make it the proper strength, apply it to the rose-bush, with a hand-engine or syringe, with as much force as practicable, and be sure that every part of the leaves is well saturated with the liquid. What falls to the ground, in application, will do good in destroying the worms and enriching the soil, and, from its trifling cost, it can be used with profusion. A hogshead of 136 gallons costs forty-five cents,—not quite four mills per gallon. Early in the morning, or in the evening, is the proper time to apply it to the plants.

As there are many other troublesome and destructive insects the above preparation will destroy, as effectually as the Rose Slug, it may be of benefit to the community to know the different kinds upon which I have tried it with success.

The *Thrips*, often called the Vine-Fretter,—a small, light-colored or spotted fly, quick in motion, which in some places, are making the rose-bush nearly as bad in appearance as the effects of the Slug. *Aphis*, or Plant Louse, under the name of Green or Brown Fly; an insect not quick in motion, very abundant on, and destructive to, the young shoots of the Rose, the Peach Tree, and many other plants. The *Black Fly*, a very troublesome and destructive insect, that infests the young shoots of the Cherry and the Snowball Tree. I have never know any positive cure for the effects of this insect, until this time. Two varieties of insects that are destructive to, and very much disfigure, Evergreens, the Balsam or Balm of Gilead Fir in particular, one an Aphis, the other very much like the Rose Slug, the *Acarus*, or Red Spider, that well-known pest to gardeners.

The disease *Mildew*, on the Gooseberry, Peach, Grape Vine, etc., etc., is checked and entirely destroyed by a weak dressing of the solution.

The above insects are generally all destroyed by one application, if properly applied to all parts of the foliage. The eggs of most insects continue to hatch in rotation, during their season. To keep the plants perfectly clean, it will be necessary to dress them two or three times.

I remain, Sir,

Your most obedient Servant,

David Haggerston

Watertown, June 19th, 1841

Henry Ward Beecher
Nail Up Your Bugs

The words of the wise are as goads and as
nails fastened by masters of assemblies.
—SOLOMON

After a great pother about canker worms, peach-tree worms, and
other audacious robber-worms; after smoke, salt, tar, and tansy,
bands of wool, cups of oil, lime, ashes, and surgery have been set
forth as remedies, to the confusion of those who have tried them
bootlessly, it now appears that we are about to *nail* the rascals. The
Boston *Cultivator*, contains an article "On Destroying Insects on
Trees," from which we quote:

"I did not intend to give it publicity until I had fully tested it,
but as the ravages are very extensive in the West, I cannot delay
giving you the experiment, hoping that some of your western readers
may now give it a fair trial and report the result. I will give one
case which may induce the experiment wherever the evil is felt. In
conversation with a friend in Newburyport, Dr. Watson, last fall, I
mentioned the experiment; he invited me to his garden, where last
year a fruit-tree was infested with the nests of caterpillar or canker-
worms, as were his neighbors' trees; he showed me a board nailed
for convenience of a clothes-line upon one of the large limbs of the
tree; he said he noticed a little while afterward that the nests on
that limb dried up, and the worms disappeared, though the cause
did not then occur to him though apparent as it will be to any
scientific mind.

"Drive carefully well home, so that the bark will heal over, a
few headless cast iron nails, say some six or eight, size and number
according to the size of the tree, in a ring around its body, a foot
or two above the ground. The oxidation of the iron by the sap, will

evolve ammonia, which will, of course, with the rising sap, impregnate every part of the foliage, and prove to the delicate palate of the patient, a nostrum, which will soon become, as in many cases of larger animals, the real panacea for the ills of life, *via Tomb*. I think if the ladies should drive some small iron brads into some limbs of any plant infested with any insect, they would find it a good and safe remedy, and I imagine in any case, instead of injury, the ammonia will be found particularly invigorating. Let it be tried upon a limb of any tree, where there is a vigorous nest of caterpillars, and watch it for a week or ten days, and I think the result will pay for the nails."

Let our farmers take their hammers and nails and start for the orchard; if they see a bug on the tree, drive a nail, and he is a bug no more! If they see a worm, in with a nail, and the "ammonia evolved" will finish his functions!

The *Southern Planter* is out with a backer to the Boston *Cultivator*:

"A singular fact, and one worthy of being recorded, was mentioned to us a few days since by Mr. Alexander Duke, of Albemarle. He stated that whilst on a visit to a neighbor, his attention was called to a large peach orchard, every tree in which had been totally destroyed by the ravages of the worm, with the exception of three, and these three were probably the most thrifty and flourishing peach-trees he ever saw. The only cause of their superiority known to his host, was an experiment made in consequence of observing that those parts of worm-eaten timber into which nails had been driven, were generally sound; when his trees were about a year old he had selected three of them and driven a tenpenny nail through the body, as near the ground as possible; whilst the balance of his orchard has gradually failed, and finally yielded entirely to the ravages of the worms, these three trees, selected at random, treated precisely in the same manner, with the exception of the nailing, had always been vigorous and healthy, furnishing him at that very period with the greatest profusion of the most luscious fruit. It is supposed that the salts of iron afforded by the nail are offensive to the worm, whilst they are harmless, or perhaps even beneficial to the tree."

We do not wish to interrupt any experiments which the enterprising may choose to make. To be sure we regard the facts with some incredulity, and the chemical explanations with something of the mirthful superadded to unbelief. But if nails *are* an antidote to worms—a real vermifuge—let them be administered, whatever may be the explanations; whether they are an electric battery, giving the insects a little domestic, vegetable lightning, or whether they afford "salts of iron" to physic them, or "evolve ammonia" in such potent, pungent strength that vermicular nostrils are unable to endure it!

While one is fairly engaged in a campaign of experiments, we heartily hope that war will be carried to the very territory of ignorance, and we will propound several other important questions of fact and theory, which, if settled, will crown somebody's brow with laurels.

It is said that hanging a scythe in a plum-tree, or an iron hoop, or horse shoes, will insure a crop of plums. This ought to be investigated.

It is said that pear-trees that are unfruitful, may be made to bear, by digging under them, cutting the tap root, and burying a black cat there. We do not know as it makes any difference as to the sex of the cat, though we should, if trying it, rather prefer the male cat.

Lastly, that we may contribute our mite to the advancement of science, we will state that, in our youth, we were informed, that, if we would go into the wood-house once a day and rub our hands with a chip, *without thinking of red fox's tail*, the warts would all go off. We have no doubt that it would have been successful, but every time we tried the experiment, whisk came the red fox's tail into our head and spoilt the whole affair. But might this not cure warts on trees?

[*Plain and Pleasant Talk about Fruits, Flowers and Farming* (1859)]

Isaac Trimble
Appreciating Toads

"Sweet are the uses of adversity," as Shakspeare says, in alluding to the contrast between good and evil, as exemplified in the Toad. In his days it was believed that there was a stone in the head of the Toad endued with singular virtues, and this was a compensation for the venomous effects of its touch. I am a firm believer in the doctrine of compensations, but the tongue is the Toad's jewel. All gardeners know the trouble we have with some insects, and few are more provoking than the striped bug on the young Melon vines. Place one of your pet Toads (and all gardeners should have such pets) among these vines, and watch him. See how like a streak of lightning that tongue flashes out, and how the Melon Bug flashes in. If you are a collector of insects, and want those that are active at night when you are asleep, take from the Toad early in the morning the supply he has gathered to ruminate upon during the day. Many of them will be as perfect as if you had caught them with your own gauze net. And what a variety! Yes, the toad is ugly and venomous— to insects, but has a jewel in his head for us.

The Toad is a funny creature, and if you look at him as a philosopher should, without being angry, because he sometimes eats strawberries, you may find a great deal of amusement in him. I have seen animals go backwards into their burrows, but except the Toad, I have never seen any make their burrows backwards. Find one a little belated in the early morning—confront him, and watch sharply as if you suspected he had been eating strawberries or lady bugs, and his eyes will begin to wink and blink; soon his head will be averted, as if he were ashamed, but all this time he will be settling away, going down as a canal boat does in a lock; his hind feet have been throwing out the earth from under him, reminding you of the description of the first steamboat—"a grist-mill afloat, with the water getting out from under."

Toads are fond of strawberry beds. The partial burrow beneath and the broad leaves of the Hoveys above; the hosts of insects and the ripening fruit around make such a residence comfortable. I know a little girl who is a great lover of fruit. She watches the strawberries. Some very large ones are taken in the hand in the evening—turned all round and carefully examined—but not being quite ripe are allowed to remain. In the morning they are gone. She asks me why? I say it is hard to know what has been in the garden in the night. Near by is a mutilated strawberry; the mark of a bite is plainly to be seen, and close by, under a broad leaf, I observe something like the eye of a Toad—a crescent-shaped streak of white just disappearing. Could that concave wound in the strawberry be brought into juxtaposition with the convex mouth of that Toad, there would probably be found a remarkable adaptation between the two; but nothing is said about it. This little girl is old enough to appreciate strawberries, but not old enough to appreciate Toads.

When I was young I was told that if I killed the Toads the cows would give bloody milk. Children in the country are fond of milk, and the fear of such a catastrophe saved the Toads.

[*A Treatise on the Insect Enemies of Fruit and Fruit Trees* (1865)]

William N. White
Insects and Vermin

To these numerous and most destructive foes all our gardens are
exposed. No plant and no part of a plant is exempt from their attacks.
One devours its tender leaf as it issues from the ground; another
preys upon the root, and the plant perishes; another burrows into
the stem, boring it in every direction until it is broken off by the
wind. The caterpillar preys upon the leaves when it gets more
mature, while the black grub cuts off the young plant just as it is
shooting into growth. Some feed upon the flowers, while others
devour the matured fruit or seed.

Insects are on the increase in American gardens, partly from
the fact that the destruction of forest trees and wild plants has driven
them to the cultivated ones for food, (the apple tree borer, for
instance, originally subsisting on the thorn,) partly from being constantly imported from all other countries from which seeds and
plants are brought, and partly from the diminution of birds and
other enemies by which they are naturally held in check.

Insects are the most extensive class of animals. They are destitute of an internal skeleton, but possess a sort of external one,
serving both for skin and bones, and divided into numerous segments connected together by slender points of attachment. They
all have six or more articulated legs, and are generally oviparous,
or produced from eggs. They possess sight, hearing, smell, and touch
at least,—senses in common with those of the superior animals.
They do not breathe through the mouth or nostrils, but through

vessels, for the reception of air, called spiracula, placed along each side of the body.

Nearly all insects have four stages of existence. First, eggs which hatch into larvæ; these change into pupæ, where they remain dormant for a longer or shorter period, and from which they emerge at last as perfect insects. Some insects, however, bring forth their young alive, as well as deposit eggs. In others, as the Orthoptera, or grasshopper family, the young has nearly the form of a perfect insect. Some insects are injurious to plants only in one stage of their existence, others at all times, when not in a dormant state.

A knowledge of the habits and transformations of insects is necessary to detect how and at what period of their existence they can best be destroyed, or in what manner vegetation can best be shielded from their attacks.

By many insects plants are at once destroyed; by others wounds are inflicted that end in a diseased condition of the parts affected, which is communicated to the whole plant. Plants in a weak or diseased state are far more liable to be attacked by insects than those which are healthy and vigorous.

Various remedies are proposed when plants are attacked by insects, among which those most generally applicable are dusting the leaves with quicklime, sulphur, snuff, soot, dust impregnated with the oil of turpentine. Also sprinkling or washing the plants with water heated to 130°; or with infusions of aloes, tobacco, quassia, China berries; also with soapsuds, especially that made from whale oil soap, guano dissolved in water, fumigating with tobacco smoke, etc.

A camphor and aloes preparation is also found serviceable for sprinkling plants, and was first recommended by Dr. Batty, of Georgia, in the *Southern Cultivator*, and is thus prepared: Put into a barrel of water a quarter of a pound of camphor, in pieces the size of a hickory nut; fill with water and let it stand a day, and with this water your plants, and fill the barrel for the next watering. The camphor is slowly dissolved, and will last a long time. If the camphor water is too weak, add to a barrel of water a cupful or more of strong lye, and more will dissolve. Add also a pound of cheap cape aloes to a gallon of lye (or water in which a pound of saleratus or potash has been dissolved); add a pint of this to a barrel of water, and use as the camphor water. Camphor and aloes (especially the former) are offensive to most insects.

Preventive measures are of more value than remedial, in protecting plants from insects. Among those most likely to be of value, are the following:

Rotation of crops.—Each species of insect generally feeds on the same species of plant, or at least on plants of the same natural family; hence a constant change of crop prevents the forthcoming brood from finding their proper food, and many of them perish. This is, however, more applicable in the case of field crops, than in orchards and gardens.

Decaying Trees.—Destroy all decaying trees in the neighborhood of orchards and gardens, as they are often a refuge, and tend to propagate insects destructive to the neighboring crops.

Scraping of the rough bark of trees, and washing them with tobacco water, lime water, or a wash of lime, sulphur and clay, or a solution of potash, destroys the hiding places of insects, and many of the insects themselves, which infest trees.

Birds and other Animals.—The encouragement of insectivorous birds and other animals, instead of their thoughtless and injurious destruction, is one of the most promising methods of lessening the insect tribes. A single pair of breeding swallows, Bradley has calculated, destroy over three thousand worms in a week. Toads live almost entirely upon insects, and do not injure plants. A large class of insects also live entirely upon insects that are injurious to plants, and should be encouraged.

Lime and Salt.—Dressing the soil with lime, sowing in autumn six or eight bushels of salt to the acre, turning over the soil and exposing it to frost just before winter, or during the winter months when the ground is open, are all found to be beneficial. Rolling the surface soil smooth when crops are planted destroys the hiding places of many insects, and renders them less destructive.

Any insect peculiarly injurious must be watched, as to its habits, mode of feeding, and its transformations, in order to discover where it may be most successfully attacked.

As healthy plants are less subject to attack, keep the ground in good order, sow good seed, cultivate thoroughly, and the crop will be less endangered.

William N. White

Fires.—Insects also may be destroyed and their increase prevented by bonfires of brush, just after dark, which will attract and destroy immense numbers of moths and beetles.

[*Gardening for the South* (1866)]

Charles Dudley Warner
Garden Pests, Including Children

The striped bug has come, the saddest of the year. He is a moral double-ender, iron-clad at that. He is unpleasant in two ways. He burrows in the ground so that you cannot find him, and he flies away so that you cannot catch him. He is rather handsome, as bugs go, but utterly dastardly, in that he gnaws the stem of the plant close to the ground, and ruins it without any apparent advantage to himself. I find him on the hills of cucumbers (perhaps it will be a cholera-year, and we shall not want any), the squashes (small loss), and the melons (which never ripen). The best way to deal with the striped bug is to sit down by the hills, and patiently watch for him. If you are spry, you can annoy him. This, however, takes time. It takes all day and part of the night. For he flieth in darkness, and wasteth at noonday. If you get up before the dew is off the plants,—it goes off very early,—you can sprinkle soot on the plant (soot is my panacea: if I can get the disease of a plant reduced to the necessity of soot, I am all right); and soot is unpleasant to the bug. But the best thing to do is to set a toad to catch the bugs. The toad at once establishes the most intimate relations with the bug. It is a pleasure to see such unity among the lower animals. The difficulty is to make the toad stay and watch the hill. If you know your toad, it is all right. If you do not, you must build a tight fence round the plants, which the toad cannot jump over. This, however, introduces a new element. I find that I have a zoölogical garden on my hands. It is an unexpected result of my little enterprise, which never aspired to the completeness of the Paris Jardin des Plantes. [. . .]

I scarcely dare trust myself to speak of the weeds. They grow as if the devil was in them. I know a lady, a member of the church, and a very good sort of woman, considering the subject condition of that class, who says that the weeds work on her to that extent that, in going through her garden, she has the greatest difficulty in keeping the ten commandments in anything like an unfractured condition. I asked her which one, but she said, all of them: one felt like breaking the whole lot. The sort of weed which I most hate (if I can be said to hate anything which grows in my own garden) is the "pusley," a fat, ground-clinging, spreading, greasy thing, and the most propagatious (it is not my fault if the word is not in the dictionary) plant I know. [. . .]

There is another subject which is forced upon my notice. I like neighbors, and I like chickens; but I do not think they ought to be united near a garden. Neighbors' hens in your garden are an annoyance. Even if they did not scratch up the corn, and peck the strawberries, and eat the tomatoes, it is not pleasant to see them straddling about in their jerky, high-stepping, speculative manner, picking inquisitively here and there. It is of no use to tell the neighbor that his hens eat your tomatoes: it makes no impression on him, for the tomatoes are not his. The best way is to casually remark to him that he has a fine lot of chickens, pretty well grown, and that you like spring chickens broiled. He will take them away at once.

The neighbors' small children are also out of place in your garden, in strawberry and currant time. I hope I appreciate the value of children. We should soon come to nothing without them, though the Shakers have the best gardens in the world. Without them the common school would languish. But the problem is, what to do with them in a garden. For they are not good to eat, and there is a law against making away with them. The law is not very well enforced, it is true; for people do thin them out with constant dosing, paregoric, and soothing-syrups, and scanty clothing. But I, for one, feel that it would not be right, aside from the law, to take the life even of the smallest child, for the sake of a little fruit, more or less, in the garden. I may be wrong; but these are my sentiments, and I am not ashamed of them. When we come, as Bryant says in his *Iliad*, to leave the circus of this life, and join that innumerable caravan which moves, it will be some satisfaction to us that we have never, in the way of gardening, disposed of even the humblest child unnecessarily. My plan would be to put them into Sunday-schools

The American Gardener

more thoroughly, and to give the Sunday-schools an agricultural turn; teaching the children the sacredness of neighbors' vegetables. I think that our Sunday-schools do not sufficiently impress upon children the danger, from snakes and otherwise, of going into the neighbors' gardens.

[*My Summer in a Garden* (1870)]

Celia Thaxter
A Mass of Sooty, Shapeless Slime

It seems to me the worst of all the plagues is the slug, the snail without a shell. He is beyond description repulsive, a mass of sooty, shapeless slime, and he devours everything. He seems to thrive on all the poisons known; salt and lime are the only things that have power upon him, at least the only things I have been able to find so far. But salt and lime must be used very carefully, or they destroy the plant as effectually as the slug would do. Every night, while the season is yet young, and the precious growths just beginning to make their way upward, feeling their strength, I go at sunset and heap along the edge of the flower beds air-slaked lime, or round certain most valuable plants a ring of the same,—the slug cannot cross this while it is fresh, but should it be left a day or two it loses its strength, it has no more power to burn, and the enemy may slide over it unharmed, leaving his track of slime. On many a solemn midnight have I stolen from my bed to visit my cherished treasures by the pale glimpses of the moon, that I might be quite sure the protecting rings were still strong enough to save them, for the slug eats by night, he is invisible by day unless it rains or the sky be overcast. He hides under every damp board or in any nook of shade, because the sun is death to him. I use salt for his destruction in the same way as the lime, but it is so dangerous for the plants, I am always afraid of it. Neither of these things must be left about them when they are watered lest the lime or salt sink into the earth in such quantities as to injure the tender roots. I have little cages of fine wire netting which I adjust over some plants, carefully heaping the earth about them to leave no loophole through which the enemy may crawl, and round some of the beds, which are inclosed in strips of wood, boxed, to hold the earth in place, long shallow troughs of wood are nailed and filled with salt to keep off the pests. Nothing that human ingenuity can suggest do I leave untried to save my beloved flowers! Every evening at sunset I pile lime and salt about my pets, and every morning remove it before I sprinkle them at sunrise. The salt dissolves of itself in the humid sea air and in the dew, so around those for whose safety I am most solicitous I lay rings of pasteboard on which to heap it, to be certain of doing the plants no harm. Judge, reader, whether all this requires strength, patience, perseverance, hope! It is hard work beyond a doubt, but I do not grudge it, for great is my reward. Before I knew what to do to save my garden from the slugs, I have stood at evening rejoicing over rows of fresh emerald leaves just springing in rich lines along the beds, and woke in the morning to find the whole space stripped of any sign of green, as blank as a board over which a carpenter's plane has passed.

In the thickest of my fight with the slugs some one said to me, "Everything living has its enemy; the enemy of the slug is the toad. Why don't you import toads?"

I snatched at the hope held out to me, and immediately wrote to a friend on the mainland, "In the name of the Prophet, Toads!" At once a force of only too willing boys was set about the work of catching every toad within reach, and one day in June a boat brought a box to me from the far-off express office. A piece of wire netting was nailed across the top, and upon the earth with which it was half filled, reposing among some dry and dusty green leaves, sat three dry and dusty toads, wearily gazing at nothing. Is this all, I thought, only three! Hardly worth sending so far. Poor creatures, they looked so arid and wilted, I took up the hose and turned upon them a gentle shower of fresh cool water, flooding the box. I was not prepared for the result! The dry, baked earth heaved tumultuously; up came dusky heads and shoulders and bright eyes by the dozen. A sudden concert of liquid sweet notes was poured out on the air from the whole rejoicing company. It was really beautiful to hear that musical ripple of delight. I surveyed them with eager interest as they sat singing and blinking together. "You are not handsome," I said, as I took a hammer and wrenched off the wire cover that shut them in, "but you will be lovely in my sight if you will help me to destroy mine enemy"; and with that I turned the box on its side and out they skipped into a perfect paradise of food and shade. All summer I came upon them in different parts of the garden, waxing fatter and fatter till they were as round as apples. In the autumn baby toads no larger than my thumb nail were found hopping merrily over the whole island. There were sixty in that first importation; next summer I received ninety more. But alas! small dogs discover them in the grass and delight to tear and worry them to death, and the rats prey upon them so that many perish in that way; yet I hope to keep enough to preserve my garden in spite of fate.

In France the sale of toads for the protection of gardens is universal, and I find under the head of "A Garden Friend," in a current newspaper, the following item:—

"One is amused, in walking through the great Covent Garden Market, London, to find toads among the commodities offered for sale. In such favor do these familiar reptiles stand with English market gardeners that they readily command a shilling apiece. . . . The toad has indeed no superior as a destroyer of noxious insects, and as he possesses no bad habits and is entirely inoffensive himself, every owner of a garden should treat him with the utmost hospitality. It is quite worth the while not only to offer any simple inducements which suggest themselves for rendering the premises attractive to him, but should he show a tendency to wander away from them, to go so far as to exercise a gentle force in bringing him back to the regions where his services may be of the greatest utility."

[*An Island Garden* (1894)]

Celestine Sibley
Garden Pests

*According to the record of the rocks, in-
sects preceded man on this planet by quite
some time, and pessimists contend that they
will be the last to leave it.*

—RALPH B. SWAIN

There's a theory circulating among my friends and neighbors that I
don't rise up and do battle against the creeping, crawling, hopping,
flying, boring, sucking wild life that makes free with my garden
because I'm either too lazy or too squeamish.

And while there's an element of truth in this theory, it's not
the whole truth. The whole truth is that I'm too ignorant and too
scared. I don't know enough about insect life to dare to tamper with
it . . . much.

My friend Mrs. Ralph Sauls, a lady now in her seventies, once
told me a story out of her own childhood that made a big impression
on me. She said she was visiting an aunt who raised chickens and
for the first time saw the miracle of an egg hatching. Somebody had
explained to her that the little pecking sound she heard within an
egg was a baby chicken trying to make his way out into the world.

To the gentle little girl the shell seemed to be a prison and
when nobody was around she decided to help the tiny prisoners
escape. She cracked and pulled away egg shells and all the little
chickens died from premature freedom—exposure.

Overwhelmed by shock and grief she held out sticky little hands
to her aunt and cried inconsolably. Her cry was the cry of benevolent
meddlers the world over: "I was just trying to *help!*"

Her aunt comforted her and then gave her a piece of stern
advice all of us need at times.

"Alberta," she said, "always remember this: *Keep your hands off what you don't understand!*"

I don't understand garden pests.

The last United States Department of Agriculture tome I saw on the subject estimated that there may be as many as 1,500,000 different kinds of insects in the world and the injurious species in the United States could run between 6,500 and 10,000.

The catch is that some of these are harmful in one stage and beneficial in another, and it takes time to wait around and see if a leaf-gnawing worm may grow up, go legit and earn his keep by becoming an aphid-eating beetle. The suspense is debilitating and all that getting up at night and running through the garden with the flashlight to see what is happening under the tomato leaves and in the innermost heart of the cabbage certainly takes its toll of the next day's work.

But it does seem to me that we have an obligation to know what we're doing, whom we are killing, when we grab up a bottle of spray or a packet of lethal dust. It's perfectly obvious that without insect life on earth things would come to a pretty pass. There might not be any vegetation at all. And although I don't for a minute imagine that my ninety-eight-cent can of poison spray will annihilate a whole species of insect and thereby throw what the ecologists call "the totality of interrelationships" out of kilter, I do worry that I might kill villains and heroes indiscriminately, repay the kindness of my invaluable friends, the birds, with a case of acute gastritis and possibly even jeopardize the health and well-being of those great gardening assistants, my grandchildren.

If I had vast acreage at stake I might feel differently. In fact I might make so much money off my broad airplane-dusted fields that I could afford to haul my family and friends off to some pollution-free spot (if there is any left) to wait until the poison cloud settled. But in my little patch if the eggplant turns to lace-and-drawn work—and it does—I just take eggplant off the menu and when I have dinner guests I let 'em eat squash. (This is a terrible deprivation, too, because thanks to Julia Fitch and Ben Pace, a peerless vegetable grower and eater, I have two eggplant recipes that turn that bland vegetable into something sumptuous.)

When one of my red rose buds, whose unfolding I await with great excitement, doesn't unfold at all but looks like it was scorched with a hot iron I'm not exactly serene and accepting. I stomp around looking for the culprit and swearing vengeance. And when great ripening tomatoes, just hours from the table, come down with cancerous sores, the sound of my weeping, wailing and gnashing of teeth rends the country quiet.

Nevertheless, before I launch chemical warfare I feel compelled to know more about what I am doing. The experts, although saving us from plagues of locusts and boll weevil and potato famines in the past, have had their moments of doubt and error. Remember how jubilant we all were about the way DDT disposed of flies and other household pests? (In South Alabama I know old-timers who still sing hosannas to it for giving us a generation or two of freedom from bedbugs alone.) The trouble was that the few pests that escaped the spray fled to bosky dells somewhere where they regrouped and promptly produced DDT-resistant offspring. So it looks like the only recourse is bigger and more deadly sprays. To be followed by bigger and more resistant pests? It's a grim prospect.

There must be a better way and I believe it begins with studying insects well enough to be able to identify them. The handiest book I have for this is Ralph B. Swain's *The Insect Guide: Orders and Major Families of North American Insects.* The pictures really look like the insects I encounter in life and the text is easy, concise and oddly enjoyable. In addition to telling you which of your crops the chewer or sucker is likely to attack, it adds nice little gossipy notes about the minute monster's home life. For instance, Bessybugs. They are members of the prominent Passálidae family and, it occurred to me, probably in the South called Betsybug, which your relatives frequently say, "You haven't any more sense than." These citizens live under rotten logs and "bestow great care upon the young," even chewing the wood before their babies eat it. And the larvae of carpet beetles, officially *Dermestes maculatus*, are sometimes used by museum workers "to clear the dried flesh from the delicate skeletons of small animals."

In fact, if this book has a fault it's that when you tear into the house sweating and breathing fire to look up some strange bug you might get so absorbed in reading about why the scarab was sacred in Egypt or how fireflies use their lights as a signal for mating that you forget entirely about the critter waiting in the jelly glass for identification.

Once you have identified the bug—and a magnifying glass is good for this—and know what to expect of it, if it prefers cabbage to carrots, for instance (and most insects eat one kind of plant, ignoring other kinds), then you can decide for yourself how far you want to go in poisoning him and his relatives and, incidentally, some of the air and the earth.

To me there are other routes that are appealing because they seem less drastic, more imaginative and just plain interesting.

My neighbors Jerry and Polly Eaves, notable for building the settlement's first swimming pool, are also impressive because they leave insect control to a family of potracking guineas. Guineas never touch a vegetable or a flower, they tell me, because they sate themselves on juicy bugs. Even better, they make such an infernal racket that the young Eaveses practically never see a snake. Snakes, being lovers of peace and quiet, take to the tall timber to avoid the clatter of guineas.

For some time I've thought of installing a few guineas at Sweet Apple, but recently bantam chickens have taken my eye. They are peerless when it comes to insect pests, my neighbors tell me, amazingly prolific and hardly ever touch garden truck unless a low-growing and flamboyant tomato takes their eye. The care needed by domestic fowls has deterred me so far, but my neighbor Olivia Johnson says she will give me a start of banties—a rooster and two hens—out of her very next setting of eggs. And I'll take them, I think, because my mother says a country place doesn't seem furnished if you don't have at least one rooster to crow and a few hens to supply eggs for the table and fertilizer for the garden.

Somewhere I read that turkeys are highly recommended as garden police and if they eat *their* weight in bugs, as birds are said to do, it would be an orgy to end all orgies. Ducks and geese have been used in some places to eat the insects and weed strawberry beds and cotton fields. Generally they have a reputation for sticking to business and leaving garden crops alone, but I've heard that ducks have a secret yen for young onions, especially in the spring, and since I only plant one row of onions, one row of shallots and a small bed of chives it wouldn't take a duck on a spree long to decimate my entire crop. Funny, while ducks relish young onions, rabbits, they tell me, abhor them and won't even darken the garden that is surrounded with onions.

Enlisting the aid of fowls to handle weed and pest control appeals as a simple and direct approach. So is hand-picking the bugs from the plant and dropping them in a bucket of kerosene but ah, how I hate that job, particularly those big soft green horned cutworms. It seems easier to make paper-cup or foil collars for the tomato plants when they are young and it works. I've noticed that if you can get a young tomato plant up some size it doesn't seem attractive to cutworms. Other things move in, of course, but there's a saying among organic gardeners that if the soil is good and the plant is strong and healthy it will probably survive, and I believe it. The idea is maximum biological efficiency in your department to throw off the effect of insect attackers, as human beings in the pink frustrate disease germs.

Gardening lore is full of all kinds of safe home remedies for pest control, some of them time tested and some of them, I suspect, old wives' tales. Since I am in the midst of trying some of them for the first time I can't vouch for their effectiveness. I can say they add a new element of excitement to gardening.

There are hideous brews, of course, which I won't try except as a desperate, last-ditch measure—urine to repel grasshoppers, for instance, and an evil potion made by picking off the most troublesome bugs, putting them in a bottle containing a little water and letting them decompose. The resulting juice is said to be very efficacious as a spray because most insects have a superstitious way of avoiding the dead bodies of their own kind. You try it if you like, but I lost my license to practice witchcraft.

My sage, which Olivia planted for me back of the woodpile one spring day when I thought it was too hot for the young plants to survive, flourishes on neglect. But watch it, warns another neighbor, there are certain people whose very touch will kill sage. These include menstruating women.

The nicest and most interesting garden health measures are plant repellents or the practice of companionate planting. Janet Gillespie advanced the cause of marigolds in her book, *Peacock Manure and Marigolds*. This smelly little beauty affects some insects as it does some people. They turn up their sensitive noses and move out of its range. Its roots are also said to excrete something which kills soil nematodes. So I edge my garden with dwarf marigolds and plant the tall beauties anywhere I can find a spot to stick them.

They have blossoms almost as big as football-season chrysanthemums and one package of seed, started early in a flat in the house, goes further than practically anything you can buy.

Garlic is also said to be as effective in holding some insects at arm's length as it does some people. I planted a bulb beside each rosebush, and next year I'm hoping to have enough to stick them around every peach tree to see if they will turn back the borers.

Up at Chadwick's, the old-time general store which has served the people of this area for more than a hundred years, when you buy your turnip and mustard seeds loose from the big seed bins, instead of in the more expensive packages with pictures on them, they will throw in a scoop of radish seed. It's the custom of the country to sow them all together, counting on the radishes to save the mustard and turnips from lice. So far I have a good stand of young greens without a sign of trouble anywhere. Radishes are also said to protect squashes from squash bugs.

The stinging nettle school interested me. This powerful plant (advocated as an aphrodisiac in old herbals) is said by old gardeners to repel aphids and to enrich the soil. So I left a few plants in my salad-green bed expecting great results. Olivia is so kindhearted she hated to tell me that those stalwart nettles I was counting on weren't stinging nettles at all but another kind of scratchy weed which was not only of no value but could become a pest itself.

Anything that is strong smelling seems to excite or disgust bugs. Even a fragrant hand lotion will draw so many bees, yellow jackets and gnats on a summer morning that you have to come in the house and wash with yellow soap. The herb fragrances which are a delight to people—mint, rosemary and sage—are said to disgust the cabbage butterfly. Corn borers, according to some observers, can't work within range of geranium or marigold smell. Santolina and southernwood, which I have planted on the rock wall near the porch, should by all accounts be in the garden to keep away moths. And let's see, there are moth balls which will keep away rabbits if scattered around the lettuce patch and black pepper which, if sprinkled around squash vines, will repel squash borers. (An old recipe for keeping houseflies, blowflies and those nasty green bottle flies away from the gardener is to wash your clothes in soap suds to which oil of anise has been added.)

Just as there are plants that jog along together happily neigh-

boring, there are many others that seem to offend each other. Tomatoes are good neighbors to asparagus, they say, repelling the
asparagus beetle, but poor neighbors to peppers and corn, drawing
the same kind of pests.

Wood ashes, which I have in abundant supply in fireplace
weather, go on my garden automatically and I don't have any way
of knowing if they turn back hordes of maggot flies and scab, as they
are supposed to do. I put them there because of the somewhat vague
assurance of most of my gardening friends that they are "good for
the soil." Since I haven't seen any maggot flies or beet scab I like
to believe it's true. It may be that maggot flies and scab didn't see
anything that interested them in my small patch and passed on to
better pickings.

Anyhow, I have to put the ashes somewhere and I like the idea
that they are working in the garden. The same is true of mint. After
years of being unable to grow mint I suddenly found myself going
down for the third time in oceans of spearmint, lemon, pineapple
and peppermint, not to mention their cousin, catnip. I started pulling it out of flower beds with a heavy hand and hauling it to the
raw clay bank across the road where I'm trying to get something—
anything—to grow.

"You know, they say snakes won't go around mint," Laura
Dorsey remarked casually.

"They *won't*?" I cried.

Being of a scientific bent, Laura wasn't about to give me any
gold-plated guarantee but she did tell me this story. When they
first settled their old house on the hill in Cherokee County they
kept finding snake skins on the fireboard in the living room and this
struck cold terror to the hearts of the young girls in the family, as
it would to mine if I knew a snake was sneaking into my house
unbeknownst to me to make his seasonal change of clothes.

"I planted mint around all the foundations and by the steps
and the snake skins didn't appear again," Laura related.

However, the snake himself showed up in the tool house. He
was harmless, a kind of pest repellent in fact, but he also repelled
Laura so she planted mint around the tool house. She never saw
the snake there again.

"Where did he go, I wonder?" I mused, thinking of distant
mintless regions.

"To the privy," said Laura. "I'm planting mint around it now."
I'm planting mint, too, everywhere there's an untenanted inch
of ground and in some places where I have to pull up other things.

[*The Sweet Apple Gardening Book* (1973)]

Eleanor Perényi
Pests and Diseases

Central to organic gardening is the belief that plants so grown are healthier to begin with, hence more able to cope with attacks from whatever quarter; that preventive measures are better than drastic attempts at cure; and that natural remedies must be substituted for those man-made ones that are 90 percent toxic in one way or another. As a corollary, nature left alone will strike a tolerable balance among the predators. And we organic gardeners had better be right, because time is running out on the indiscriminate users of chemicals. A point of no return has already been reached in several parts of the world where more and more deadly pesticides are deployed against insects more and more able to resist them, natural controls are destroyed, and the ecology is in ruins. Diseases aren't being cured either. On the contrary, as more land is devoted to single, high-yield, high-profit crops like wheat and soybeans planted in the same soil year after year, blights are both more frequent and more devastating. Finally (and this may save us where missionary work has failed), the whole appalling array of chemicals (pesticides, herbicides, fungicides, etc.) is now so expensive that the cost may soon be prohibitive to farmers and home gardeners alike.

You would expect the agricultural establishment, dominated as it is in large part by the petrochemical industry, to set its face against change and to loose a barrage of defensive propaganda—and it has. What you ought *not* to expect is for the gardening press, with so much less to lose, to follow suit—as *it* has. Gardening books, newspaper columns, radio programs devoted to answering gardeners' questions, continue to give the impression that sprays (and chemical

fertilizers) are the answer to everything, with no hint that alternatives exist, let alone that there is a school of thought totally opposed
to both. Even the U.S.D.A., until recent years the faithful servant
of the commercial interests, knows better than that and is in fact
examining and testing alternatives to chemical extermination, while
gardening editors as a whole seem blissfully unaware of what is
happening or what can be done about it. I sometimes wonder if
they read the news in their own papers.

Take the recent banning of the pesticide aldicarb or Temix, a
favorite with Long Island potato farmers. It was banned because it
was belatedly found to be contaminating wells and streams—and,
one would infer, the potatoes themselves. Yes or no? The question
was asked and the official reply was that while it may have, most
people don't eat potatoes every day and that therefore the level of
the poison consumed could be considered safe. A leading newspaper, and the one I judge by, ran this story on the front page, then
let it drop. The gardening editor never referred to it—though it
was surely of concern to home vegetable gardeners who have also
been using aldicarb on their potatoes for many years. (My own
reaction was to conduct a small poll on who *does* eat potatoes every
day, and anyone could have predicted the result: People living on
limited incomes eat potatoes once and often twice a day—they are
a staple food. Only the diet-conscious with money to spend on meat
do not. So much for that—except that it didn't occur to the newspaper to pursue the obvious point.)

Even so, it didn't surprise me that this story was ignored, not
only, be it said, by newspaper gardening columns but by most of
the gardening press. Worse things have happened, most notoriously
with the herbicide 2,4,5-T, which the Environmental Protection
Agency only got around to outlawing some eight years after the
Vietnam war, in which it did horrendous damage not only to the
wretched Vietnamese peasants and their land but, it now develops,
to the American soldiers who handled the stuff: 2,4,5-T is an ingredient of the infamous Agent Orange. But it was also an ingredient
of the herbicides American gardeners were spreading on their lawns,
and how many knew that? How many know it now? The casualness
with which the whole affair has been handled is staggering, and the
gardening editor of the newspaper referred to above is, once again,
typical. She is as high on herbicides as ever and only the other day

listed no fewer than five to be applied to lawn weeds, beginning with 2,4-D and something called Banvel. Then apparently a warning light flickered, and she added a footnote for the benefit of those who might be frightened by that sequence of numbers. Noting that the E.P.A. has suspended the sale of 2,4,5-T, she wrote: "The herbicide 2,4,5-T was an ingredient of the Agent Orange and is not to be confused with 2,4-D." No comment on her own past recommendation of 2,4,5-T, and no reason given for why we should now unquestioningly accept 2,4-D. Are we not entitled to know what the significant difference between them is?

She might reply that the responsibility for guaranteeing the safety of these products rests with the United States government, not with a newspaper, and up to a point she would be right. But as a reporter and adviser to the public she surely has a responsibility of her own to go beyond a supine acceptance of whatever the government may be saying at the moment. She can't be unaware of how often and how disastrously we have been misled on everything from atomic fallout to chemical dumping. 2,4,5-T isn't an isolated case. For decades the government ignored the evidence against the commonly used pesticides in the group called chlorinated hydrocarbons, which includes DDT, dieldrin, aldrin, heptachlor, endrin, lindane and chlordane. These have been denounced for years by independent scientists as indiscriminate killers of a broad range of life forms. They don't break down into nontoxic materials soon after application and are suspected carcinogens. The first four have now been taken off the market. The others haven't, though they may be at any moment. Meanwhile they are still being recommended in the gardening press without a caveat to innocent readers. The general attitude seems to be that it's our funeral—as indeed it will be —and when it is you can be sure there will be no expressions of regret. It is one of the nastier features of the chemical world that repentance is never forthcoming for past errors, however lethal they may have proved.

The organic gardener can't be detached about the situation, which will enrage or depress him according to his temperament. But it doesn't affect him directly. (I have had to check the spelling of all those sinister names and have some trouble keeping them straight since none has ever entered my gates.) He is under no obligation to produce blemish-free crops of fruit and can put up with a mild case of powdery mildew on the lilacs, knowing that neither is fatal. He can do himself nothing but good when he banishes chemicals from the premises, and I guarantee that if he then takes certain measures he needn't look forward to insect invasions or epidemics of disease. (I have no experience of either—Japanese beetles excepted, and I will get to those in a moment.) All he has to do is to follow the simple rules of good husbandry, and instead of trying to keep up with the latest in chemical extermination, educate himself a little on how to run a garden without an array of bags, bottles and aerosol cans in his shed.

Compost of course is basic. Aside from its fertilizing and soil-conditioning properties, it teems with antibiotics and is thus the best insurance against disease. Keep the garden clean: Get rid of anything that looks really sick and compost the rest. Old stalks and litter lying around aren't organic so much as a sign of laziness. Bugs and blights can multiply in trash as opposed to the compost heap. Then, if you are growing vegetables, rotate the crops—no matter how small the kitchen garden may be. This is important protection against root rots and nematodes, which are tiny, eel-like worms that attack root systems. Compost is a help here too because it is a breeding-ground for certain fungi that devour nematodes. Rotation discourages the pest from building up a population in the spot where their favorite vegetables grow year after year. Give them something they don't like and they starve. What they like best are the mid-summer vegetables such as tomatoes, pepper, eggplant, okra, melons, etc., so be careful never to grow these more than once every three years on the same land. (I make a note in my garden book of what went where—I can remember for one year but not for two.) Stay away from all plants after a heavy rain—moving around among wet leaves spreads any diseases that may be about—and don't embark on wet-weather weeding for the same reason. Some vegetable diseases breed on weeds and are conveyed from plant to plant by moisture.

Plants imported to the garden may, of course, be infected too, and this is one of the best arguments for raising your own if you can. If not, do at least stay away from those emporia whose stock comes from a distant source they can't vouch for, and try to find a local nurseryman you can trust. Seed catalogues make a point of noting which varieties are disease-resistant, and these would be the ones to order if you were having troubles. On the other hand, catalogues dealing in perennials, bulbs, shrubs or trees are apt to be reticent on this subject—though some of the species they are selling are notoriously susceptible to disease and to insect attack as well. You must do your own homework. Ask a neighbor who has a tree you are interested in, or look it up. Had I had the sense to do this some years ago, I would have spared myself the expense of a row of Lombardy poplars, installed under the influence of romantic European memories, only to be removed a few years later in disgrace. Had I inquired, I would have learned of the poplar's propensity to canker and scale, which attacked mine more or less simultaneously. Thus bitten, I am now shy of ordering, say, English hawthorns, though I long for a dense pink hedge of them. But I now know that in this part of the country they, too, have a bad name and must be regularly sprayed if they are to do well.

There are other secrets to a healthy garden, and one of them (though we had no idea of this when our original layout was made) is to have it full of a number of things: vegetables, flowers, herbs, small fruits and berries, rather than the sparsely planted modern plot. The kitchen garden in particular oughtn't to consist of a limited number of vegetables in segregated rows. This may satisfy a sense of order but is an invitation to predators and diseases to demolish a crop overnight. Short rows of different vegetables interspersed with herbs and flowers have a contrary effect. Not only do they limit the spread of a blight, they discourage methodical attack by insects whose appetite for one kind of plant can be deflected by the near presence of another they dislike. In other words, the cottage garden, which in one form or another has flourished the world over since the beginning of time, is now seen to be scientifically sound. It remains to sanctify its procedures with a name and to find an explanation of how it works that will be acceptable to the agricultural establishment.

The name is companion planting (or interplanting), and the practice is based on the observable fact that plants in cultivation, as in nature, seem to reinforce one another when grown in mixtures. Partly, this is because some plants are naturally repellent to certain insects and can therefore protect their neighbors, though what the repellent properties may consist of is only now being seriously investigated. But there can be no doubt that they exist. Marigolds and garlic are perhaps the most famous all-purpose deterrents to a variety of pests from root nematodes to borers, and it at once occurs to the rationalist that it was on just such simple foundations that the whole Gothic edifice of plant mythology was built. (What more natural than to deduce from the effect of garlic on sucking insects that it would also work on vampires?) But however off-putting that edifice may be to some of us, the original thesis does prove out in practice. Besides marigolds and garlic, geraniums, nasturtiums, petunias, and many herbs—notably tansy, the mints, rosemary, and summer savory—actually do behave as claimed and repel a wide variety of pests. Still other plants are useful in specific situations. Snap beans and horseradish are distasteful to potato bugs; and the wormwoods to cabbage butterflies. (Hemp, i.e., marijuana, is said to be the most powerful deterrent of all to these pests. Dutch cabbage beds were surrounded with it throughout the nineteenth century, but I haven't been willing to risk a police raid to prove the point.) A comprehensive list of insect-repelling plants would be too long to give here. Those inclined to join the faithful can consult *The Encyclopedia of Organic Gardening* or the excellent *Companion Planting* by Louise Riotte.

There is more to companion planting than putting in marigolds to ward off the Mexican bean beetle. Subtle patterns of interaction between the plants themselves are manifested in curious friendships and antipathies, and in this area I am bound to say I think the organic press has done a terrible job of explication. It is all very well to say that such relationships exist—to assert that potatoes don't do well in proximity to tomatoes, squash, or cucumber but get along beautifully with beans, corn, and cabbage, while cabbage doesn't want to be near beans or tomatoes, which in turn are compatible with onions but inimical to potatoes and cabbage, and so on, ad infinitum. Such assertions seem on the face of it to countermand the premise that mixtures of plants are a good idea. Furthermore, the gardener who tried to accommodate so many likes and dislikes would be in the position of a hostess making out a guest list and trying to remember out of half a hundred people who is or isn't on good terms with whom—and going out of her mind. And the more so in this case because the "rules of" compatibility are often in conflict with those of crop rotation, and those at odds with others applying to insect control. (Example: Flea beetles are repelled by tomatoes interplanted with cole crops, but tomatoes, we are else-where told, don't *like* cole crops.) Lastly, I question whether all this juggling accomplishes anything. My experience doesn't verify the quaint vision of vegetables turning from one another or alternatively falling into each other's arms. It seems to me they rub along pretty well together, and if they don't I haven't noticed. There are, to be sure, variations from year to year, but I can't determine that they have any connection with my having introduced a tomato, say, to a fennel—which according to *Companion Planting* is so unpopular with so many other vegetables it shouldn't be asked to the party at all but planted outside the kitchen garden.

I have other objections to what is called trap-cropping. This consists in growing a bug's favorite meal next to something you want to protect from its depredations, and it has a prominent place in organic literature. I don't see the sense of it, not because it doesn't work but because it does. It is quite true that eggplants next to potatoes will be more attractive to the potato beetle than the po-tatoes are; that zinnias (especially in white or pale colors), white roses and white geraniums will lure Japanese beetles away from other plants; and that dill charms the tomato hornworm into de-serting the tomatoes. What of it? What of the eggplants, zinnias, white roses, dill, I have lost in the process? Even more to the point, what if I also prefer the beetle's first choice to its second, would rather have the eggplants than the potatoes, the white roses than the beans? Trap-cropping may serve a practical purpose for the farmer or the orchardist. To me, it is an exercise in futility.

In any case, and whatever you do, insects of some sort are going to visit you sooner or later. Deciding what constitutes an infestation is then the beginning of wisdom. It also helps to know what the insect is. So distant are most Americans from the natural world, so thoroughly have they been brainwashed on this topic, that the ma-jority fear anything that flies or crawls. Should you encounter an object some five inches long that seems to be constructed of wire and toothpicks, which turns a tiny triangular face in your direction, you may be slightly unnerved even when you know perfectly well what it is: a praying mantis, of course, so greatly valued for its consumption of aphids, tent caterpillars, leaf hoppers, locusts, chinch bugs and half a dozen other menaces that organic gardeners order its egg cases by mail and carefully attach them to the branches of shrubs and trees in hopes that a population of mantises will emerge. Or perhaps you notice a congregation of ladybugs on a rose stalk. Don't invoke the old nursery saying and ask them to fly away home. Their house is not on fire. Your roses are, with aphids, which the ladybugs are feeding on—and you can bless yourself that they have come to your rescue. Ladybugs are a boon, and another insect the organic gardener takes pains to import if he hasn't got them already.

These are examples of the famous "balance of nature" we're always talking about, and the principle is the same as that of the old balance-of-power politics. Every harmful insect has a mortal enemy. Cultivate that enemy and he will do your work for you. Observe the tomato hornworm. Bright green and stuck all over with white pins as often as not, this decorative creature is on its last legs when you see it: those pins are the larvae of a wasp and they are eating the worm alive. Wasps are, in fact, one of our more valuable allies owing to their parasitic habits. The trichogramma wasp lays eggs inside the eggs of other insects such as the corn borer, the cabbage looper, the codling moth, and once hatched the baby wasps consume their hosts. Organic apple growers rely on them for help in producing worm-free harvests, and like mantises and ladybugs, the trichogramma is sold commercially. But try telling that to those who panic at the sight of any flying object. Strong men in my employ have been incapacitated by a single sighting. I recall one idiotic youth who arrived panting at the back door. "Have you," he demanded, "ever seen a *white-faced wasp?*" "I have now," was my reply—which attempt at humor didn't stop him from buying a gas bomb to destroy these imaginary enemies. He had, of course, to go. Had he chanced to lay eyes on one of those insects that go by the names of ambush, assassin and damsel bug (fierce devourers of caterpillars and grubs) he would probably have fainted away. Even the lovely lacewing (a predator of aphids, mites, mealybugs, etc.) might have been too much for him.

I make fun of him, but really there is nothing funny about the prevailing fear of insects and the indiscriminate use of sprays it leads to. It can't be said too often that spraying is like using a bomb instead of a bullet, killing the good along with the bad; and the psychology of those who defend it is perilously close to that of the general who wanted to destroy the village in order to save it. In the end it isn't even effective. The history of the Japanese beetle in this country is instructive. Accidentally introduced in 1916, it quickly became one of the worst of garden pests. Yet it hadn't been in Japan. Why? As early as 1933, government entomologists isolated a bacterial organism that produces a fatal disease in Japanese beetle grubs. They called it milky spore disease after the whitish look of infected insects, and it then turned out that it is naturally present in the soils of Japan. Here, it wasn't, and the beetles were soon out of control. In the 1950's and early 1960's, we were engulfed in beetles, but nobody told us about milky spore disease. Spray and spray some more was the advice handed out, and it was worse than useless. The beetles quickly developed immunity. Nor, I have to admit, did I succeed in knocking them off with garlic planted in the rose beds. Praying mantises couldn't seem to get a grip on the situation either. Not until milky spore disease became available in powder form sold commercially were the beetles finally routed. (Several laboratories produce it under license from the U.S.D.A. and market it under the names Doom or Japonex.) It is applied mostly to lawns, where the beetle grubs are hatched, is harmless to everything but the beetles, and once established is said to last indefinitely. Why, then, did it take so long to appear on the market? Why isn't it sold, even now, at every garden center? One may well ask.

Milky spore disease (*Bacillus popilliae*) is called a biological control. Another such is *Bacillus thuringiensis*, or simply BT (trade names are Thuricide, Biotrol and Dipel), which is fatal to the larvae of many serious pests, particularly tent caterpillars, peach tree borers, cabbage worms, codling moth worm and the gypsy moth caterpillar. The last is of special interest at the moment because, and not for the first time, it is infesting large sections of the northeast. But in spite of the availability, safety and known effectiveness of BT, and still more to the point, past experience with mass spraying of this caterpillar that killed birds, bees, small animals and deer in large numbers without having much effect on the gypsy moths, the battle is still being fought between those who insist on spraying and the environmentalists begging that BT be used instead. The lesson is never learned.

There are other forms of biological control but they are too sophisticated for the ordinary gardener, who anyway doesn't need them. For us, the simplest measures usually suffice: a blast of water from the hose to dislodge the aphids, a saucer of beer for the thirsty slugs to drown in, a small tin can or a paper collar around young plants to foil the cutworm. The squeamish brush visible pests into a can of kerosene carried about for the purpose. I crush beetles and aphids between thumb and forefinger and leave the victims on the battlefield as a caution. Coming across the mangled remains of one's kin is evidently as unpleasant to bugs as it would be to human beings, and they usually leave the scene. (On the same principle, some organic gardeners grind them to a pulp in a blender, dilute the strained juice with water and use it as a spray.)

Organic gardeners are enthusiastic concocters of homemade sprays—infusions of hot peppers, wormwood, a medicinal bark called quassia, garlic, horseradish and other nippy substances, but although these are probably harmless, *The Encyclopedia of Organic Gardening* takes rather a dim view of them since they, too, might upset the balance of nature in some unforeseen way. Ideally, one should use no sprays at all unless in extremis, but one or two organic products are considered acceptable: rotenone (but not if adulterated with synthentic toxins—read the label); dormant oil spray (without additives); pyrethrum, the least toxic of any.

Most gardeners, I think, come to organic gardening through the kitchen door. Their first concern is fresh, uncontaminated vegetables, and it may seem less important to apply the same principles to trees, shrubs, lawns and flowers. But it doesn't make much sense to keep the kitchen garden free of poisons if you apply herbicides to the lawn and something that smells like boiled rubber to the flowers. A garden is a world, and its parts are not separable.

[*Green Thoughts: A Writer in the Garden* (1981)]

Roger Swain
Gypsy Moths

I may be accused of being soft on caterpillars, but gypsy moths are here to stay and we'd best learn to live with them. Gypsy moths have never been well received, and when their numbers increase, as they do periodically, people become alarmed and begin to talk about an end to the landscape as we know it. Throughout the Northeast this year, people have been getting up at town meetings and demanding to know what preventive measures are being taken, while privately they worry about property values going down.

I have been asked what I think of gypsy moths by people whose bumper stickers proclaim their love of four-legged animals. On occasion, they know I have spoken enthusiastically of six-legged ones, and they wonder whether my enthusiasm extends to gypsy moths. They themselves, of course, are horrified—horrified by the thousands of dark, hairy caterpillars with their blue and red warts, horrified by the incessant leaf chewing, and revolted by the steady drizzle of caterpillar droppings from the branches overhead. Gypsy moths have aroused such enormous enmity that anyone even suggesting coexistence with them faces the modern equivalent of being ridden out of town on a rail. And yet the zeal with which some people call for their eradication provokes me to suggest just that.

Shortly after Patriots' Day, that celebration of the alarm spread by Paul Revere, William Dawes, and Samuel Prescott, a similar tocsin is sounded about gypsy moths. The morning papers begin to describe this year's infestation, calling the reader's attention to the silk tents in the crotches of cherry trees along the highway. The silk tents aren't built by gypsy moths, however. They are the nests of the Eastern tent caterpillar, a native American insect that differs from the gypsy moth in both its construction of tents and its gregarious nature. At night, dozens of these caterpillars cluster together within each tent, venturing out by day to eat the leaves of wild cherry and apple trees. Although the tents are unsightly, tent caterpillars, with their white midstripe and rows of blue ovals, are seldom numerous enough to cause serious damage. Another caterpillar, the fall webworm, builds similar, but larger, tents late in the summer on the ends of branches. Within these tents, yellow green caterpillars feed. But since the leaves they are eating would have been shed shortly, their feeding does little damage to trees. Unlike the fall webworm or the tent caterpillar, gypsy moths do not make tents. But because tent caterpillar eggs hatch at about the same time as gypsy-moth eggs, tent caterpillars are invariably victims of mistaken identity.

In late April or early May, or when the white flowers of the shadbush are open and the oak leaves are just beginning to unfurl, the eggs of *Lymantria dispar*, the gypsy moth, hatch. Although it was cold throughout the Northeast last winter, the mercury rarely reached the minus 25 degrees Fahrenheit needed to kill them. The newly emerged gypsy-moth caterpillars, buff-colored at birth, turn black in a few hours. They remain on the light brown, furry egg mass that is plastered to a tree trunk as long as the temperature is below 40 degrees Fahrenheit, or as long as it is raining. Then, with fair skies and warmer air, each tiny caterpillar, a mere eighth of an inch long, begins to ascend the tree on which it was born. As it travels, the young caterpillar lays down a trail of silk excreted by glands in its head. Reaching the topmost twig of the tree, the caterpillar keeps going, paying out the silken lifeline as it falls. Stopping abruptly in midair, the caterpillar begins to ascend the line, but before it regains that top twig, a breeze usually snaps the silk and the caterpillar—kept aloft by the length of silk and its own unusually long body hairs, which act as sails—is blown sidewise onto the branch of another tree. Here it climbs and falls once more until, after several such repetitions, the caterpillar settles down to feed hundreds of yards from where it hatched.

This ballooning is the gypsy moth's natural means of dispersal, the way it moves into new territory. Although most of the caterpillars being wafted about are not yet feeding, some people are already upset, irritated by skin rashes where the windblown caterpillars have bumped their bare arms. Others are bothered by having to pick caterpillars off the backs of their necks when they come in for lunch.

First-stage, or first-instar, larvae—as these caterpillars are called—chew small holes in the middle of leaves. After about a week of feeding, the larva stops, preparing to shed its skin. Twenty-four hours later, the skin suddenly ruptures behind the head and the caterpillar steps out of its old skin. It swings its body from side to side a few times, its long hairs straighten out, and in a few hours it begins to feed again. Second-instar larvae are larger and proportionately hungrier, and they begin to consume whole leaves, starting at the leaf's margin.

By the time the caterpillars have shed their skin twice more, at intervals of four to ten days, depending on temperature, and become fourth-instar larvae, their feeding behavior changes again. Instead of occasionally moving to the underside of a leaf or branch to rest, the caterpillars now travel down the trunk of the tree at dawn and spend the day hidden beneath a flap of bark, in a crevice in the trunk, or in some sheltered spot on the ground. At dusk, they climb to the foliage and resume feeding.

Two months after they have hatched, or about the first week in July, the caterpillars stop feeding for good. The largest caterpillars, resplendent with five pairs of blue spots followed by six pairs of red ones, are now as long as 2½ inches. The males have gone through five instars; the females, six. Both sexes have also gone through a lot of leaves. A late-instar caterpillar can convert 12 square inches of leaf into gypsy moth and gypsy-moth droppings in twenty-four hours. The caterpillars have their preferences. Oak leaves are their favorite, but they will also eat leaves of apple, basswood, beech, gray birch, hawthorn, poplar, and willow. Less preferred but still acceptable are paper birch, cherry, elm, hickory, hornbeam, maple, and sassafras. Late-instar larvae will even devour things the earlier ones avoid, such as hemlock, pine, and spruce.

The good news is that there are a few plants that the caterpillars tend to avoid—ash, butternut, black walnut, catalpa, flowering dogwood, American holly, locust, sycamore, tulip tree, and such evergreens as arborvitae, balsam fir, mountain laurel, and rhododendron. At least these used to be avoided, but with every new outbreak there are reports of the caterpillars eating things they are not supposed to like. Evolution marches on.

When caterpillars have finished with one tree, they move on to the next. A grove of pure pine may be spared because there is not enough food in it to keep the young fed, but a single white pine surrounded by oaks is almost certain to be defoliated when older caterpillars have eaten all the oak leaves nearby.

To see a tree that was in full leaf in May suddenly bare in late June is a startling sight—or horrifying, depending on your point of view. What is just as startling is to see what happens three weeks later. Buds open and a second set of leaves appears. These leaves are often smaller and a lighter shade of green than the first ones, but the tree is in leaf and most definitely alive. Responding to the loss of its first set, the tree has merely dug down into its reserves of stored energy and manufactured a second set. Independence Day rumors that the trees are all dead have usually been forgotten by Labor Day.

Some of the trees do die—if not this year, then the next. Hemlocks that have lost all their needles usually die at once. Most other trees that die, however, are already in poor condition: Their roots were cut off when the driveway was built; they have absorbed too much road salt; they are diseased; they are growing in too much shade; they have been defoliated three years running. When a tree has no energy left and it is attacked by gypsy moths, it dies. But most trees do not. Even white pines have a 75 percent chance of surviving the loss of all their needles. Most other species—especially if they are growing on moist, fertile soil instead of dry rock—have an even better chance of survival.

Certain people, notably the manufacturers of pesticides, speak of the gypsy moths' "substantial alteration of the ecology," and they claim that "the balance of nature is radically upset." They are joined by campers whose campsites have been skeletonized, by drivers whose scenic vistas are not so scenic. Yet I can't see that gypsy moths have prevented the forest from returning to New England. The foresters I talk to don't regard the gypsy moth as apocalyptic. They tell me that the first time a forest is hit by gypsy moths, a sizable percentage of trees are killed—especially if there are successive years of defoliation—but subsequent outbreaks never kill as

many. The weak trees have been weeded out. In many cases, the
trees that die would die anyway before they reached maturity. Defoliation simply compresses the mortality into fewer years. Even if
all the susceptible species were to be killed outright, species that
the gypsy moth *didn't* eat would be favored. But so far, after one
hundred years, there isn't much evidence that gypsy moths have
affected forest composition. When asked about the importance of
controlling gypsy moths, one forest economist put it simply, "Losses
just aren't high enough to justify any effort."

Why, then, has more than $100 million been spent over the
years on trying to stop the gypsy moth? The gypsy moth isn't really
a pest of trees, it's a pest of people. People are disgusted when
caterpillars cover the shingles of their house. They'd sooner have a
rat crawl up their pants leg. People don't even like stepping on
caterpillars as they stroll down the sidewalk. If the gypsy moth
resided only in deep forest, no one would notice—but it flourishes
in suburbia.

People in suburbia see trees differently than foresters do. They
cherish every one. It is useless to speak of the probability that a
certain tree will die when the tree is in someone's backyard.

"It shades the house."

"Where else would we hang the swing?"

"Great Aunt Myrtle's ashes are buried underneath."

You are talking about a personal asset, a friend, a monument,
not about board feet of lumber. And so county agents are consulted,
and arborists are hired to spray the trees. Among the insecticides
they may use are carbaryl (Sevin), acephate (Orthene), or trichlorfon
(Dylox). These sprays kill lots of different kinds of insects. Some
people are concerned about this, especially about its effect on honeybees and on the food supply for birds. So next year they start
earlier and hire someone to spray BT (*Bacillus thuringiensis*), a
bacterium that kills all kinds of butterfly and moth larvae but not
much else. It has to be applied shortly after the eggs hatch, and
perhaps a second time, and it's more expensive, but at least it spares
the honeybees.

Others, caught between extreme environmentalism and concern for their white oak, resort to manual eradication. They try to
scrape off all the egg masses into kerosene, or paint them over with

creosote or diluted shellac. The larvae that hatch, they pick off and squash. A strip of burlap tied around the trunk traps the ones that are looking for a place to rest. A band of Tanglefoot, one of several commercially available sticky substances, keeps caterpillars from climbing the tree, but tree-lovers are careful to spread it on a strip of tar paper and tie the tar paper around the tree with cotton stuffed beneath, lest the sticky stuff cause the trunk to develop a canker. Keeping trees well watered and fertilized also helps them to survive.

By early July, when people are just beginning to get desperate, the eating stops. The caterpillars, after spinning the flimsiest of cocoons, pupate, transforming themselves into large brown teardrops, the female's larger than the male's. Even the most beleaguered homeowners begin to relax and recover. The caterpillars may be missing, but, of course, the gypsy moth's life cycles on. Ten to fourteen days later, the pupae split open and the moths emerge. The males, which emerge first and are slightly smaller, are brown; the females are white speckled with black. Neither merits being collected for its looks.

The female cannot even fly. Instead, she waits near the spot where she pupated and releases from her abdomen a pheromone —a sex attractant that has been identified as cis-7,8 -epoxy -2-methyloctadecane. To a male gypsy moth, this spells love. Hundreds of yards away, he detects a few molecules of the scent with his fernlike antennae and begins to fly upwind in a pattern that has earned him the French nickname *le Zigzag*.

Shortly after mating, the female lays from 75 to 1,000 eggs in a single mass and covers them over with the buff hairs from her abdomen. Two to four days after emerging from their pupae, and without ever having fed as adults, both males and females die. The embryo in each egg reaches full development in three weeks but, instead of hatching in August, remains quiescent until spring.

In nature, the egg masses stay put, but in suburbia, it's another story. People move during the summer. A family in New York State packs up to relocate in Wisconsin. Being thrifty, they take everything with them: the clothespole, the doghouse, the picnic table, even the leftover firewood. They don't see the furry tan patches stuck to their belongings.

Next spring, the eggs hatch, and, a few years later, gypsy moths are well established where they never were before. If the town is lucky, some of the male moths will be captured in one of the 150,000 small, sticky traps, baited with synthetic sex attractant, set out by the Department of Agriculture all over the country to monitor the spread of the gypsy moth. This brings in the exterminators. Sometimes the exterminators are successful, sometimes they aren't. In 1973, a house trailer carried eggs from Connecticut to Michigan, and in spite of intense efforts to get rid of them, the moths seem to be there to stay.

This close association between humans and gypsy moths dates back to the moth's introduction to this country. Leopold Trouvelot, astronomer, naturalist, and entrepreneur, was apparently trying to breed a disease-resistant silkworm for the silk industry of his native France by crossing the gypsy moth with the silk moth. Since the gypsy moth is native to Europe (and North Africa and Asia), he should have conducted his experiments there, but in 1868 he happened to be living outside Boston, at 27 Myrtle Street, in the suburb of Medford. In the two-story clapboard house with a picket fence in front and a grape arbor out back, he began to rear gypsy moths. No one knows how it happened, but within a year some of his charges had escaped.

However much we may regret his actions today, we should note that his motives were as well intentioned as—and considerably more sensible than—those of Eugene Scheifflin, a wealthy New York City drug manufacturer who introduced forty pairs of starlings into Central Park in 1890 because he wished to establish in this country every species of bird mentioned by Shakespeare. It is to Trouvelot's credit that he recognized the omnivorous appetites of his escapees and notified the authorities. Scheifflin, on the other hand, released forty more starlings a year later, and now the pests infest the entire United States.

With an abundance of food, the escaped gypsy moths prospered, and, by 1880, their descendants occupied 400 square miles. Around the Trouvelot house they were especially troublesome, but Trouvelot had returned to Paris and the caterpillars were assumed to be some native species. It was not until 1889 that the first major outbreak occurred. There have been many population explosions since then, but none will be remembered like the summer of '89, when the caterpillars rampaged through Medford.

Mrs. F. T. Spinney, the wife of Medford's postmaster, remembered what happened: "I lived on Cross Street in 1889. In June of that year, I was out of town for three days. When I went away, the trees in our yard were in splendid condition, and there was not a sign of insect devastation upon them. When I returned, there was scarcely a leaf upon the trees. The gypsy-moth caterpillars were over everything."

"The caterpillars were so thick on the trees," added J. P. Dill, "that they were stuck together like cold macaroni."

Mrs. Thomas F. Mayo, living at 25 Myrtle Street, joined the women on the street and together they made a regular business of killing caterpillars. "The caterpillars used to cover the basement and clapboards of the house as high as the windowsill. They lay in a solid black mass. I would scrape them off into an old dishpan holding about 10 quarts. When it was two-thirds full, I poured kerosene over the mass of worms and set them on fire. I used to do this a number of times a day. It was sickening work."

The official response was immediate, and on March 14, 1890, the Massachusetts legislature appropriated $25,000 to control the gypsy moth. Men were sent aloft to scrape egg masses off even the highest branches of the largest elms. Stone walls were burned, trees were burlapped, Paris green (a compound of copper and arsenic) was sprayed from horse-drawn wagons.

The results are history. A "barrier zone" 30 miles wide was established between Long Island Sound and the Canadian border in 1923, and it failed completely. Even C-47 transport planes spraying 150 gallons of DDT a minute in 600-foot-wide swaths couldn't kill all the caterpillars. Like a scoop of ice cream melting on a summer sidewalk, the gypsy moths have continued to spread. On the map of gypsy-moth distribution, the shaded portion now extends west nearly to Ohio and south to Maryland.

In 1980, five million acres were defoliated by gypsy moths. Of course, these acres were not all contiguous. Damage tends to occur in a mosaic, a moth-eaten patchwork quilt. Adjacent to a patch of forest that has been heavily grazed, there may be another virtually untouched. How abundant the caterpillars are depends partly on the recent local history of the moth. Where moths have been particularly abundant, epidemics of disease are likely to cause their numbers to decline. In other areas, where the moths used to be scarce, their numbers suddenly increase at irregular intervals for currently inexplicable reasons—a phenomenon that bedevils scientists trying to understand the ecology of gypsy moths.

The Department of Agriculture is in charge of preventing the gypsy moth's spread, of identifying and eradicating those pockets of gypsy moths that appear regularly way out beyond the major front. But these efforts are only a holding action. There is no reason to believe that the gypsy moth will not someday occur everywhere that there is deciduous forest, from Florida to California.

Central to the success of the gypsy moths in this country is the fact that they have escaped from their natural enemies. Throughout the species' natural range from Portugal to Japan, there are places where the population periodically explodes, but such outbreaks tend to be infrequent and short-lived. The gypsy moths are always at the mercy of parasites, predators, and disease, and for years at a stretch are too scarce to cause any problems.

From the first, the importation of natural enemies was part of gypsy-moth control. "Civilized man should have the advantage of the savage in being able to use one force of nature against another," wrote Edward R. Farrar, the tree warden of Lincoln, Massachusetts, in 1906; and since then, more than forty-five natural enemies of the gypsy moth have been introduced in the United States. Most have died out, in some cases because of the lack of an intermediate host, but at least ten parasites and one predator, a greenish black ground beetle, are now established here.

In a given season, a female of *Oencyrtus kuvanae*, a tiny wasp from Japan, can destroy two hundred gypsy-moth eggs, while a female *Apanteles melanoscelus*, a wasp from Europe, can kill 1,000 caterpillars. The tachinid fly, *Blepharipa pratensis*, is even more destructive, laying 5,000 or more eggs on the foliage of infested trees. Gypsy-moth caterpillars accidentally swallow these tiny time bombs when they are feeding. The eggs hatch and the maggots consume the caterpillars from within.

All but one of these parasites were successfully introduced before 1930. Misplaced optimism that DDT was going to eradicate gypsy moths once and for all led to a reduced interest in biological control. But the questionable effectiveness of aerial spraying and its unquestionably high cost have prompted a renewed interest in the gypsy moth's natural enemies. Laboratories in Paris and Sapporo, Japan, are devoted to searching for new parasites. Hundreds are thought to exist, and all of China remains to be explored.

The best-known disease that afflicts the gypsy moth is wilt disease, so-named because of the inverted V in which the dying caterpillar hangs. The disease was accidentally introduced to this country and epidemics of it have caused dense populations to crash. Laboratory-reared caterpillars are being infected with the nuclear polyhedrosis virus that causes the disease, and their bodies are then freeze-dried and ground up to produce a spray called Gypchek that the Forest Service hopes will cause premature collapse of exploding populations.

Finally, there are predators. A host of native animals have developed tastes for gypsy moths. Chickadees, blue jays, and robins will all feed on sparse populations, while flocking species such as crows, grackles, and red-winged blackbirds are attracted to areas where there are dense ones. Even Eugene Scheifflin's starlings, reviled for their bullying of smaller birds and their clogging of jet engines, deserve some credit for eating large numbers of caterpillars, pupae, and adult moths.

People like having birds in their backyards, but they are less fond of mice. Yet the white-footed mouse, the most common small mammal in the Northeast, eats enormous numbers of gypsy-moth caterpillars, carefully rolling back the skin like a sock to avoid the sharp hairs.

Unfortunately, mice like to live where there are brush piles, dense leaf litter, and stone walls. So do many other animals that feed on gypsy moths: chipmunks, squirrels, shrews, moles, skunks, raccoons, and opossums. Yet in most backyards, what might become predator habitat is sawed up and burned or raked up and dumped into plastic trash bags. Gypsy moths flourish in a well-manicured backyard. Their predators do not.

It is now clear that the gypsy moth will cross any artificial barrier we create, and that it will survive every attempt at extermination. I don't like gypsy moths, I never have. But since we have failed to repel the beast, I propose that we make every effort to convert it from a foreign visitor to a naturalized citizen. If its presence here becomes normal, its numbers may, too. Let us burden the gypsy moth with all the life-shortening benefits of citizenship, with the insect equivalents of such things as military service and taxation. Constant pressure from predators, parasites, and disease offers the best chance to control the number of gypsy moths. This will mean continuing to scour Europe and Asia for pests of the gypsy moth. It will mean refraining from poisoning the gypsy-moth pests we already have with the indiscriminate use of insecticides. It may also mean leaving the grass long, the leaves unraked, and the skunk nesting under the back steps.

This is not to suggest a passive policy of letting nature take its course. We never have and probably never will. Right now, dirty tricks are popular—using synthetic sex attractants to confuse male gypsy moths or releasing laboratory-reared sterile males to fool the females. This sort of activity is fine so long as it doesn't hinder the efforts of the other organisms, many of whom are better equipped to kill gypsy moths than we will ever be. We should concentrate on encouraging the gypsy moth's natural enemies, seeing to it that gypsy moths are subject to every predator, parasite, and disease there is. The wild swinging of the population pendulum will diminish once the gypsy moth is truly established in this country.

As the leaves disappear, and as caterpillar droppings rain down, many people may think that the gypsy moth is already too well established. It isn't. Not yet. But soon, when wilted caterpillars begin to appear, pupae fail to hatch, and egg masses have only 200 instead of 1,000 eggs in them, it will be a sign that the population is about to crash. Biological controls will bring the gypsy moths within bounds, and only biological controls can keep them there. What's needed at a time like this is to extend our love of animals to every snake, toad, or ant that feeds on gypsy moths. Someday there may come a time when gypsy-moth caterpillars are so uncommon that children will collect them, bringing them home in glass jars to keep as pets.

[*Field Days* (1983)]

Patti Hagan
Going Buggy

I am descended from organic gardeners. Around our place the praying mantis hatch was a blessed event and Rachel Carson was patron
saint. Immunized early against the chemical quick fix, when I came
into a garden and an appreciable pest population of my own a few
years back, I declared this small, urbane patch of green a pesticide-
free zone—a safe haven to birds, butterflies, fireflies, dragonflies,
worms, not to mention aphids, leafhoppers, mites, scale, mealybugs.

One season of natural free-for-all took me from organic pacifism
to biological war. I read the *Rodale Encyclopedia of Natural Insect
& Disease Control*. I read the *Common Sense Pest Control Quar-
terly*. The word "insectary" entered my vocabulary, and I got myself
on the mailing lists of several of these insect nurseries, including:
Unique Insect Control and Rincon-Vitova, "the world's oldest &
largest grower of beneficial insects" in California. The Necessary
Catalogue ("biological farm and garden supplies") and the Natural
Gardening Research Center catalog found me.

My backyard ordnance now ranges from positive parasitism to
positive predatorism. My mail-order bugs are called "beneficials."
This spring, while the Environmental Protection Agency has declared pesticide pollution its most urgent problem, my bio-war pro-
curement sheet reads: ½ pint ladybugs, 1 vial trichogramma wasps,
2,000 green lacewings, three praying mantis egg clusters. Of course,
accepting allies of this sort into my gardening regime has meant
giving up the idea of tight border control. These are free-foraging

animals and there is no way to corral them, which is why the Rodale encyclopedia terms certain ones "somewhat overrated."

Nevertheless, among garden entomologists, most-favored-insect status belongs at the moment to the ladybugs, the trichogrammas and the lacewings. These good bugs are mailed under a government "beneficial insect permit." Ladybugs arrive in cotton drawstring bags along with "ladybug release instructions." One should "try to maintain a balance of a few pests for food and enough ladybugs to keep them in check. This management of both the good and the bad insects is the way to achieve biological control of insects."

A half pint of ladybugs—some 4,500 of them—will do for a modest-sized garden. The ladies can be refrigerated and doled out over several weeks, by dolloping "about a tablespoon on each shrub" after sundown in a freshly sprinkled garden so that they will drink and dine immediately. (De-fatted or low-fat ladybugs are preferable, since they arrive hungry, ready to reproduce and are more likely to stay on location.) The adult ladybug puts away about 45 insects a day, and 1,500 adults weigh one ounce. (In time-trials last spring, two tablespoonfuls cleaned a Cecile Brunner rose and a large bleeding heart of aphids in under four hours.) The ladybug larva, however, has a reputation as a wolf ("aphidwolf") in beetle's clothing, doing in 40 aphids per hour. To keep them around, plant pollen-rich flowers (Queen Anne's lace is ideal) that induce the beneficials to confine their life cycles to your premises.

Less straightforward, the tiny trichogramma wasp operates parasitically, laying its eggs in the eggs of some 200 kinds of pestilential insects. Upon hatching, the tricho larva feeds on the surrounding host egg, pre-empting another pest hatch. The trichogramma vial, which on arrival appears to hold a square of fine-grained sandpaper, soon erupts with specks of life, whereupon it can be walked to a pest-riddled place in the garden and opened. "This tiny wasp does not sting or bother beneficial insects or humans," states the Necessary Trading Company, purveyor of "practical biological tools for the farmer, gardener or homeowner."

Lacewings, the beautiful, iridescent "nerve-winged" insects of the order Neuroptera, produce larvae that specialize in aphidicide, though they won't pass up mites, thrips, scale, mealybugs, leafhopper nymphs, or caterpillar eggs, while downing something like 100 aphids a day. Nicknamed aphidlions, the larvae are born ravenous. Not all beneficials are as omnivorous as lacewings. It is generally useful to suit the predator to the prey. Predatory mites eat spider and greenhouse mites; Cryptolaemus beetles munch mealybugs; Encarsia formosa parasitizes the white fly. But a lack of prey specificity has caused some biological controllers to question the alleged garden efficacy of that great glamour bug, the praying mantis, since the mantis is a cannibalistic carnivore and will devour anything, kin included, that moves into its preying range. However, this otocyclops (a single ear in the thorax has just recently been discovered) is fascinating to observe. From the moment of hatch when hundreds of minute, pallid nymphs spill out of the eggcase and begin triangulating on the world, to their diaspora throughout the garden in "early morning with dew on leaves" (as per instructions from the insectary), to the day a bright green adult turns up, very businesslike, on your neighbor's front stoop.

I have watched long minutes as a mantis perched on a blue spike of Veronica, waiting for a meal to fly by. Mantids have fast-moving front legs for catching high flies and mosquitoes and pull moths out of the air by night. Four eggcases per quarter acre are recommended.

None of this insect warfare costs much. Ladybugs can run $4.95 for 4,500, trichogrammas $4.10 for 12,000, three praying mantis eggcases yielding 600 nymphs for $3.75, lacewings $4.10 for 1,000. These bundles are also lightweight, easily mailed, require little tending, no shepherding, and almost no equipment beyond a tablespoon for ladybug dispersal and a needle and thread for sewing praying mantis eggcases to shrubs.

But to garden without pesticides does take more thought than broadcasting poison and more knowledge of the complex natural systems you are trying to aid and abet. It means getting actively involved in insect I.D. and pest demographics, since good timing is of the essence. Insectaries provide clear, at times poetic, release directions and their products give you a non-toxic way to fight the good fight for Mother Nature, while adding lots more life-interest to your immediate habitat.

Here are some mail-order sources for beneficials: Natural Gardening Research Center, Hwy. 46, P.O. Box 149, Sunman, Ind.

47041; Necessary Trading Company, 639 Main Street, New Castle, Va. 24127; Rincon-Vitova Insectaries, P.O. Box 95, Oak View, Calif. 93022; Unique Insect Control, 5504 Sperry Drive, Citrus Heights, Calif. 95621.

[*The Wall Street Journal* (June 11, 1986)]

Roy Barrette
War

By the Fourth of July the gardener feels that summer is finally here, and all is well with the world. The tomatoes are looking sturdy, the corn is coming, the beets and carrots are up, and he won't have to buy any plastic salad makings from the supermarket until November. All in all, he is feeling pretty satisfied with himself. He has even forgotten the cutworms that decimated the beet seedlings and lopped off the tomatoes, peppers, and eggplants. But pride goeth before a fall.

Four pests that can do more damage to a garden in a single night than all the cutworms, aphids and caterpillars, and bean and potato beetles in existence are deer, woodchucks, porcupines, and raccoons. (Of course, there are also rabbits, cats, dogs, and small children, not to mention the cyclones, windstorms, rain, hail, frost, drought, and other Acts of God that are visited upon us for our manifold sins and wickedness.)

The particular pest that afflicts one depends to a large degree upon where one gardens. The penthouse gardener is unlikely to suffer from the depredations of deer or porcupines, but cats, coming suddenly upon soft soil in which to establish sanitary facilities, will go out of their minds with joy. And English sparrows and starlings, no particular problem in the country, look upon young green sprouts on a rooftop as the Israelites beheld manna falling from heaven.

Although their gardens are bounded by paved roads and fences, suburbanites have long known that rabbits—supposedly inhabitants of a more rural scene—can clean out a row of lettuce overnight. They know, too, that rabbits are happy to build nests in which to raise more rabbits in gardens enclosed by houses on three sides and a railroad track on the fourth. And in recent years, raccoons have discovered that garbage in suburban refuse cans is just as tasty as that to be found in the country, and there is more of it.

Where I live, there is no pest on two, four, or any other number of legs that is is not waiting in the wings ready to assault whatever I grow. I have been able to keep deer out of my kitchen garden only by surrounding it with a six-foot-high pig-mesh fence, the interest on which investment probably exceeds the annual value of the produce it protects, but even this does not deter the coons. To a coon, six feet of wire fence is merely a jungle gym upon which it can work up an appetite before raiding the corn.

Last summer we stretched an electrically charged wire, the sort that is used to keep cows in a pasture, along the top of the fence. Were our raiders dismayed? I'll say not. In fact, I think they enjoyed being tickled. We then strung three more strands around the corn patch itself, which proved equally ineffective. Finally, we hung lighted oil lanterns on posts at the end of the rows. This did puzzle them for a few days, but then I think they figured we were just being considerate and lighting the night for them. We gave up and decided we would advise our guests (who are used to enjoying our frozen corn in midwinter) that, as the seedsmen often say, we had suffered a crop failure.

The only way I know to beat coons, and this goes for woodchucks too, is with a gun. The trouble with this method is that coons are nocturnal and groundhogs (woodchucks) are very early risers. Besides, in suburban areas, though not around here, the blast of a shotgun in the dark of night, or in the first faint light of dawning day, will bring all the police cars within five miles screaming into the neighborhood.

I merely mention this *en passant* because in the country, or in this part of Maine anyway, the sound of a gun or rifle between sunset and dawn just indicates that someone is jacking deer. Most of us never investigate such sounds of warfare. Who knows? One might run across a friend. Every time I hear a rifle shot I associate it with an unknown benefactor who is defending that part of my garden that is not fenced.

Porcupines can climb down fences, though they seldom do. They can climb up a forty-foot spruce with the greatest ease, and about the only way they can be prevented from completely killing a tree once they have started on it is by banding it with a three-foot strip of steel or aluminum. A couple of years ago porcupines decided they enjoyed a yellow willow near my barn, and before I took notice of what they were up to they had ripped it to pieces. After I banded it a branch still lived, a testament to the hold on life inherent in a willow, but it looks like something out of a picture of Belleau Wood or Guadalcanal.

If your garden is where porcupines can raid it, they will keep it as bare as the Sahara. I once knew a lady, a schoolteacher, who devoted most of her summers to internecine warfare with porcupines. It is said that the female is more deadly than the male, and if an example were needed she would provide it. After school closed each year Elizabeth came to her family farm in Maine, where she spent her summers. In the fullness of time small green things sprouted and grew, for Elizabeth was a first-rate gardener. But unhappily, and concurrently, porcupines appeared out of the woods.

It was a far stretch from the woods to the garden. Our pedagogue spent her summers, or most of them, on her back porch reading, knitting, drinking tea, and, because she was an ardent fisherwoman, thinking about the bass that had eluded her that morning but that she was sure she would catch for supper that night. During all of these sedentary musings she kept by her side a good, stout, battle-scarred two-by-three with one end whittled down to form a smooth handle for her delicate, schoolteacherly hand. She never wore shoes during the summer, perhaps because Diana is usually portrayed with her toes sticking out of sandals.

As soon as she noticed a "porky" emerge from the woods, she would keep him under strict surveillance until he had reached a point of no return in his journey toward the cabbage patch. At that moment, at that precise moment, she would light out, barefoot, skirts billowing behind her like those of a pioneer woman chasing an Indian who has stolen her child. Brandishing her club, she cut off the porky's retreat to the woods.

A porcupine's defense lies in its quills. It locomotes at about the same speed as a drunken man and with approximately the same gait. It is not built for speed. Elizabeth would stand, terrible in her wrath, and wait; when her prickly prey came in range she would fetch him a smart crack on the nose with her club, turn him over, and with her sharp little paring knife extract his liver and cut off his feet. The liver she ate, and the feet she delivered to the game warden to collect the porcupine bounty.

I don't know how many she disposed of during the course of a summer, but it must have been considerable. Come to think of it, perhaps her reason for going barefoot was to show her contempt for her victim. So far as I know, she never stepped on a quill and she was careful to stay out of range of the tail, which is what a porcupine will smite you (or your dog) with if you venture too close. Sadly for fiction, they cannot "shoot" their quills, which for those of us who inhabit their territory is just as well.

Not being geared to pursuing porcupines in my bare feet, I keep a .22 close at hand. When anyone sees a porky heading toward the garden he yells "Mark!" and I head off in a long reach to starboard and then come about on the other tack to head him off. When he is so close I can see the whites of his eyes, I shoot between them. If the bullet strikes a glancing blow from a distance, the porky's quills will deflect it, and you will have wasted your ammunition.

But I have forgotten the coons. A friend who had been having coon trouble (they had murdered twenty ducks he was keeping safely—he thought—in a pen) told me that the way to solve my problem was to buy a Havahart trap. Bait it, he said, with stinking fish or any old garbage, set it, and in the morning you will have caught something. He was quite right, but the difficulty is that what you catch may not be what you are setting your cap for.

There are other vagrants abroad at night besides coons. Sooner or later you are bound to find your neighbor's cat—or your own, if you have one—a prisoner. The cat will be indignant, but it won't have learned a thing. You are going to have to tally "cat" on your scoreboard regularly, unless or until the cat mysteriously disappears. Sometimes you will find larger game, say a skunk or a woodchuck, or even the coon you have been hoping for. The woodchucks and coons you can dispose of as your conscience allows. (My friend heaves them, trap and all, on the end of a line into the deepest part of his pond; when there are no more bubbles there is no more coon.) But a skunk is a different matter. Skunks present a problem that I have never been able to cope with. It has been my fixed habit to treat *Mephitis mephitis* with considerable respect. I suggest you turn the job over to someone lower on the ladder of seniority.

If you find it difficult to execute these night raiders as a matter of principle, lug them off and turn them loose where they can gorge themselves on someone else's garden, which they will ultimately do even if you think you have found a nice "woodsy" spot for them. They don't enjoy eating spruce trees and skunk cabbage any more than we do.

I must confess that I find it difficult to understand the logic of those who weep over a dead raccoon but employ paid assassins to work in the Chicago stock yards so that they can order "a sirloin, very rare, please," or enjoy the smell of a portion of dead pig roasting in the oven. Well, each to his own. Pork and beans are pretty tasty too, but if you want any beans next winter you had better keep the woodchucks out of your bean patch.

[*A Countryman's Bed-Book* (1987)]

Ann Lovejoy
Slug Boots
The Northwest's Answer to Pesticides

I recently read a delightful account of gardening in the Deep South in which the wise gardener never set foot into the garden patch without the protection of a sturdy pair of snake boots. Where snakes are plentiful, irritable and poisonous, it clearly pays to have half an inch of shoe leather between you and those curving fangs. Not only is your calf covered, you have a fairly deadly weapon of your own, right at foot. When deadly snakes rear their ugly little heads, you simply stomp them to belt material. Now, here in the Northwest, venomous snakes are not everyday fare, but another sinister and slimy character lurks beneath every leaf, waiting to attack the unsuspecting gardener. Anybody who has ever stepped barefoot on a large and squashy slug will immediately see both the charm and the application of this concept. Slug Boots. I like it.

Northwesterners would do well to emulate this custom, modified to the peculiar rigors and pests of our climate. To be really practical, slug boots must not be made of leather, which is unimproved by constant immersion in water, but of sleek, shining, supple, and sensuous plastic. The pair I finally settled on are fire engine red, with a determined little heel and a nicely patterned tread— not too deep, or it would defeat the whole purpose. Those slithery little buggers would curl up and hide in a deep tread. They are very sneaky, and very determined. Many people don't know just how serious a pest they can be. The day we found one exploring the depths of our Melitta coffeepot was the day I realized the extent of the problem. We all read the newspaper article about the electrical blackout up in Lakewood. A whole community lost its power thanks to the slime-trail of an errant slug making its leisurely way across a circuit board. We read it and chuckled; electricity, big deal. But nobody messes with my coffeepot. I got out those slug boots, tromped on that slug, and a few more I found lying around, and I was sold. You do need that tread, though, since the little suckers are slippery. I soon got into the rhythm, something like clog dancing, and have been practicing assiduously ever since.

Now, we don't stoop to using much poison around here, since that would be politically and environmentally incorrect, but any of the widely available baits based on metaldehyde are acceptable, especially for those who simply can't dance. It attracts with the powerful allure of a blend of bran (which slugs find irresistible) and an alcohol analog that is fatally intoxicating. It is well known that slugs love to party; just leave a beer bottle in the garden overnight if you want proof. Set it on its side near the infant lettuce, with a tablespoon or so of beer left in it (any more would be a waste of B-vitamin complex). You are sure to find half a dozen crocked and reeling gastropods whooping it up in there in the morning. In my book, slugs are born to die anyway; surely this is an essentially thoughtful and gracious way to usher them out of this world?

If all this grisly death talk is too painful, you can simply speed slugs on their merry way, getting them out of your garden, but not necessarily all the way into slug heaven in one swoop. Just scoop one up, loosen up the old throwing arm and let fly. Slugs are great travelers, and any sensible one would quickly decide to skip the return trip to your yard, given such treatment. If you can't bear the idea of handling slugs, take advantage of a natural and symbiotic partnership; pick them up with a mollusk. It is not widely known that snails and slugs are mutually adhesive, but such is the case. Many squeamish souls who would sooner lose their lettuce than touch a slimy creature can toss a snail over the fence without much trouble. Next time you do this, look around for a baby slug, moosh it with the sticky part of your snail, and wish them bon voyage.

Since slugs are migratory, it isn't enough to empty the yard once a year. More will creep over the border at night, eluding the most vigilant patrols, to sup well at your salad bar before moving on. Snails have a less restless spirit. They are little homebodies;

when they find a cozy place to sleep, in the crown of your favorite
daylily, nestled among the agapanthus, or snuggled deep into the
heart of a bulb, they develop a fondness for it and are very apt to
return there day after day. You can take advantage of this habit by
leaving a few bricks or boards around on the garden paths. Before
too long, such spots become social centers, and you in your slug
boots are the star turn.

There are a number of patented little fences and barriers which
purport to be slug-proof, but nothing is really proof against the
depredations of this slippery little character except the full weight
of your disapproval. Actually, there are a few good tricks to try,
other than the above-mentioned commercial bait, the most environmentally acceptable one around. Diatomaceous earth, generously sprinkled around the plants you want to keep, can keep those
howling and snapping slugs at bay. It is particularly useful if pets
or kids seem interested in the metaldehyde bait. (Both are fascinated
by those little green plastic huts in which the bait is supposed to
be protected from rain, which makes them more dangerous than
useful.) The diatomaceous earth is made of the crushed exoskeletons
of diatoms, tiny fossilized critters that are as brittle and sharp-edged
as glass when pulverized. Harmless to humans and pets, the stuff
punctures slugs and snails with hundreds of pinpricks as they crawl
through it. That causes them to leak out all their innards, which is
fairly final. It is, however, expensive.

An acquaintance of the family has earned his doctorate studying
the ecology of banana slugs, and he has shown us a series of pictures
which are really quite endearing. In them, a saucer of milk is set
down, and one by one, the slugs approach, bending their little horns
curiously, tasting the milk, at first cautiously, then avidly dipping
in to the dish. The final shot of a whole tiny herd of slugs slurping
is absolutely cute. A gardening friend recounts a fascinating tale of
the courtship and mating ritual of slugs, as she observed it one fine
day. Apparently as slugs merge, a clear and crystalline droplet forms,
dangling on a long thread and spreading slowly into a scalloped,
pulsating sac. As the embrace is completed, the bag of living water
is drawn up and reabsorbed. The process is lengthy, and as our
friend describes it, lovely and moving, almost lyrical. Perhaps we
ought to reconsider, make room in our hearts for these little creatures, defenseless and guileless.

Well, maybe. But when I see another crop of promising seedlings mown down wholesale, a brand-new and long-awaited plant
gnawed to the bare and quivering roots, the glossy new leaves of
my miniature hostas tattered and ragged, I give no quarter. Let
them eat metaldehyde! After all, it's not as if slugs are an endangered
species. I do make a few concessions; I don't bait routinely, just
when seedlings are rowed out, when seeds are sown, or when fragile
treasures are transplanted. However, when I uncover a nest of
gastropod eggs, round and shimmering like tiny pearls, those future
sluglets and snailings go straight under the fierce little heels of my
slug boots.

[*The Year in Bloom* (1987)]

LAWNS... OR
ENCLOSED GARDENS?

Andrew Jackson Downing
On Lawns

November, 1846

Landscape gardening embraces, in the circle of its perfections, many *elements* of beauty; certainly not a less number than the modern chemists count as the simplest conditions of matter. But with something of the feeling of the old philosophers, who believed that earth, air, fire and water, included every thing in nature, we like to go back to plain and simple facts, of breadth and importance enough to embrace a multitude of little details. The great elements then, of landscape gardening, as we understand it, are TREES and GRASS.

TREES—delicate, beautiful, grand, or majestic trees—pliantly answering to the wooing of the softest west wind, like the willow; or bravely and sturdily defying centuries of storm and tempest, like the oak—they are indeed the great "princes, potentates, and people," of our realm of beauty. But it is not to-day that we are permitted to sing triumphal songs in their praise.

In behalf of the grass—the turf, the lawn,—then, we ask our readers to listen to us for a short time. And by this we do not mean to speak of it in a moral sense, as did the inspired preacher of old, when he gravely told us that "all flesh is grass"; or in a style savoring of the vanities of costume, as did Prior, when he wrote the couplet,

> *Those limbs in* lawn *and softest silk arrayed,*
> *From sunbeams guarded, and of winds afraid.*

Or with the keen relish of the English jockey, whose only idea of "the turf," is that of the place nature has specially provided him upon which to race horses.

[315]

Neither do we look upon grass, at the present moment, with the eyes of our friend Tom Thrifty, the farmer, who cuts "three tons to the acre." We have, in our present mood, no patience with the tall and gigantic *fodder*, by this name, that grows in the fertile bottoms of the West, so tall that the largest Durham is lost to view while walking through it.

No—we love most the soft turf which, beneath the flickering shadows of scattered trees, is thrown like a smooth natural carpet over the swelling outline of the smiling earth. Grass, not grown into tall meadows, or wild bog tussocks, but softened and refined by the frequent touches of the patient mower, till at last it becomes a perfect wonder of tufted freshness and verdure. Such grass, in short, as Shakespeare had in his mind, when he said, in words since echoed ten thousand times,

> *How sweet the moonlight sleeps upon that bank;*

or Ariosto, in his Orlando—

> *The approaching night, not knowing where to pass,*
> *She checks her reins, and on the* velvet grass,
> *Beneath the umbrageous trees, her form she throws,*
> *To cheat the tedious hours with brief repose.*

In short the ideal of grass is a *lawn*, which is, to a meadow, what "Bishop's lawn" is to homespun Irish linen.

With such a lawn, and large and massive trees, one has indeed the most enduring sources of beauty in a country residence. Perpetual neatness, freshness and verdure in the one; ever expanding beauty, variety and grandeur in the other—what more does a reasonable man desire of the beautiful about him in the country? Must we add flowers, exotic plants, fruits? Perhaps so, but they are all, in an ornamental light, secondary to trees and grass, where these can be had in perfection. Only one other grand element is needed to make our landscape garden complete—*water*. A river, or a lake, in which the skies and the "tufted trees" may see themselves reflected, is ever an indispensable feature to a perfect landscape.

[*Rural Essays* (1854)]

Frank J. Scott
The Lawn

Whether we look, or whether we listen
We hear life murmur, or see it glisten;
Every clod feels a stir of might,
   An instinct within it that reaches and towers,
And, groping blindly above it for light,
   Climbs to a soul in grass and flowers.
   —JAMES RUSSELL LOWELL

On each side shrinks the bowery shade,
Before me spreads an emerald glade;
The sunshine steeps its grass and moss,
That couch my footsteps as I cross.
   —ALFRED B. STREET

A smooth, closely shaven surface of grass is by far the most essential element of beauty on the grounds of a suburban house. Dwellings, all the rooms of which may be filled with elegant furniture, but with rough uncarpeted floors, are no more incongruous, or in ruder taste, than the shrub and tree and flower-sprinkled yards of most home-grounds, where shrubs and flowers mingle in confusion with tall grass, or ill-defined borders of cultivated ground. Neatness and order are as essential to the pleasing effect of ground furniture as of house furniture. No matter how elegant or appropriate the latter may be, it will never look well in the home of a slattern. And however choice the variety of shrubs and flowers, if they occupy the ground so that there is no pleasant expanse of close-cut grass to relieve them, they cannot make a pretty place. The long grass allowed to grow in town and suburban grounds, after the spring gardening fever is over, neutralizes to a certain degree all attempts of the lady or gentleman of the house to beautify them, though they spend ever so much in obtaining the best shrubs, trees, or flowers the neighbors or the nurseries can furnish. It is not necessary to have an acre of pleasure-ground to secure a charming lawn. Its extent may always be proportioned to the size of the place; and if the selection of flowers and shrubs and their arrangement is properly made, it is surprising how small a lawn will realize some of the most pleasing effects of larger ones. A strip twenty feet wide and a hundred feet long may be rendered, proportionately, as artistic as the landscape vistas of a park.

And it needs but little more to have room to realize by art, and with shadowing trees, the sparkling picture that the poet Alfred B. Street thus presents in his "Forest Walk."

> *A narrow vista, carpeted*
> *With rich green grass, invites me tread;*
> *Here showers the light in golden dots,*
> *There sleeps the shade in ebon spots,*
> *So blended that the very air*
> *Seems net-work as I enter there.*

[*The Art of Beautifying Suburban Home Grounds* (1870)]

Frank J. Scott
Relative Beauty of Lawn, Trees, Shrubs, and Flowers

The true lover of nature is so omnivorous in his tastes, that for him to classify her family into different grades of usefulness or beauty, is about as difficult a task as to name which of her vegetable productions is the best food. But though a variety is better than any one, there is, in both cases, strong ground for a decided choice; and we repeat what has already been suggested, that, of all the external decorations of a home, a well kept LAWN is the most essential. Imagine the finest trees environing a dwelling, but everywhere beneath them only bare ground: then picture the same dwelling with a velvet greensward spreading away from it on all sides, without a tree or shrub upon it, and choose which is the most pleasing to the eye. The question of value is not to be considered, but simply which, in connection with the dwelling, will make the most satisfactory impression on the mind. The fine trees are vastly the more valuable, because it requires half a life time to obtain them, while the lawn may be perfected in two or three years.

The comparative value of trees and shrubs depends much on the extent of the ground and the taste of the occupants. If the lot is small, and the family has a decided appreciation of the varied characteristics of different shrubs, they will have much more pleasure from a fine collection of them than from the few trees which their lot could accommodate. But if the occupants are not particularly appreciative of the varied beauties of smaller vegetation, then a few trees and a good lawn only, will be more appropriate for their home. Larger lots can have both, but the foregoing consideration may govern the preponderance of one or the other. When once the planting fever is awakened, *too many of both are likely to be planted*, and grounds will be stuffed rather than beautified.

One full grown oak, elm, maple, chestnut, beech, or sycamore will cover with its branches nearly a quarter of an acre. Allowing seventy feet square for the spread of each tree (all the above varieties being occasionally much larger), nine such trees would completely cover an acre. But as we plant for ourselves, instead of for our children, it will be sufficient in most suburban planting to allow for half-grown, rather than full-grown trees. Grounds, however, which are blessed with grand old trees should have them cherished lovingly—they are treasures that money cannot buy—and should be guarded with jealous care against the admission of little evergreens and nursery trees, which new planters are apt to huddle under and around them, to the entire destruction of the broad stretches of lawn which large trees require in order to reveal the changing beauty of their shadows. Where such trees exist, if you would make the most of the ground, lavish your care in enriching the soil over their vast roots, and perfecting the lawn around them; and then arrange for shrubs and flowers away from their mid-day shadows. Even fine old fruit trees, if standing well apart on a lawn, will often give a dignity and a comfortable home-look to a place that is wanting in places which are surrounded only with new plantings.

But it is an unfortunate fact that nine-tenths of all the town and suburban lots built on are bare of trees, and therefore, after the attainment of a fine lawn, the lowly beauties of shrubs and flowers, with all their varied luxuriance of foliage and fragrant bloom, must be the main features of the place, while the trees are also growing in their midst which may eventually over-top and supersede them. If one could imagine Americans to live their married lives, each pair in one home, what a pleasing variety might the changing years bring them. An unbroken lawn around the dwelling should typify the unwritten page in the opening book of earnest life. Young trees planted here and there upon it would suggest looking forward to the time when, under their grand shadows, the declining years of the twain may be spent in dignity and repose. Flowers and shrubs meanwhile repay with grateful beauty all their care, until, overshadowed by the nobler growth, they are removed as cumberers of the ground, and give way to the simplicity that becomes "a fine old home."

Most small places can be much more charmingly planted with shrubs alone, than with trees and shrubs mingled. Indeed, it is one of the greatest blunders of inexperienced planters to put in trees where there is only room enough for shrubs. A small yard may be made quite attractive by the artistic management of shrubs and flowers whose size is adapted to the contracted ground; but the same place would be so filled up by the planting of a cherry tree or a horse-chestnut, that no such effect could be produced.

Where the decorative portion of the grounds do not exceed a half acre, there can be little question of the superior beauty of shrubberies to the very small collection of trees that such narrow limits can accommodate. The greatly increased beauty of shrubs when seen upon a lawn without any shadowing of trees, nor crowded one side or another "to fill-up," can only be appreciated by those who have seen the elegance of a tastefully arranged place planted with shrubs alone.

The part which annuals and low growing flowers should have in home surroundings may be compared with the lace, linen, and ribbon decorations of a lady's dress—being essential ornaments, and yet to be introduced sparingly. Walks may be bordered, and groups pointed, and bays in the shrubbery brightened by them; or geometrically arranged groups of flower-beds may be introduced in the foreground of important window views; but beware of frequently breaking open stretches of lawn for them. Imagine bits of lace or bows of ribbon stuck promiscuously over the body and skirt of a lady's dress. "How vulgar!" you exclaim. Put them in their appropriate places and what charming points they make! Let your lawn be your home's velvet robe, and your flowers its not too promiscuous decorations.

[*The Art of Beautifying Suburban Home Grounds* (1870)]

Frank J. Scott
Neighboring Improvements

Small is the worth of beauty from the light retired.
—TENNYSON

There is no way in which men deprive themselves of what costs them nothing and profits them much, more than by dividing their improved grounds from their neighbors, and from the view of passers on the road, by fences and hedges. The beauty obtained by throwing front grounds open together, is of that excellent quality which enriches all who take part in the exchange, and makes no man poorer. As a merely business matter it is simply stupid to shut out, voluntarily, a pleasant lookout through a neighbor's ornamental grounds. If, on the other hand, such opportunities are improved, and made the most of, no gentleman would hesitate to make return for the privilege by arranging his own ground so as to give the neighbor equally pleasing vistas into or across it. It is unchristian to hedge from the sight of others the beauties of nature which it has been our good fortune to create or secure; and all the walls, high fences, hedge screens and belts of trees and shrubbery *which are used for that purpose only*, are so many means by which we show how unchristian and unneighborly we can be. It is true these things are not usually done in any mere spirit of selfishness: they are the conventional forms of planting that come down to us from feudal times, or that were necessary in gardens near cities, and in close proximity to populous neighborhoods with rude improvements and ruder people. It is a peculiarity of English gardens, which it is as unfortunate to follow as it would be to imitate the surly self-assertion of English travelling-manners. An English garden is "a love of a place" to get into, and an Englishman's heart is warm and hospitable at his own fire-side; but these facts do not make it less uncivil to bristle in strangers' company, or to wall and hedge a lovely garden against the longing eyes of the outside world. To hedge out deformities is well; but to narrow our own or our neighbor's views of the free graces of Nature by our own volition, is quite another thing. We have seen high arbor-vitæ hedges between the decorated front grounds of members of the same family, each of whose places was well kept, and necessary to complete the beauty of the other and to secure to both extensive prospects! It seems as if such persons wish to advertise to every passer, "my lot begins here, sir, and ends there, sir," and might be unhappy if the dividing lines were not accurately known. "High fences make good neighbors," is a saying often repeated by persons about walling themselves in. The saying has some foundation in fact. Vinegar and soda, both good in their way, are better kept in separate vessels. If a man believes himself and his family to be bad neighbors, certainly they ought to fence themselves in, thoroughly. Or if they have reason to believe their neighbors are of the same sort, they may well be sure of the height and strength of the divisions between them. But we prefer to imagine the case reversed; and that our neighbors are kindly gentlemen and women, with well-bred families, who can enjoy the views across others' grounds without trespassing upon them. These remarks are intended to apply to those decorative portions of home-grounds which, in this country, and especially in suburban neighborhoods, are usually in front of the domestic offices of the house. The latter must necessarily be made private and distinct from each other. One of the most fertile sources of disagreements between families having grounds opening together, are incursions of boisterous children from one to another. Now it is suggested that children may be trained to respect and stop at a thread drawn across a lawn to represent a boundary, just as well as at a stone wall. Every strong high barrier challenges a spirited boy's opposition and enterprise, but what costs no courage or strength to pass, and a consciousness of being where he don't belong, generally makes him ashamed to transgress in such directions. A well-defined line will, in most cases, be all that is necessary. This may be simply a sunk line in the grass [. . .] or it may be a row of low, small cedar or iron posts, with a chain or wires running from one to another, or some very low, open, and light design of woven-wire fencing; anything, in short, which will leave the eye an unbroken range of view, and still say to the children, "thus far shalt thou go, and no farther." If parents on both sides of the line do their duty in instructing the children not to trespass on contiguous lawns, less trouble will result from that cause than from the bad feelings engendered by high outside boundary walls, that so often become convenient shields to hide unclean rubbish and to foster weeds.

An interesting result, that may be reached by joining neighboring improvements, is in equalizing the beauties of old and new places. Suppose B. has bought an open lot between A. and C., who have old places. The grounds of A., we will suppose, are filled, in old village style, with big cherry trees, maples, lilacs, spruce trees, roses, and annuals; and C.'s grounds may have a growth of noble old trees, which had invited a house to make its home there. Between the two is Mr. B.'s bare lot, on which he builds a "modern house," which is, of course, the envy of the older places. But Mr. B. and his family sigh for the old forest trees on the right, and the flowers, and verdure, and fruit trees on the left. Not having them to begin with, we advise him to make a virtue of necessity, and cause his neighbors to envy him the superior openness and polish of his own grounds. A. has a yard cluttered with the valuable accumulations of years; a fine variety of trees, shrubs, and flowers; yet nothing shows to advantage. The shade, the multiplicity of bushes, the general intertanglement of all, make it very difficult to grow a close turf, and keep it mown as a lawn. Mr. B., on the other hand, can begin, as soon as his ground is enriched and set to grass, to perfect it by constant cutting and rolling till it is a sheet of green velvet. Cut in the lawn, here and there near his walks, small beds for low and brilliant flowers may sparkle with sunny gayety; at the intersection of walks, or flanking or fronting the entrances, low broad-top vases (rustic or classic, as the character of the house or their position may require) may be placed, filled with a variety of graceful and brilliant plants. In two or three years, if Mr. B. shall thus have made the most of his open ground, ten chances to one both of the neighbors will be envying the superior beauty of the new place. It will, probably, really be the most charming of the three; not, however, by virtue of its open lawn alone, but by the contrast which his neighbor's crowded yard on one side, and the forest trees on the other, serve to produce. Each of their places forms a back-ground for his lawn; while, if the three places are allowed to open together, his lawn is a charming outlook from the shades of theirs. *Neither one of these places would, alone, make landscape beauty; yet the three may make charming combinations from every point of view.*

[*The Art of Beautifying Suburban Home Grounds* (1870)]

Donald Mitchell
On Gateways

I have often wondered why the professional writers on landscape gardening have so little to say of gateways. Among the more pretentious authors of this class I find sketches of gate-lodges, very charming in their details, many of them; but I find little or no mention of those modest gates which must hang at every man's door-yard—those unpretending swinging barriers, by which every country house-holder is shut off from the world, and by which he is joined to the world. They may be made to give a good deal of expression to a place; they have almost as much to do with it, in fact, as a man's mouth has to do with the expression of his face.

There was once a gate called "Beautiful," by which a lame man lay—we all remember that; there was once too a certain "wicket-gate" (with a great light shining somewhere beyond it) which Evangelist pointed out to Christian, whereby the pilgrim might enter upon the path to the Celestial City—we all remember that gate; and there was another gate, belonging to our days of roundabouts and satchels, by which we went out, noon and morning, by which we returned, noon and evening—on which we swung upon stolen occasions—a gate whereat we loitered with other philosophers, in other roundabouts and with other green satchels, and discussed problems of marbles, or base-ball, or of the weather,—a gate through which led the path to the first home; well, I think everybody remembers such a gate. And thus it happens that the subject has a certain poetic and romantic interest which cannot be wholly ignored, and which I wonder that the landscapists have so indifferently treated.

Fancy, if you can, a rural home,—without its gateway—lying

all abroad upon a common! The great charm of privacy is gone utterly; and no device of shrubbery, or hedge, can make good the loss of some little wicket which will invite approach, and be a barrier against too easy familiarity. The creak of the gate-hinge is a welcome to the visitor, and as he goes out, the latch clicks an adieu.

But there are all sorts of gates, as there are all sorts of welcomes; there is, first, your inhospitable one, made mostly, I should say, of matched boards, with a row of pleasant iron spikes running along its top, and no architectural decorations of pilaster or panel can possibly remove its thoroughly inhospitable aspect. It belongs to stable-courts or jail-yards, but never to a home or to a garden.

Again, there are your ceremonious gates, of openwork indeed, but ponderous, and most times scrupulously closed; the very open-ing of them is a fatiguing ceremonial, and there is nothing like a lively welcome in the dull clang of their ponderous latches.

Next, there is your simple, unpretending, rural gate, giving promise of unpretending rural beauties—homely in all its aspect, and giving foretaste of the best of homeliness within. And I make a wide distinction here between the simple rurality at which I have hinted, and that grotesqueness which is compassed by scores of crooked limbs and knots wrought into labyrinthine patterns, which puzzle the eye, more than they please. All crooked things are not necessarily charming, and the better kind of homeliness is measured by something besides mere roughness.

Lastly, there is your hospitable gate, with its little rooflet stretched over it, as if to invite the stranger loiterer to partake at his will of that much of the hospitalities of the home. Even the passing beggar gathers his tattered garments under it in a sudden shower and blesses the shelter. [. . .] Yet who does not see written all over it—plain as it is: Loiter if you like! Come in, if you like! And I love to think that some little maid, under it—in some by-gone year—said her good-night to some parting Leander. Who shall laugh at this, that has ever been young? Are not the little maids and the Leanders always growing up about us? I always felt sure when I found such covered wickets that no curmudgeon lived within.

[*Rural Studies* (1897)]

Alice Morse Earle
Front Dooryards

There are few of us who cannot remember
a front yard garden which seemed to us a
very paradise in childhood. Whether the
house was a fine one, and the enclosure
spacious, or whether it was a small house
with only a narrow bit of ground in front,
the yard was kept with care, and was
different from the rest of the land alto-
gether . . . People do not know what they
lose when they make way with the reserve,
the separateness, the sanctity of the front
yard of their grandmothers. It is like writ-
ing down family secrets for anyone to read;
it is like having everybody call you by your
first name, or sit in any pew in church.

—SARAH ORNE JEWETT
Country Byways, 1881

Old New England villages and small towns and well-kept New England farms had universally a simple and pleasing form of garden called the front dooryard. A few still may be seen in conservative communities in the New England states and in New York or Pennsylvania. I saw flourishing ones this summer in Gloucester, Marblehead, and Ipswich. Even where the front yard was but a narrow strip of land before a tiny cottage, it was carefully fenced in, with a gate that was kept rigidly closed and latched. There seemed to be a law which shaped and bounded the front yard; the side fences extended from the corners of the house to the front fence on the edge of the road, and thus formed naturally the guarded parallelogram. Often the fence around the front yard was the only one on the farm; everywhere else were boundaries of great stone walls; or if there were rail fences, the front yard fence was the only painted one. I cannot doubt that the first gardens that our foremothers had, which were wholly of flowering plants, were front yards, little enclosures hard won from the forest.

The word yard, not generally applied now to any enclosure of elegant cultivation, comes from the same root as the word garden. Garth is another derivative, and the word exists much disguised in orchard. In the sixteenth century yard was used in formal literature instead of garden; and later Burns writes of "Eden's bonnie yard, Where yeuthful lovers first were pair'd."

This front yard was an English fashion derived from the forecourt so strongly advised by Gervayse Markham (an interesting old English writer on floriculture and husbandry), and found in front of many a yeoman's house, and many a more pretentious house as well in Markham's day. Forecourts were common in England until the middle of the eighteenth century, and may still be seen. The forecourt gave privacy to the house even when in the centre of a town. Its readoption is advised with handsome dwellings in England, where ground-space is limited,—and why not in America, too?

The front yard was sacred to the best beloved, or at any rate the most honored, garden flowers of the house mistress, and was preserved by its fences from inroads of cattle, which then wandered at their will and were not housed, or even enclosed at night. The flowers were often of scant variety, but were those deemed the gentlefolk of the flower world. There was a clump of Daffodils and of the Poet's Narcissus in early spring, and stately Crown Imperial; usually, too, a few scarlet and yellow single Tulips, and Grape Hyacinths. Later came Phlox in abundance—the only native American plant,—Canterbury Bells, and ample and glowing London Pride. Of course there were great plants of white and blue Day Lilies, with their beautiful and decorative leaves, and purple and yellow Flower de Luce. A few old-fashioned shrubs always were seen. By inflexible law there must be a Lilac, which might be the aristocratic Persian Lilac. A Syringa, a flowering Currant, or Strawberry bush made sweet the front yard in spring, and sent wafts of fragrance into the house-windows. Spindling, rusty Snowberry bushes were by the gate, and Snowballs also, or our native Viburnums. Old as they seem, the Spiræas and Deutzias came to us in the nineteenth century from Japan; as did the flowering Quinces and Cherries. The pink flowering Almond dates back to the oldest front yards, and Peter's Wreath certainly seems an old settler and is found now in many front yards that remain.

The glory of the front yard was the old-fashioned early red "Piny," cultivated since the days of Pliny. I hear people speaking of it with contempt as a vulgar flower,—flaunting is the conventional derogatory adjective,—but I glory in its flaunting. The modern varieties, of every tint from white through flesh color, coral, pink, ruby color, salmon, and even yellow, to deep red, are as beautiful as Roses. Some are sweet-scented; and they have no thorns, and their foliage is ever perfect, so I am sure the Rose is jealous. [. . .]

I am pleased to note of the common flowers of the New England front yard, that they are no new things; they are nearly all Elizabethan of date—many are older still. Lord Bacon in his essay on gardens names many of them. Crocus, Tulip, Hyacinth, Daffodil, Flower de Luce, double Peony, Lilac, Lily of the Valley.

A favorite flower was the yellow garden Lily, the Lemon Lily, *Hemerocallis*, when it could be kept from spreading. Often its unbounded luxuriance exiled it from the front yard to the kitchen dooryard. Its pretty old-fashioned name was Liricon-fancy, given, I am told, in England to the Lily of the Valley. I know no more satisfying sight than a good bank of these Lemon Lilies in full flower. Below Flatbush there used to be a driveway leading to an old Dutch house, set at regular intervals with great clumps of Lemon Lilies, and their full bloom made them glorious.

The time of fullest inflorescence of the nineteenth century front yard was when Phlox and Tiger Lilies bloomed; but the pinkish-orange colors of the latter (the oddest reds of any flower tints) blended most vilely and rampantly with the crimson-purple of the Phlox; and when London Pride joined with its glowing scarlet, the front yard fairly ached. Nevertheless, an adaptation of that front-yard bloom can be most effective in a garden border, when white Phlox only is planted, and the Tiger Lily or cultivated stalks of our wild nodding Lily rise above the white trusses of bloom. These wild Lilies grow very luxuriantly in the garden, often towering above our heads and forming great candelabra bearing two score or more blooms. It is no easy task to secure their deep-rooted rhizomes in the meadow. I know a young man who won his sweetheart by the patience and assiduity with which he dug for her all one broiling morning to secure for her the coveted Lily roots, and collapsed with mild sunstroke at the finish. Her gratitude and remorse were equal factors in his favor.

The Tiger Lily is usually thought upon as a truly old-fashioned flower, a veritable antique; it is a favorite of artists to place as an accessory in their colonial gardens, and of authors for their flower-beds of Revolutionary days, but it was not known either in formal garden or front yard, until after "the days when we lived under the King." The bulbs were first brought to England from Eastern Asia in 1804 by Captain Kirkpatrick of the East India Company's Service, and shared with the Japan Lily the honor of being the first Eastern Lilies introduced into European gardens. A few years ago an old gentleman, Mr. Isaac Pitman, who was then about eighty-five years of age, told me that he recalled distinctly when Tiger Lilies first appeared in our gardens, and where he first saw them growing in Boston. So instead of being an old-time flower, or even an old-comer from the Orient, it is one of the novelties of this century. How readily has it made itself at home, and even wandered wild down our roadsides!

The two simple colors of Phlox of the old-time front yard, white and crimson-purple, are now augmented by tints of salmon, vermilion, and rose. I recall with special pleasure the profuse garden decoration at East Hampton, Long Island, of a pure cherry-colored Phlox, generally a doubtful color to me, but there so associated with the white blooms of various other plants, and backed by a high hedge covered solidly with blossoming Honeysuckle, that it was wonderfully successful.

To other members of the Phlox family, all natives of our own continent, the old front yard owed much; the Moss Pink sometimes crowded out both Grass and its companion the Periwinkle; it is still found in our gardens, and bountifully also in our fields; either in white or pink, it is one of the satisfactions of spring, and its cheerful little blossom is of wonderful use in many waste places. An old-fashioned bloom, the low-growing *Phlox amœna*, with its queerly fuzzy leaves and bright crimson blossoms, was among the most distinctly old-fashioned flowers of the front yard. It was tolerated rather than cultivated, as was its companion, the Arabis or Rock

Cress—both crowding, monopolizing creatures. I remember well how they spread over the beds and up the grass banks in my mother's garden, how sternly they were uprooted, in spite of the pretty name of the Arabis—"Snow in Summer."

Sometimes the front yard path had edgings of sweet single or lightly double white or tinted Pinks, which were not deemed as choice as Box edgings. Frequently large Box plants clipped into simple and natural shapes stood at the side of the doorstep, usually in the home of the well-to-do. A great shell might be on either side of the doorsill, if there chanced to be seafaring men-folk who lived or visited under the roof-tree. Annuals were few in number; sturdy old perennial plants of many years' growth were the most honored dwellers in the front yard, true representatives of old families. The Roses were few and poor, for there was usually some great tree just without the gate, an Elm or Larch, whose shadow fell far too near and heavily for the health of Roses. Sometimes there was a prickly semidouble yellow Rose, called by us a Scotch Rose, a Sweet Brier, or a rusty-flowered white Rose, similar, though inferior, to the Madame Plantier. A new fashion of trellises appeared in the front yard about sixty years ago, and crimson Boursault Roses climbed up them as if by magic.

One marked characteristic of the front yard was its lack of weeds; few sprung up, none came to seed-time; the enclosure was small, and it was a mark of good breeding to care for it well. Sometimes, however, the earth was covered closely under shrubs and plants with the cheerful little Ladies' Delights, and they blossomed in the chinks of the bricked path and under the Box edges. Ambrosia, too, grew everywhere, but these were welcome—they were not weeds.

Our old New England houses were suited in color and outline to their front yards as to our landscape. Lowell has given in verse a good description of the kind of New England house that always had a front dooryard of flowers.

> *On a grass-green swell*
> *That towards the south with sweet concessions fell,*
> *It dwelt retired, and half had grown to be*
> *As aboriginal as rock or tree.*
> *It nestled close to earth, and seemed to brood*

O'er homely thoughts in a half-conscious mood.
If paint it e'er had known, it knew no more
Than yellow lichens spattered thickly o'er
That soft lead gray, less dark beneath the eaves,
Which the slow brush of wind and weather leaves.
The ample roof sloped backward to the ground
And vassal lean-tos gathered thickly round,
Patched on, as sire or son had felt the need.
But the great chimney was the central thought.

* * *

It rose broad-shouldered, kindly, debonair,
Its warm breath whitening in the autumn air.

Sarah Orne Jewett, in the plaint of *A Mournful Villager*, has drawn a beautiful and sympathetic picture of these front yards, and she deplores their passing. I mourn them as I do every fenced-in or hedged-in garden enclosure. The sanctity and reserve of these front yards of our grandmothers was somewhat emblematic of woman's life of that day: it was restricted, and narrowed to a small outlook and monotonous likeness to her neighbor's; but it was a life easily satisfied with small pleasures, and it was comely and sheltered and carefully kept, and pleasant to the home household; and these were no mean things. [. . .]

When the fences disappeared with the night rambles of the cows, the front yards gradually changed character; the tender blooms vanished, but the tall shrubs and the Peonies and Flower de Luce sturdily grew and blossomed, save where that dreary destroyer of a garden crept in—the desire for a lawn. The result was then a meagre expanse of poorly kept grass, with no variety, color, or change,—neither lawn nor front yard. It is ever a pleasure to me when driving in a village street or a country road to find one of these front yards still enclosed, or even to note in front of many houses the traces of a past front yard still plainly visible in the flourishing old-fashioned plants of many years' growth.

[*Old-Time Gardens* (1901)]

Neltje Blanchan
Rudely Exposed to Public Gaze

In an emotional moment of "civic improvement" we were advised to take down our front fences and hedges, throw open our lawns and share with the public all the beauty of our home grounds, or be branded as selfish and undemocratic. The family life that should be lived as much as possible under the open sky, when rudely exposed to public gaze, must become either vulgarly brazen or sensitively shy, in which latter case it withdraws to the vine-enclosed piazza or to the house itself. There is a vast difference between the Englishman's insultingly inhospitable brick wall, topped with broken bottles, and an American's encircling belt of trees around his home grounds, or the tall hedge around his garden room to ensure that privacy without which the perfect freedom of home life is no more possible than if the family living-room were to be set on a public stage. The busy mistress of the house needs every encouragement to run out and work a while among her flowers without feeling that her unfashionable dress and tucked up petticoat are exciting the comment of passers-by. Thanks to the shielding evergreens, the young people may have rough and tumble play on the lawn, the father may feel free to don overalls and paint the garden chairs if the humour seize him, and the entire family, safely sheltered from curious eyes, may frequently enjoy a meal out of doors with perfect freedom and naturalness. The plainest fare has zest when eaten *al fresco*.

[*The American Flower Garden* (1909)]

George Washington Cable
The American Garden

As to manners, our incipient American garden has already developed
one trait which distinguishes it from those beyond the Atlantic. It
is a habit which reminds one of what somebody has lately said about
Americans themselves: that, whoever they are and whatever their
manners may be, they have this to their credit, that they unfailingly
desire and propose to be polite. The thing we are hinting at is our
American gardens' excessive openness. Our people have, or until
just now had, almost abolished the fence and the hedge. A gard,
yard, garth, garden, used to mean an enclosure, a close, and implied
a privacy to its owner superior to any he enjoyed outside of it. But
now that we no longer have any military need of privacy we are
tempted—are we not?—to overlook its spiritual value. We seem to
enjoy publicity better. In our American eagerness to publish everything for everybody and to everybody, we have published our gardens—published them in paper bindings; that is to say, with their
boundaries visible only on maps filed with the Registrar of Deeds.

Foreigners who travel among us complain that we so overdo
our good-natured endurance of every public inconvenience that we
have made it a national misfortune and are losing our sense of our
public rights. This obliteration of private boundaries is an instance.
Our public spirit and our imperturbability are flattered by it, but
our gardens, except among the rich, have become American by
ceasing to be gardens.

I have a neighbor who every year plants a garden of annuals.
He has no fence, but two of his neighbors have each a setter dog.
These dogs are rarely confined. One morning I saw him put in the

seed of his lovely annuals and leave his smoothly raked beds already a pleasant show and a prophecy of delight while yet without a spray of green. An hour later I saw those two setter dogs wrestling and sprawling around in joyous circles all over those garden beds. "Gay, guiltless pair!" What is one to do in such a case, in a land where everybody is expected to take everything good-naturedly, and where a fence is sign of a sour temper? Of course he can do as others do, and have no garden. But to have no garden is a distinct poverty in a householder's life, whether he knows it or not, and—suppose he very much wants a garden?

They were the well-to-do who began this abolition movement against enclosures and I have an idea it never would have had a beginning had there prevailed generally, democratically, among us a sentiment for real gardening, and a knowledge of its practical principles; for with this sentiment and knowledge we should have had that sweet experience of outdoor privacy for lack of which we lose one of the noblest charms of home. The well-to-do started the fashion, it cost less money to follow than to withstand it and presently the landlords of the poor utilized it.

The poor man—the poor woman—needs the protection of a fence to a degree of which the well-to-do know nothing. In the common interest of the whole community, of any community, the poor man—the poor woman—ought to have a garden; but if they are going to have a garden they ought to have a fence. We in Northampton know scores of poor homes whose tenants strive year after year to establish some floral beauty about them, and fail for want of enclosures. The neighbors' children, their dogs, their cats, geese, ducks, hens—it is useless. Many refuse to make the effort; some, I say, make it and give it up, and now and then some one wins a surprising and delightful success. Two or three such have taken high prizes in our competition. The two chief things which made their triumph possible were, first, an invincible passion for gardening, and, second, poultry-netting.

A great new boon to the home gardener they are, these wire fencings and nettings. With them ever so many things may be done now at a quarter or tenth of what they would once have cost. Our old-fashioned fences were sometimes very expensive, sometimes very perishable, sometimes both. Also they were apt to be very ugly. Yet instead of concealing them we made them a display, while

the shrubbery which should have masked them in leaf and bloom
stood scattered over the lawn, each little new bush by itself, visibly
if not audibly saying—

You'd scarce expect one of my age—

etc.; the shrubs orphaned, the lawn destroyed.

If the enclosure was a hedge it had to be a tight one or else it
did not enclose. Now wire netting charms away these embarrass-
ments. Your hedge can be as loose as you care to have it, while
your enclosure may be rigidly effective yet be hidden from the eye
by undulating fence-rows; and as we now have definite bounds and
corners to plant out, we do not so often as formerly need to be
reminded of Frederick Law Olmsted's favorite maxim, "Take care
of the corners, and the centres will take care of themselves."

Here there is a word to be added in the interest of home-lovers,
whose tastes we properly expect to find more highly trained than
those of the average tenant cottager. Our American love of spaciousness leads us to fancy that—not to-day or to-morrow, but somewhere in a near future—we are going to unite our unfenced lawns
in a concerted park treatment: a sort of wee horticultural United
States comprised within a few city squares; but ever our American
individualism stands broadly in the way, and our gardens almost
never relate themselves to one another with that intimacy which
their absence of boundaries demands in order to take on any special
beauty, nobility, delightsomeness, of gardening. The true gardener—who, if he is reading this, must be getting very tired of our
insistent triteness—carefully keeps in mind the laws of linear and
of aerial perspective, no matter how large or small the garden. The
relative stature of things, both actual and prospective; their breadth;
the breadth or slenderness, darkness or lightness, openness or den-
sity, of their foliage; the splendor or delicacy of their flowers, whether
in size or in color; the season of their blooming; the contour of the
grounds—all these points must be taken into account in determining
where things are to stand and how be grouped. Once the fence or
hedge was the frame of the picture; but now our pictures, on almost
any street of unpalatial, comfortable homes, touch edge to edge
without frames, and the reason they do not mar one another's effects
is that they have no particular effects to be marred, but lie side by

side as undiscordantly as so many string instruments without strings. Let us hope for a time when they will rise in insurrection, resolved to be either parts of a private park, or each one a whole private garden.

[*The Amateur Garden* (1914)]

Grace Tabor
In Defense of Privacy

Our present system of regulated building [. . .] is wasteful, vulgarly frank and ostentatious, and utterly destructive of garden opportunities as well as of the fine instinct of home reserve and privacy that is such a priceless human asset.

We have not grown old enough as a nation, however, to shrink from personal publicity; we still cherish the infantile instinct to cry "hello!" to the passer-by, to lift up our possessions to his gaze—which will be flatteringly covetous if these are striking enough—and shake them triumphantly before him with an exultant "see!" So we have the veranda-stage whereon our little dramas are to be played before this audience; and we plan all the settings around about to capture the admiration of the street.

Consequently the suburbs of American cities are said to be the most beautiful in the world—*to drive through.* Could there be a more eloquent qualification of praise than that final clause? I think not, when it is remembered that these are colonies of homes, not public parks. They are not for the man who drives through. They are for the man who stays there, and for his wife and his sons and his daughters. Yet the streets are the most attractive part of them!

There are few at the present time, I grant, who would have the courage to break away from what has come to be a traditional style or plan here, even if convinced of its advantages, both ethical and material; yet I am going to suggest what a colony which adopted the other older and better ways might gain, and the very real beauties which would remain in its streets even though they were deprived of their domestic panoramas.

In the first place, every foot of his ground is available to the man whose house forms a part of his boundary walls and whose boundary *is walled*. If he buys forty by one hundred feet, he has forty by one hundred feet to use—not forty by one hundred less forty by twenty-five, or one quarter of the whole, which restrictions bind him to turn over to the street, to put it as actual unvarnished truth. He has space for flowers, fruits, and vegetables to an unbelievable amount—unbelievable at least to those who have never thought about it or figured it out or tried it—and within his own garden beauty and interest and recreation and diversion, instead of in the street.

It is a reversal that is very complete, for instead of a front porch overlooking the throng and the dust and invaded by both, figuratively in the first instance, actually in the second, this outdoor room will open at the rear—or side, depending upon the proper weather exposure, which must always be the determining factor—and looks over the fruits growing upon the wall, the green things everywhere, flowers in their trim borders, a tennis court, perhaps, or a bowling green, a pool in the sunlight where water lilies bloom and gold fish rest in the shadows, a hammock in the distance under the trees with table and chairs, and *al fresco* breakfasts on fine mornings—where grocers' carts and delivery wagons cannot adventure, where all the privacy and lounging indolence of indoors is possible, out under the blue in the fragrant sweetness of a true garden.

Yet in the street there is the same cool shade that there has always been, from trees along the curb; the same refreshing strips of emerald turf beneath them; a flicker of light and shadow in the vines growing on garden walls and house façades; gleams of color from blossoms in window boxes; and glimpses beyond into delightful garden retreats—glimpses that are infinitely more alluring than the endless bits of lawn that stretch monotonously back from the sidewalk to the inevitable clotheslines of present day back yards. And finally there is restful unity of purpose taking the place of what is to-day, at best, lack of harmony and uncertainty—an uncertainty that is inevitable when the appearance and general effect of each place from the ground up is so dependant upon the general effect of its neighbors, and of all the others in its block, standing as they do in the open and all together.

I am inclined to think that we have departed so far from the sensible, reasonable arrangement practiced by older peoples—by our own ancestors here, indeed, in early times, as old villages in many parts of the country still bear witness—through a fundamental misconception of the town, village, or suburban home, its possibilities and its limitations. We have not recognized that it is definitely a type, alone and by itself; as distinct as the city home; *widely different* from the country home. Right here, indeed, is just where the most serious error has slipped in, for all the effort has been to treat the suburban grounds along the same lines which the large estate admits, to build the suburban house according to the same plans from which the house in the midst of acreage rises.

So a kind of landscape gardening has been attempted, in a loose fashion, to which boundary fences and walls and many other rational features have been sacrificed in the vain hope of creating an illusion of the spaciousness and splendor which the town or suburban place cannot, in the very nature of things, possibly enjoy. For it has its very definite limitations, fixed and unalterable, of which it cannot be rid. Not until these are recognized and, being recognized, are turned to account in the distribution and ornamentation of its grounds, will its highest possibilities, both esthetic and practical, be realized.

[*Come into the Garden* (1921)]

Frank A. Waugh
The Ideal American Home

"There's no place like home," and "it's not a home until it's planted."

This combination of slogans drives well in double harness. The two go together, and in combination they express a great truth.

It is only fair to say that the home is the greatest institution in America—greater than the Republican party and the Democratic party combined—greater than any seven kinds of religious sects which might be named—more important than intercollegiate football—worth more to the country than votes for women—in short, standing above every known cause or institution.

Now, the ideal American home means a single house for each family, with a little plot of ground about it, said plot of ground to include a front yard between the house and the street with some sort of garden behind the house. This formula is universally accepted even if not always followed. While it seems to be the trend of the times for more families to live in apartment houses, still nobody considers such an apartment a home. Much less do we look upon such an institution as the ideal American home.

Everyone who is patriotic, therefore, and wants to do something for his country, will promote to the utmost of his ability the development of such ideal American homes. A small house and a small garden both protect and express the family life.

It is well and sadly known, of course, that tens of thousands of individual house lots have not been planted. In other words these houses have not been converted into homes. We may all accept the further patriotic duty, therefore, of promoting this campaign of planting.

In the Old Country the primary planting which gives a home its individuality is a hedge all along the street front. The American home is characteristically different in that it is open to the street. The plantings, instead of forming a hedge on the street line, are pushed back against the foundations of the house. They are foundation plantings.

This type of planting is therefore fundamental to the whole of American domestic landscape architecture in a double sense. It is hardly too much to say that this is altogether the most important branch of landscape architecture, socially considered, in the entire field of practice.

There are several definite purposes which are served by the foundation plantings about the home when they are properly made. It may be worth while to run over these briefly.

First of all, the foundation planting should connect the house with the grounds and with the other plantings. Suppose we look at a new house on a new lot where no planting has been done. It is quite clear that the whole house could be picked up and moved to another lot. Any contractor will do the job for a reasonable fee. Or the house might be moved forty feet to one side, or ten feet back on the same lot. Perhaps our judgment would indicate that such a move would be desirable.

But if we see the same place three years later, after the foundation plantings have become established, the house then seems to have grown out of the ground. It could not be taken away without leaving a serious scar. The house and grounds have grown together into a permanent unity. This result is one of great moral value quite beyond the enormous addition of beauty to the place.

Secondly, the foundation plantings should soften harsh architectural lines of the house. We might say that no architect is going to make harsh achitectural lines in his design. Still he does. The architect himself recognizes this fact. He never sends out to his client even a preliminary sketch of his house elevations without marking in some foundation plantings. Even the merest pencil sketch needs to be broken up in this way in order to make it look cozy and homelike.

In the third place, the foundation plantings help to screen objectionable features. Again we might say that the architect and landscape architect should not leave any objectionable features on the home grounds. Still the Monday washing has to be hung out somewhere; the children have to have a playground; there may be a kennel for the dog or a coopful of chickens. Not one of these things is sinful or seriously objectionable in itself; still no householder wishes to publish them to the street. They are better if they are screened away from public view. This screening effect of foundation plantings, therefore, may come to have a very important role.

Finally, the foundation plantings help to dress up the whole place. As we have already said it makes it seem more cozy and homelike. The difference between an unplanted place and one decently furnished with trees and shrubs is so great that even the dullest mind can see it. The only wonder is, with these facts so obvious, that any one should keep a house without planting it and planting it well.

[Preface to Leonard H. Johnson, *Foundation Planting* (1927)]

Henry Beetle Hough
Renascence of the Fence

What there is behind this cycle of fences we do not know. But there certainly is a cycle, which should be satisfying to the countless theorists to whom the recurrences of human history are more important than anything else. In this present instance, the fences are more engrossing to us than the cycle, but since there is a cycle we feel justified in pointing it out.

Thirty years ago people were taking down their fences, here on the Vineyard, at least, and leaving their grounds open and plain before the public view. The destruction of pickets was terrific. Probably it was considered modern to do away with the white slats and pickets, and to come out from behind historic barriers. Of course they really were not barriers; perhaps they were merely conventions, and exceedingly attractive ones as we see it now, offering contrast with green lawns and crimson ramblers, introducing parallels and diagonals into a scheme of natural irregularity and rumpus.

Now people are putting up fences again. Occasionally they are content with privet hedges, but few are satisfied without some line of demarcation, materially emphasized, to restore the convention swept away in an earlier decade. White fences once again match white houses, and the hollyhocks have something to tower above, and pedestrians find it pleasant to see gardens framed in yards to which fences add a touch of the chaste and prim.

As to the reason for these changes, we prefer to await the judgment of the theorists. It may be that the new era of fences means an effort to shut out a dismaying and rapidly moving civilization; or human retreat from looming problems; or a pursuit of some father image through fantasies of time. Anyway, it is probably adequate to say, in the words of certain sages, that there was an unfenced generation and there is now a fenced generation.

However it may be, the rebirth of the fences contributes a thrifty dignity to the Island scene, a running theme of decoration joined with order. Seldom may good taste be materialized with the use of such plain materials—posts, stringers, slats, and, most of all, white paint.

[*Singing in the Morning* (1951)]

Celestine Sibley
My Thicket

*Americans must be far more brotherly-
hearted than we are, for they do not seem
to mind being over-looked. They have no
sense of private enclosure.*

—V. SACKVILLE-WEST

Amateur gardeners need all the confidence they can get and the
best device I know for shoring up one's belief in one's own aspi-
rations, if not achievements, is to seek out the authorities. Just as
they say the devil can quote scripture for his own evil purposes
(they *do* say that, don't they?), it's possible for the fledgling gardener
to find some expert to advocate whatever he wants to do.

Take thickets. I love being enclosed by walls of green growing
things. I have not the slightest desire to see or be seen by the people
passing my door on the dirt road. In fact, it seems to me that one
of the great needs of the human spirit nowadays is for privacy—a
spot of earth where you can be alone.

Time was, I know, when aloneness was the condition of country
living and not too desirable. My predecessors at Sweet Apple had
to fight their way through a wilderness to get here and a symbol of
home was a clearing—a little space where you could see the approach of enemy or friend, a swept area wild animals would be
reluctant to cross, a clean spot where even the smallest snake track
would be visible. The landscaping in those days didn't include foundation planting, which is to say flowers and shrubs around the walls
of the cabin. Whatever ornamental bushes and trees the householder
got were set off at a distance. Boxwood, if any, grew in the middle
of the yard. The old clump of mock orange which was here when I
came was up the slope and halfway to the garden.

The cabin itself was built close to the road—for company, I suppose, as well as for convenience. Transportation was difficult at best and people wanted to be as near to the public roads as possible. If anybody passed, the family with no telephone or automobile wanted to be at least within hailing distance. Even better, the passing traveler might stop and share a bed or a meal and relate all the news from the world beyond.

The need to be near passing traffic no longer exists but habit is strong. People who have small lots necessarily build cheek by jowl to their neighbors. But even with space to spare you'll see new houses going up, all barefaced and exposed, next to the paved road. And then when the craving for privacy hits, you'll see a redwood-enclosed patio going up in the back.

The style for the "uncluttered" came along a few years ago and throughout the land you saw householders taking down picket fences and the wonderful old iron fences. They uprooted their hedges, whacked down their dark cedars and hauled away old and fat ligustrum bushes. (And a good thing that last was, too!) The fashion was for sweeps of unblemished lawn and maybe a few low-growing hollies around the eaves to sort of anchor the house to the land. (I had a friend who planted the thorniest holly she could find under all her windows to repel burglars.)

Everybody in the world went crazy about sun and the old passion for shade trees—for elm- and oak-lined streets—languished. With air conditioners humming away at every window, who needed trees to cool the air and shade the roof? We all spoke feelingly of openness and light and the joys of having the sun shine in our windows.

There were holdouts, of course, and my mother, Muv, was one of them. When everybody else in her little town took down their fences on the ground that there was no longer any wandering livestock in the streets, Muv painted hers and trained a wisteria along its top runner. When her neighbors, lately come from yards hard swept with gallberry brush brooms, went in for wide and treeless lawns, Muv cut swatches out of hers to allot to a magnolia tree, a new water oak, a mimosa, a jacaranda, a tea olive, and assorted beds and borders of azaleas, camellias and roses. Further offending the eyes of her neighbors, she planted a screen of vines and bridal wreath stage center so she would have a hiding place to sit unseen and sip her coffee in the early morning.

Newcomers to her street made the mistake of thinking Muv lived in this jungle because she was getting along in years and lacked the strength to prune. So when she went to the hospital for a few days once they generously got together and trimmed up her trees and leveled her bushy tangle of coral vines and bridal wreath to the ground.

It suited me very well not to be present when they came for their thanks.

By the time I got there she had replanted. The result is not one to gladden the eye of a landscape architect and draw photographers from *House & Garden* magazine, but it is right for Muv and her birds and her cats.

When she wanders forth with her coffee in the mornings she has, even on her smallish lot, some place to *go*, something to see. There are crooks and turns, little paths to follow, minute views to surprise the eye. You don't take it all in at once. There's a small patch of open lawn big enough for a bird bath and a feeder but not so big it taxes the strength of the man who comes twice a month to cut the grass for her. There are caverns of coolness beneath the bushes for her cats and a bench here or a chair there for Muv to rest upon.

Oddly enough, the crowding doesn't seem an impediment to most of Muv's plants. The pomegranate tree by the kitchen wall puts out blazing flowers all summer and an occasional harvest of fruit. Her tea olive by the screened porch sweetens the late winter and early spring air with its fragrance and a magnolia between her and her neighbor's fence perfumes the late spring and summer. Defying all the rules for growing roses as to spacing and pruning, Muv still manages to have something blooming all the time. Her camellias are a wonder and when all else peters out quantities of lilies lift pristine, gold-filled cups above an untidy green snarl of foliage, their own and other plants'.

Naturally, being a child of the uncluttered garden era, I didn't plan to emulate my mother's jungle. The first thing I did at Sweet Apple was to skin the front yard bare of everything except four spindly pine saplings, a seedling peach and one wild plum. Then we set about planting grass, wonderful grass. The winter rye popped up promptly, looking in sere November like a lush carpet of artificial green spread by an unctuous undertaker to hide an honest grave. I really hated that glorious, phony greensward but comforted myself that it was nurturing the earth and, come spring, we would plant real grass that would be green only in season and decently brown in season.

Whatever we planted—and I mercifully forgot—was all wrong. It languished and died. Manure was needed, we decided, and enlisted the services of Herb Hawkins, whose family runs a Roswell seed-feed store. One hot summer day young Mr. Hawkins arrived in a mighty truck equipped with a fan, which blew chicken litter all over the yard. Back and forth he drove and what my son called "the material" hit the fan and then the yard.

Anybody who has smelled chicken litter—the stuff that comes from the floor of the chicken houses—under the hot Georgia sun will comprehend my dedication to the dream of a good lawn. The idea, Mr. Hawkins said, was to get it out before the rain. It would, he admitted, smell a little until we had a good rain to wash the rich and pungent scent into the earth.

That was the understatement of the century. That chicken litter stank. It was not a mildly offensive odor that you could sniff and forget. It was a stench, oppressive, pervasive, overpowering.

And that was the summer it didn't rain.

One night my son, Jimmy, and I drove into the yard from town and the aroma of chicken litter reached out and got us—not just strong enough to scorch our noses but strong enough to craze the enamel on the car.

It was hot and we knew we would have to sleep with the windows open. *Sleep?* We'd be asphyxiated!

The impulse hit us simultaneously. We rushed in and grabbed up some blankets and headed north to camp out. The mountain camp was eighty miles away but at that point eighty miles seemed scarcely far enough.

Eventually, of course, it rained and time and the weather dissipated the chicken litter. The grass began to grow and so did the weeds. My dream of a velvet stretch of uncluttered lawn went a-glimmering. I had chick weed, dock, plantain, dandelions and thousands of other little wildings that were nameless to me. At first our neighbor Doc comforted me by saying that it was all green and if you kept it cut who was to know that it wasn't grass?

But keeping weeds mowed is harder than keeping grass mowed. They are not content to creep along the earth but must reach for the sky and I guess they have more dominant personalities than effete, citified, cultivated grass blades. Anyhow, with a resignation born of desperation, I began to look, really look, at those weeds and they began to strike me as more interesting than grass.

For one thing, most weeds are herbs and are good for something. You can't make a poultice or a tea with grass. At least, I never heard that you could. But weeds . . . ah, country lore is full of stories about their magical healing properties. Cocklebur, for instance, can be steeped in a tea, sweetened with honey and served up for sore and husky throats. (One ounce of dried leaves to one pint of boiling water, honey to taste, an old herbal says.)

Ground ivy, the tenacious little plant with the sharp, aromatic odor, filled me with despair when it got in flower beds and spilled over and snuffed out grass, until I read that the scent of its crushed foliage inhaled deeply will cure headaches when all other efforts have failed. It is also good for poultices for "abcesses, gatherings and tumours" and valued by gypsies for making ointments for cuts or sprains. Now I leave it where it grows and enjoy the scent it gives off when I walk or push the lawn mower over it.

Plantain, which took a stand in my yard, sending big turnipy roots down to China, didn't look at all ornamental to me until I learned its other name is "Englishman's foot." This is said to have been given to it by the Indians because it seemed to spring up everywhere the white man went. Romeo in *Romeo and Juliet* recommended it "for your broken shin" and all sorts of authorities have found use for it in poultices to draw out poison, in infusions for diarrhea and ointments for sore eyes.

But you really can't turn your front yard into a weed patch without offending the taste of all your neighbors and any random passerby. Which brings me back to the need of privacy. A woman's log cabin should be her castle and she should feel free, even comfortable, to have a lawn, mown or unmown, a weed patch or a jungle, if it suits her. I wouldn't go as far as to say she could have a fence made of old tires painted silver or a gate of old bedsteads. But on the other hand, if she wanted such in her yard and kept it hidden from the general view . . . ?

It was a very appealing idea to me and I talked about it off and on for years but rather hopelessly. Sweet Apple *is* close to the road and traffic is increasing every day. A dozen new houses have been built within two miles of us within the last eight years and 750 others are going up in the beautiful pasture three miles away. Time will come when a respectable woman dare not wander around in the cool of the evening in her shimmy or sit under a tree in her pajamas to drink her morning coffee.

The pines in the front yard were growing, of course, and three of the nine dogwoods that we planted in a zigzag line across the front had plumped out. When the road crews stopped hacking it back we turned out to have quite a nice stand of sumac and an old crape myrtle tree that some long-ago owner planted here. The Dorothy Perkins rose ran rampant over the yard and into the trees before we cleared it out and threw it on the road bank. Now it runs rampant on the road bank and sprawls all over the rail fence, offering bouquets of pink shattery blooms for about two weeks out of the year and growing, growing, growing the rest of the time. In summer there are blackberries and Queen Anne's lace and daisies to turn the dust; in the fall, goldenrod. On the whole, an unsightly mess, my family and friends tell me, and why don't I clear it away and plant grass?

Lacking the courage of my convictions, I didn't shout, "Never!" or even try to defend my burgeoning fence row. That is, I didn't until I found my authority.

In her book *A Joy of Gardening*, V. Sackville-West has something to say about the advantages of a thicket. She says the American attitude of "All is open. Walk in, walk in!" probably illustrates an admirable democratic spirit but it isn't likely to be emulated in Britain.

"It is entirely at variance with our traditional idea that our own bit of ground surrounding our house, our home, be it large or small, is sacred to ourselves," she writes.

So the plan, advanced by an acquaintance, of going beyond planting "a mere hedge" and planting a thicket strikes her as "a very useful idea."

"Thickets," she points out, "can be planted anywhere, can be of any shape, and can be composed of any plants to your choice. If I had room for a thicket myself and had enough span of life to look forward to it twenty years hence, I know what I should do: I should plant it far too thickly and extravagantly to start with, and then should thin it gradually as my shrubs and trees developed in size, crowding one another out. . . . You could remove, and add, and alter, indefinitely. There would be no end to the fun and interest and variety."

I have never been to Sissinghurst Castle but I have a feeling Miss Sackville-West's estate is at least slightly bigger than mine and anybody would say that she had more room for a thicket. But no matter. The need for a thicket can live in the heart of a log cabin dweller as well as in the heart of the chatelaine of an English castle.

It's the privacy that we covet, the sense of being enclosed by greenness, secure from the public gaze. If V. Sackville-West says a thicket is horticulturally sound and esthetically proper, who's to answer nay?

So, emboldened by my authority, I have embarked on my thicket. You can have free rein in dreaming up a thicket. (The planting is a bit more difficult.) How about holly trees? A weeping willow? More dogwood? Sourwood, that gem of a little tree that is laden with panicles of white beloved by the bees all summer and a blazing bonfire of brilliant, lacquered red in the fall? Althea, the little summer-blooming tree whose other name is Rose of Sharon? You could plant more sumac. That exotic-looking wilding called "shoemake" in the rural South is handsome with its stag horns of deep red berries and its flaming autumnal foliage. There are shrubs— all the viburnums, wild azaleas, sweet shrub, mock orange. How about a crab apple tree for springtime fragrance and heart-stopping pink blossoms?

All the experts not in accord with your yearning for a thicket will tell you that these trees and bushes need space. They will warn you to visualize the grown tree and allow room accordingly. I have but to look out my window at one of nature's thickets and know that they are not necessarily right. I see pines and young maples, dogwood, hickories, sweetgums and wild plums clumped together, making an impenetrable wall to the west of me. Why not in front?

An artist friend warned me that it would spoil the view of Sweet

Apple cabin from the road but from the inside looking out, what could be pleasanter than a thicket, a real *thick* thicket?

Now when opposition arises I do what I advise all neophyte gardeners to do. I drop a name: "V. Sackville-West says . . ."

[*The Sweet Apple Gardening Book* (1973)]

Biographical Notes
Bibliography

Biographical Notes

Roy Barrette, after his retirement as an insurance company executive in 1962, moved to a farm in Maine and became weekly columnist for the *Ellsworth American* and the *Berkshire Eagle*. His books include *A Countryman's Journal* (1981) and *A Countryman's Bed-Book* (1987).

Catharine Esther Beecher (1800–78) was the oldest daughter of Lyman Beecher, a noted preacher, and the sister of Henry Ward Beecher and Harriet Beecher Stowe. She was co-founder of the Hartford Female Seminary, an ardent Abolitionist, and a frequent writer on women's issues. Her books include *A Treatise on Domestic Economy* (1841) and *The True Remedy for the Wrongs of Women* (1851).

Henry Ward Beecher (1813–87), a Congregationalist preacher, was the brother of Catharine Beecher and Harriet Beecher Stowe. A frequent journalist on agricultural topics, he also wrote *Summer in the Soul (1858)* and *Evolution and Religion* (1885).

Neltje Blanchan is the pen name of Neltje DeGraaf Doubleday (1865–1918). Born in Chicago, she married the publisher Frank Nelson Doubleday in 1886. She wrote books on birds, American Indians, and antiques, as well as on gardening. She died in China in 1918 while there with her husband on a Red Cross mission.

Joseph Breck (1794–1873), a Boston seedsman, was one of the founders of the Massachusetts Horticultural Society. His book *The Flower Garden* went through five editions between 1851 and 1866. He also wrote *The Young Florist* (1833).

George Washington Cable (1844–1925) was born in New Orleans. A soldier in the Confederate Army, Cable lived in New England from 1879 on. His books include *Old Creole Days* (1879) and *Lovers of Louisiana* (1918).

Rosetta E. Clarkson founded with her husband, Ralph P. Clarkson, *The Herb-Grower Magazine*. She was a collector of rare herbals, many of which, such as William Coles's *The Art of Simpling* (1657), she published in facsimile editions.

Thalassa Cruso was born in Great Britain, but has lived and gardened in Boston since 1935. Her television series, *Making Things Grow*, enjoyed great popularity from its first appearance in 1967, as did her book of the same title. She also wrote *To Everything There Is a Season* (1973).

Mrs. William Starr Dana (1862–1952) was born Frances Theodora Smith. After her first husband, a naval officer, died of influenza early in their marriage, she was moved by the writings of John Burroughs and the advice of a friend, Marian Satterlee, to take up nature study. The first edition of her classic, *How to Know the Wildflowers* (1893), sold out almost immediately, and 65,000 copies sold within a decade. Her second husband was James Russell Parsons, and some editions of her wildflower book give its author as Frances Theodora Parsons.

Andrew Jackson Downing, who was born in 1815 and who died in a steamboat accident on the Hudson River in 1852, was the foremost authority on fruit trees in nineteenth-century America, as well as the country's first important landscape designer. His staunch advocacy of public parks was influential in bringing New York's Central Park into being.

Alice Morse Earle (1851–1911) was born in Worcester, Massachusetts. She moved to Brooklyn Heights, New York, after her marriage in 1874 to Henry Earle, a broker. Her first book, *The Sabbath in Puritan New England*, went through seventeen editions. Her books include *Curious Punishments of Bygone Days* (1896), *Child Life in Colonial Days* (1899), *Old-Time Gardens* (1901), and *Sun Dials and Roses of Yesterday* (1902).

Helena Rutherfurd Ely's *A Woman's Hardy Garden* (1903) was a bestseller soon after it was published. She also wrote *The Practical Flower Garden* (1911). In 1913 she was one of the founders of the Garden Club of America.

Robert Finch is a naturalist on Cape Cod. Many of the "Soundings" columns he wrote for four local newspapers were collected in *Common Ground* (1981).

Jeanne Goode, who writes frequently for several horticultural magazines, is a member of the herbarium staff of the New York Botanical Garden.

Patti Hagan is the garden columnist for *The Wall Street Journal*.

Harland J. Hand is an artist and former high-school teacher who lives in El Cerrito, California, where his garden has become internationally famous for its strong design.

Pamela J. Harper was born in Great Britain, where she published *The Story of a Garden* (1972) before moving to the United States. She is a leading international specialist in horticultural photography, the author of numerous articles on gardening, and co-author of *Perennials: How to Select, Grow, and Enjoy* (1986).

Henry Beetle Hough (1896–1985) was for many years the editor of the Martha's Vineyard *Gazette*. He wrote many books on New England lore and on local and natural history.

William Lanier Hunt, whose garden in Chapel Hill, North Carolina, is famous throughout the South, is the author of *Southern Gardens, Southern Gardening*.

Biographical Notes

Thomas Jefferson (1743–1826), the most horticulturally minded President of the United States thus far, encouraged his countrymen to develop a literature on gardening that would be "independent of the productions of Great Britain."

Louise Seymour Jones, who lived and gardened in Redlands, California, was a frequent contributor to *Vogue* and other magazines in the 1930s.

Mrs. Francis King (1864–1948) was born in Washington, New Jersey. Garden editor of *McCall's* and garden advisor to Montgomery Ward, she was one of the founders of the Garden Club of America in Philadelphia in 1913. A prolific writer, in 1921 she was the first woman to receive the George Robert White medal of honor from the Massachusetts Horticultural Society.

Elizabeth Lawrence (1910–85), who has been called "the Jane Austen of American gardening writers," was born in Marietta, Georgia, but grew up in Garysburg, North Carolina, and then Raleigh, where she lived and gardened for many years after receiving degrees in literature from Barnard College and in landscape architecture from the State College of North Carolina. In her later years, she lived in Charlotte, where she wrote a weekly column on gardening for *The Charlotte Observer*. Her books include *A Southern Garden* (1942), *Gardens in Winter*, *The Little Bulbs*, and *Gardening for Love: The Market Bulletins* (1987).

Alice Lounsberry wrote *The Garden Book for Young People* (1903) and *Gardens Near the Sea* (1910). She is best known for her botanical writings dealing with her travels through the mountains of southern Appalachia.

Ann Lovejoy is the garden columnist of the *Seattle Weekly*, and the author of *The Year in Bloom*.

Frederick McGourty, with his wife, Mary Ann, owns and operates Hillside Nursery in Norfolk, Connecticut. The former editor of the Brooklyn Botanical Gardens series of publications, he is co-author of *Perennials: How to Select, Grow, and Enjoy*.

Bernard McMahon (or M'Mahon) was born in Ireland in 1776 and emigrated in 1796 to Philadelphia, where he established an influential seed and nursery company. He actively promoted American native plants, both in the United States and in Great Britain and Europe. His massive treatise, *The American Gardener's Calendar* (1806), which went through many editions, is generally regarded as the first truly American book on gardening. He died in 1816.

Julian R. Meade (1909–40), a novelist who lived in Virginia, also wrote two books on gardening and the children's books *Peter by the Sea* and *Miss Couch and the Scamps*.

Lynden B. Miller, an artist who studied horticulture in England, is the director of the Central Park Conservancy.

Donald Mitchell was a nineteenth-century essayist on rural matters, best known for his books about Edgewood, his farm in New England.

Henry Mitchell writes two columns a week for *The Washington Post*, one of them on gardening. He is the author of *The Essential Earthman* (1981).

Biographical Notes

Amanda B. Morris is an enigma. Inquiries at three major horticultural libraries have produced no information about her, beyond the fact that she published *Wildflowers and Where They Grow* in Boston in 1882.

Jay Neugeboren (b. 1938) is writer-in-residence at the University of Massachusetts in Amherst. His novels include *The Stolen Jew* (1981) and *Before My Life Began* (1985).

Eleanor Perényi, a former managing editor of *Mademoiselle*, is the author of *Franz Liszt: The Artist as Romantic Hero* and *Green Thoughts: A Writer in the Garden* (1981).

Anne Raver is the garden columnist for *Newsday*.

Hanna Rion (b. 1875) wrote *Let's Make a Flower Garden* (1912) and *The Garden in the Wilderness, by a Hermit* (1909).

Frank J. Scott was one of the first landscape architects in America. His writings in the late nineteenth century were extremely influential in determining the shape the suburban landscape took on during many decades.

Celestine Sibley is a columnist for the Atlanta *Constitution*.

Harriet Beecher Stowe (1811–96), was the fourth daughter of the preacher Lyman Beecher and sister to both Catharine Beecher and Henry Ward Beecher. A prolific writer, she is best known for her extraordinarily influential novel *Uncle Tom's Cabin* (1831).

Roger Swain is science editor of *Horticulture* magazine and the author of two collections of essays, *Earthly Pleasures* (1980) and *Field Days* (1983). He regularly appears on the television series *The Victory Garden*.

Grace Tabor, a pioneering landscape architect, also wrote *The Landscape Gardening Book* (1910), *Old-Fashioned Gardening* (1913), and *Suburban Gardens* (1913).

Celia Laighton Thaxter (1835–94) was born in Portsmouth, New Hampshire, but grew up on White Island, one of the Isles of Shoals, off the New Hampshire coast, where her father was for a time a lighthouse keeper. When she was twelve, her parents moved to nearby Appledore Island, where they built a fashionable summer resort hotel. She was an extremely popular poet. In her later years, her cottage on Appledore, with its tiny garden of annuals, was a favorite haunt of such American Impressionist painters as Childe Hassam, who illustrated the first edition of her classic book, *An Island Garden*, which was published a few months before she died.

Isaac Trimble, like Amanda Morris, is enigmatic. His book *A Treatise on the Insect Enemies of Fruit and Fruit Trees* was published in New York in 1865.

Charles Dudley Warner (1829–1900), although trained in law, was co-editor of *Harper's Magazine*. A frequent writer on travel, he was co-author with Mark Twain of the novel *The Gilded Age* (1873).

Frank A. Waugh (1869–1943) was a professor of landscape architecture at the University of Massachusetts in Amherst. A prolific writer of books on fruit trees

Biographical Notes

and orchards, he also wrote *Home Pork Production* under the pseudonym John Smedley.

Candace Thurber Wheeler (1827–1923) was born in Delhi, New York. Her home on Long Island was a salon for American painters like Frederick E. Church and Albert Bierstadt. A fabric and tapestry designer, she was influential in the founding of the Society for Decorative Art in 1877. Her books include *Principles of Home Design* (1903), *The Development of Embroidery in America* (1921), and an autobiography, *Yesterdays in a Busy Life* (1918).

Katharine S. White was an editor at *The New Yorker* for thirty-four years. An avid gardener at her summer home in Ellsworth, Maine, where she later retired with her husband, E. B. White, she began writing in her final days at the magazine a series of fourteen articles for it, over a period of twelve years. These classic essays were published posthumously in 1979 as *Onward and Upward in the Garden.*

William Nathaniel White (1819–67) was born in Stamford, Connecticut, but moved to Georgia in 1847 for reasons of health. A frequent contributor to horticultural journals in both the North and the South, he bought and edited *The Southern Cultivator*, an agricultural monthly, in 1861, continuing to publish and edit it even during the Civil War, when he was in the Confederate Army. His book *Gardening for the South*, first published in 1856, was enormously influential in the Southern states.

Louise Beebe Wilder (1878–1938) was born in Baltimore. In 1902 she married Walter Robb Wilder of New York City. An avid and accomplished gardener at her home in Bronxville, New York, she wrote ten gardening books, including *My Garden* (1916) and *Adventures in a Suburban Garden* (1931).

Mabel Osgood Wright (1859–1934), a novelist and nature writer, helped found the Connecticut Audubon Society. She wrote *The Garden of a Commuter's Wife* (1901) and *Stranger at the Gate* (1913).

Linda Yang is the author of *The Terrace Gardener's Handbook* and a frequent contributor to horticultural magazines. She writes a regular column for the Thursday "Home" section of *The New York Times.*

Bibliography

Barrette, Roy. *A Countryman's Bed-Book*. Camden, Maine: Down East Books, 1987.

Beecher, Catharine, and Harriet Beecher Stowe. *The American Woman's Home*. New York: J. B. Ford, 1869.

Beecher, Henry Ward. *Plain and Pleasant Talk about Fruits, Flowers and Farming*. New York: Derby & Jackson, 1859.

Betts, Edwin Morris. *Thomas Jefferson's Garden Book*. Philadelphia: The American Philosophical Society, 1944.

Blanchan, Neltje. *The American Flower Garden*. New York: Doubleday, Page, 1909.

———. *Nature's Garden*. Toronto: William Briggs, 1900.

Breck, Joseph. *New Book of Flowers*. New York: Orange, Judd, 1866.

Cable, George Washington. *The Amateur Garden*. New York: Scribner's, 1914.

Clarkson, Rosetta E. *Green Enchantment*. New York: Macmillan, 1940.

Cruso, Thalassa. *To Everything There Is a Season*. New York, Knopf, 1973.

Dana, Mrs. William Starr. *According to Season*. New York: Scribner's, 1894.

Downing, Andrew Jackson. *The Fruits and Fruit Trees of America*. New York: John Wiley, 1845.

———. *Rural Essays*. New York: Leavitt & Allen, 1854.

Earle, Alice Morse. *Old-Time Gardens*. New York: Macmillan, 1901.

Ely, Helena Rutherfurd. *A Woman's Hardy Garden*. New York: Macmillan, 1903.

Finch, Robert. *Common Ground: A Naturalist's Cape Cod*. Boston: David Godine, 1981.

Goode, Jeanne. "In Praise of Virginia Creeper," in *Horticulture*, September 1986.

Hagan, Patti. "Going Buggy," in *The Wall Street Journal*, June 11, 1986.

Haggerston, David. Letter reprinted in Joseph Breck, *New Book of Flowers*. New York: Orange, Judd, 1866.

Hand, Harland J. "The Color Garden," in *Pacific Horticulture*, Spring 1978.

Harper, Pamela J. "It Began with Butterfly Weed," in *Pacific Horticulture*, Spring 1986.

Bibliography

Hough, Henry Beetle. "A Counsel of Prudence," in *Horticulture*, April 1985.

————. *Singing in the Morning*. New York: Simon and Schuster, 1951.

Hunt, William Lanier. *Southern Gardens, Southern Gardening*. Durham, N.C.: Duke University Press, 1982.

Jones, Louise Seymour. *Put a Feather in Your Hat*. Los Angeles: Ward Richie, 1938.

King, Mrs. Francis. *The Well-Considered Garden*. New York: Scribner's, 1915.

Lawrence, Elizabeth. *Gardening for Love: The Market Bulletins*. Durham, N.C.: Duke University Press, 1987.

————. *A Southern Garden*. Chapel Hill, N.C.: University of North Carolina Press, 1942.

Lounsberry, Alice. *Gardens Near the Sea*. New York: Frederick A. Stokes, 1910.

————. *Southern Wildflowers and Trees*. New York: Frederick A. Stokes, 1901.

Lovejoy, Ann. *The Year in Bloom*. Seattle: Sasquatch Books, 1987.

McGourty, Frederick. "Combining Perennials," in *American Horticulturist*, February 1985.

McMahon, Bernard. *The American Gardener's Calendar*. 11th ed. Philadelphia: Lippincott, 1857.

Meade, Julian R. *Bouquets and Bitters*. New York: Longmans, Green, 1940.

Miller, Lynden B. "Perennials in Urban Areas," in *Proceedings of the 1986 Perennial Plant Association Symposium*, Columbus, Ohio, 1987.

Mitchell, Donald. *Rural Studies*. New York: Scribner's, 1897.

Mitchell, Henry. *The Essential Earthman*. Indiana University Press, 1981; Farrar, Straus & Giroux, 1983.

Morris, Amanda B. *Wildflowers and Where They Grow*. Boston: B. Lothrop, 1882.

Neugeboren, Jay. "Reflections on a Family Garden," in *Horticulture*, July 1982.

Perényi, Eleanor. *Green Thoughts: A Writer in the Garden*. New York: Random House, 1981.

Raver, Anne. "Tendrils to the Heart," in *Newsday*, July 3, 1986.

Rion, Hanna. *Let's Make a Flower Garden*. New York: McBride, Nast & Co., 1912.

Scott, Frank J. *The Art of Beautifying Suburban Home Grounds*. New York: D. Appleton & Co., 1870.

Sibley, Celestine. *The Sweet Apple Gardening Book*. Garden City, N.Y.: Doubleday, 1973.

Swain, Roger. *Field Days*. New York: Scribner's, 1983.

Tabor, Grace. *Come into the Garden*. New York: Macmillan, 1921.

Thaxter, Celia. *An Island Garden*. Boston: Houghton Mifflin, 1894.

Trimble, Isaac. *A Treatise on the Insect Enemies of Fruit and Fruit Trees*. New York: William Wood, 1865.

Warner, Charles Dudley. *My Summer in a Garden*. Boston: Field, Osgood & Co., 1870.

Waugh, Frank A. Preface to Leonard H. Johnson, *Foundation Planting*. New York: A. T. DeLaMare, 1927.

Bibliography

Wheeler, Candace. *Content in a Garden*. Boston: Houghton Mifflin, 1902.

White, Katharine S. *Onward and Upward in the Garden*. New York: Farrar, Straus & Giroux, 1979.

White, William N. *Gardening for the South*. New York: Orange, Judd, 1866.

Wilder, Louise Beebe. *Colour in My Garden*. Garden City, N.Y.: Doubleday, Doran and Co., 1918.

————. *The Fragrant Path*. New York: Macmillan, 1932.

Wright, Mabel Osgood. *Flowers and Ferns in Their Native Haunts*. New York: Macmillan, 1907.

Yang, Linda. "Blueberries on a Mid-City Terrace," in *Organic Gardening*, March 1975.

ACKNOWLEDGMENTS

"Blueberries on a Mid-City Terrace," by Linda Yang, Copyright © 1975 by Linda Yang, Reprinted by permission of the author. "Going to Seed," from *Common Ground: A Naturalist's Cape Cod*, by Robert Finch, Copyright © 1981 by Robert Finch, Reprinted by permission of David R. Godine, Publisher. "Reflections on a Family Garden," by Jay Neugeboren, Copyright © 1982 by Jay Neugeboren, Reprinted by permission of the author. "A Counsel of Prudence," by Henry Beetle Hough, Copyright © 1985 by Henry Beetle Hough, Reprinted by permission of the author's estate. "Perennials in Urban Areas," by Lynden Miller, Copyright © 1986 by Lynden Miller, Reprinted by permission of the author. "A Charming Happening in the Borders," from *The Well-Considered Garden*, by Mrs. Francis King, Copyright 1915 by Charles Scribner's Sons, Copyright renewed 1943; Reprinted with the permission of Charles Scribner's Sons, an imprint of Macmillan Publishing Company. "Magenta the Maligned" and "Familiar Plant Names," from *Color in My Garden*, by Louise Beebe Wilder, Copyright 1918 by Louise Beebe Wilder, Reprinted by permission of the author's estate. "November—and the Barbaric Scarlet of Tithonia," from *A Southern Garden: A Handbook for the Middle South*, by Elizabeth Lawrence, Copyright 1942, Reprinted by permission of the University of North Carolina Press. "The Color Garden," by Harland J. Hand, Copyright © 1978 by Harland J. Hand, Reprinted by permission of the author. "Marigolds and Mass Madness," from *The Essential Earthman*, by Henry Mitchell, Copyright © 1981 by Henry Mitchell, Reprinted by permission of Indiana University Press. "Combining Perennials," by Frederick McGourty, Copyright © 1985 by Frederick McGourty, Reprinted by permission of the author. "It Began with Butterfly Weed," by Pamela J. Harper, Copyright © 1986 by Pamela J. Harper, Reprinted by permission of the author. "Pleasures of the Nose" and "Fragrant Annuals," from *The Fragrant Path*, by Louise Beebe Wilder, Copyright 1932 by Louise Beebe Wilder, Reprinted by permission of the author's estate. "I Remember, I Remember" and "Where Have All the Flowers Gone," from *To Everything There Is a Season*, by Thalasso Cruso, Copyright © 1973 by Thalassa Cruso, Reprinted by permission of Alfred A. Knopf, Inc. "Wild Flowers of June and July," from *Southern Gardens, Southern Gardening*, by William Lanier Hunt, Copyright © 1982 by William Lanier Hunt, Reprinted by permission of Duke University Press. "In Praise of Virginia Creeper," by Jeanne Goode, Copyright © 1986 by Jeanne Goode, Reprinted by permission of the author. "Now the Sweet Pepperbush" and "Renascence of the Fence," from *Singing in the Morning*, by Henry Beetle Hough, Copyright © 1951 by Henry Beetle Hough, Reprinted by permission of the author's estate. "Rosa Hicks," from *Gardening for Love*, by Elizabeth Lawrence, Copyright © 1987 by Duke University Press, Reprinted by permission of Duke University Press. "Tendrils to the Heart," by Anne Raver, Copyright © 1986 by Newsday, Inc., Reprinted by permission. "Garden Pests" and "My Thicket," from *The Sweet Apple Gardening Book*, by Celestine Sibley, Copyright © 1973 by Celestine Sibley, Reprinted by permission of the author. "Pests and Diseases," from *Green Thoughts: A Writer in the Garden*, by Eleanor Perényi, Copyright © 1981 by Eleanor Perényi, Reprinted by permission of Randon House, Inc. "Gypsy Moths," from *Field Days*, by Roger Swain, Copyright © 1983 by Roger Swain, Reprinted with the permission of Charles Scribner's Sons, an imprint of Macmillan Publishing

Acknowledgments